ECHO IN RAMADI

THE FIRSTHAND STORY OF U.S. MARINES IN IRAQ'S DEADLIEST CITY

SCOTT A. HUESING

REGNERY
HISTORY

Regnery History™ is a trademark of Salem Communications Holding Corporation; Regnery® is a registered trademark of Salem Communications Holding Corporation

Cataloging-in-Publication data on file with the Library of Congress

This paperback edition published 2019: ISBN 978-1-62157-961-8
Originally published in hardcover 2018

Published in the United States by
Regnery History, an imprint of
Regnery Publishing
A Division of Salem Media Group
300 New Jersey Ave NW
Washington, DC 20001
www.RegneryHistory.com

Manufactured in the United States of America

10 9 8 7 6 5 4 3 2 1

Books are available in quantity for promotional or premium use. For information on discounts and terms, please visit our website: www.Regnery.com.

Praise for

Echo in Ramadi

"This is a masterfully told story of brave warriors and heroic deeds in battle, but it also defines the unbreakable bonds of men who would rather die than let down their fellow Marines. Scott shares in vivid detail the challenges of leadership, his love for his men, and the pain endured from those killed or wounded in battle. Precisely details the day-to-day pressure in combat, the individual bravery, and his humility as a proven combat leader.

"During a military career, 'one must prepare himself for a moment that may never come: to thrust himself into the unchartered arena of battle.' For Huesing, that moment occurred more than once—each time he successfully rose to the occasion with courage and success."

—**Brigadier General William "Wild Bill" Weise**, USMC (Ret), commanding officer, 2d Battalion, 4th Marines, 1967–1968, Dai Do, Vietnam, recipient of the Navy Cross for Valor, Silver Star, and three Purple Heart Medals

"Absolutely perfect...Unique and captivating...Of all the books I've read on the War on Terror, *Echo in Ramadi* puts the reader on both sides of the wire with the men—seeing it through their eyes on the battlefield and back home with the families that share their pain and perception of waiting for news of their Marines. Major Huesing has delivered a timeless account of war for all to read."

—**Gunnery Sergeant Jack Coughlin**, USMC (Ret), *New York Times* bestselling author of *Shooter* and thirteen other best-selling books

"Huesing drops you into the middle of the action and shows you what fighting was like in the toughest areas of Iraq against a determined enemy at the height of the insurgency. You will feel as if you are standing side by side with these heroic Marines as they move from one firefight to the next, courageously overcoming uncertainty and dealing with the attacks, fear, and excitement. More apparent, he shows how they overcame the friction they faced on many fronts of the war."

—**Patrick Van Horne**, author of *Left of Bang*, U.S. Marine captain, and founder of the CP Journal

"Expertly told as you turn the pages. You feel the pain, cold, and heat these Magnificent Bastards endured, cheering through their experiences, only to be pulled back into the grim reality of combat. *Echo in Ramadi* is destined to be a classic narrative of men in war—not due to the great heroics often highlighted in most military works but to the lack of such grandiosity by a loyal commanding officer who provides honest and unvarnished reflections of those in his charge. It will be hard not to admire these Marines, and even harder to forget them."

—**Colin Heaton**, co-author of *Noble Warrior*, U.S. Marine, and owner of Heaton-Lewis Books

Echo in Ramadi

*To all of the brave Echo Company "Longhorns" who fought
and died defending the freedoms of our nation, both on and off the
battlefield, to all of the "The Magnificent Bastards" of 2d Battalion,
4th Marines—who battled alongside—and to the families who gave
their unyielding support to us all.*

■ ■ ■

*Corporal Dustin J. Libby USMC
Born: 4 January 1984
Killed in Action: 6 December 2006*

■ ■ ■

*Lance Corporal Emilian D. Sanchez USMC
Born: 29 May 1986
Killed in Action: 21 January 2007*

■ ■ ■

*Lance Corporal Andrew G. Matus USMC
Born: 14 September 1987
Killed in Action: 21 January 2007*

■ ■ ■

*Lance Corporal Anthony C. Melia USMC
Born: 29 August 1986
Killed in Action: 27 January 2007*

■ ■ ■

*Corporal Richard O. Quill III USMC
Born: 27 November 1984
Killed in Action: 1 February 2007*

■ ■ ■

*Sergeant Major Joseph J. Ellis USMC
Born: 8 September 1966
Killed in Action: 7 February 2007*

■　■　■

Sergeant Clinton W. Ahlquist USMC
Born: 1 December 1983
Killed in Action: 20 February 2007

■　■　■

Lance Corporal Steven M. Chavez USMC
Born: 21 November 1986
Killed in Action: 14 March 2007

■　■　■

Corporal Andrew W. Marrari USMC
Born: 26 August 1985
Died: 3 December 2009

■　■　■

Corporal Simon R. Litke USMC
Born: 27 December 1984
Died: 2 November 2015

CONTENTS

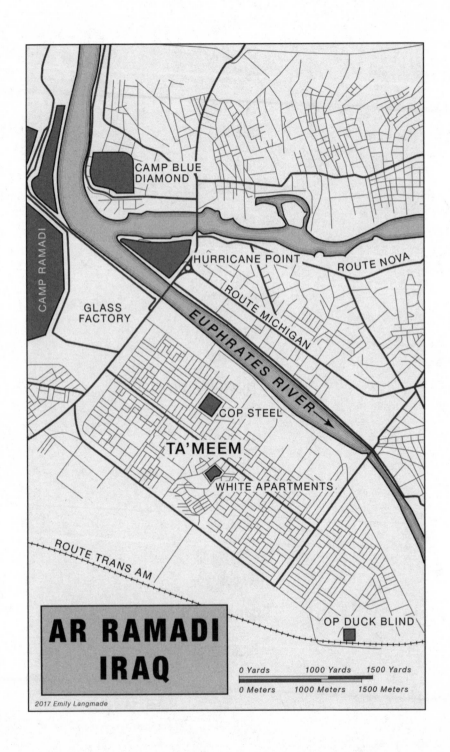

CAMP BLUE DIAMOND

CAMP RAMADI

GLASS FACTORY

HURRICANE POINT

ROUTE NOVA

ROUTE MICHIGAN

EUPHRATES RIVER →

COP STEEL

TA'MEEM

WHITE APARTMENTS

ROUTE TRANS AM

OP DUCK BLIND

AR RAMADI
IRAQ

| 0 Yards | 1000 Yards | 1500 Yards |
| 0 Meters | 1000 Meters | 1500 Meters |

2017 Emily Langmade

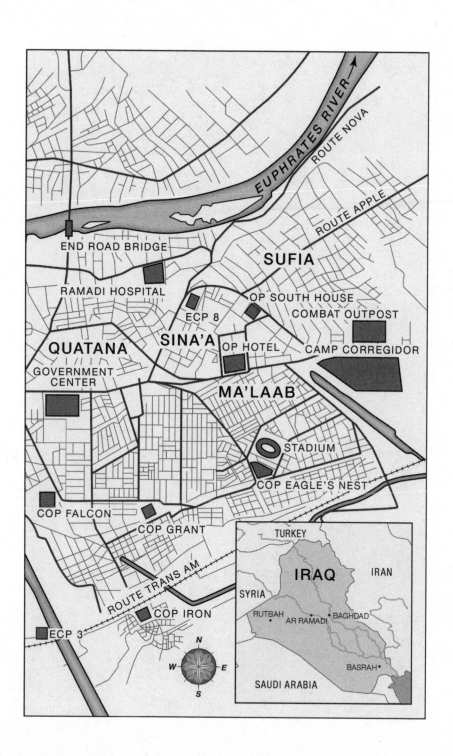

Foreword

Major General James E. Livingston, USMC (Retired), Medal of Honor Recipient

Major Scott Huesing has written a book not just about Marines in combat, but also about life as a Marine in my old command: Echo Company, Second Battalion, Fourth Marine Regiment. The narrative comes through clear and concise, and exposes the reader to the collective boredom of warfare, punctuated by moments of sheer terror that these young Marines, soldiers, and sailors endured during the second battle of Ramadi.

As a combat Marine officer and leader of warriors, I endorse this book for many reasons, not the least of which is the honest, paternalistic approach taken by the author as he details the heroism, suffering, and collective brotherhood of those Marines and sailors under his leadership.

This is a solid work written by a warrior who was there in command, which is always the best approach to writing such literary works. What I found most impressive was his clearly demonstrated admiration for his subordinates, those who carried the burden of fighting, some wounded, and others killed in action, while neglecting to mention his own valor.

Prologue

War was not an oriflamme adventure filled with noble deeds
and tilts with destiny, as believed, but a vast, uncaring universe
of butchery and attrition, in which the imaginative, the sensitive
were crippled and corrupted, the vulgar and tough-fibered aug-
mented—and the lucky were lucky and survived, and they alone.

—*Anton Myrer,* Once an Eagle

I used to think about the medals and ribbons and parades when I was a young Marine and how they were a measure of one's success. Ten deployments and multiple combat tours later, I no longer did.

In Ramadi, none of that meant shit to me.

The United States Marine Corps had seemed romantic—blue dress uniforms, shiny medals, the bumper stickers, and the Hollywood movies that glamorized war. I joined in 1989, enlisting on the advice of a high school friend who did it on a whim. I had just turned nineteen. Not having college prospects on the horizon, it seemed the right thing to do at the time. I didn't really know anything about the Marine Corps or what I was getting myself into.

It wasn't like Hollywood depictions. Within a year of enlisting, Operations Desert Shield and Desert Storm were under way. I was scheduled to deploy to the Middle East with my unit in January 1991.

After we received orders to fight in Operation Desert Storm, everybody took a week or two to spend with their families. I went home to Illinois. My mother drove me to the airport and walked me all the way to the gate ready to send her youngest son to war. Back then, there were no security checkpoints and no such thing as the Transportation Security Agency.

My mom was worried just like any other mother. She cried, but then again, she was a crier. She was always emotional, but now with the thought of her son going off to war, it hit her very hard. I remained tough and hugged her tightly as she sent me to the gate, knowing how hard it was for her, but deep inside I was excited to go because I was finally getting what every U.S. Marine is trained for—war.

My unit flew from North Carolina to Saudi Arabia on a big white commercial jet. We weren't in first-class seating, but the flight attendants treated us as if we were.

The flight took almost twenty hours. When the plane landed, we grabbed our gear and rifles and walked down the set of stairs that had been pushed up to the plane.

We stood on the tarmac in a large military formation in our "chocolate-chip" desert uniforms. A gunnery sergeant walked through it, handing each of us five little brown cardboard boxes, each containing twenty rounds of live 5.56mm ammunition to put in the 30-round magazines for our M16-A2 rifles. Very administrative and procedural— and very different from what I imagined landing in a war zone would be.

For the next several months, we set up camp, did our jobs, stood post, burned barrels of human shit with a blend of gasoline and diesel fuel, filled sandbags, cleaned weapons, and all the other monotonous tasks needed to maintain our position.

We were preparing for war, too.

We thought it would be a magnificent battle—and we were all very excited to fight. In the meantime, we waited.

We played endless games of Spades to fill our time in between the mundane day-to-day tasks. The arrival of care packages was another relief from the monotony.

I remember each one of those small, white cardboard boxes addressed to *"Any Service Member."* I can still smell the Corn Nuts snacks that filled them and the scent of crayons on the letters written from grade school kids packed inside.

Occasionally there were some enemy rocket attacks—SCUD missiles that hit close to our camp a couple of times. One night the shrapnel from the impact of a missile shredded the tent where we ate chow. Luckily, no one was in it at the time.

It was, however, the first time I experienced enemy fire.

The whining of the SCUD alarm sounded. It was an old firehouse siren with a crank handle on it, but it was loud enough for everyone to hear. Most took shelter, or were directed to, in one of the bunkers that were nothing more than massive holes covered on top by metal engineer stakes, plywood, and sandbags stacked two or three high. I thought they would be death traps if a missile hit one, so I took my chances in one of the fighting positions that our heavy machine guns occupied.

Although it wasn't close combat with the Iraqi Army—no blazing gunfire, it was still very new and thrilling to me. But not everyone was like me.

Some Marines were terrified. Some actually cried. Most just waited it out with little show of emotion.

When the air campaign commenced, and Desert Storm officially began, I was on post, manning a Browning M2 .50 caliber machine gun. I watched in awe as more than one hundred coalition aircraft took off from Shaikh Isa Air Base out of Bahrain.

It was a magnificent sight watching and listening to the planes scream over my position, knowing that they were about to deliver their deadly ordnance against Saddam's Iraqi Army.

Romantic.

At least it was to a young lance corporal.

My unit fought during that war and did its part, but it was over very quickly—just over four months. Honestly, it was a very forgettable experience for me in comparison with my future combat deployments. Nonetheless, I was proud of what we accomplished, and I still keep in touch with some of the Marines with whom I served.

■   ■   ■

Fifteen years later, I was in command of Echo Company, 2d Battalion, 4th Marines, deployed to Ramadi, Iraq. It was the third year of Operation

Iraqi Freedom, and my command was assigned to the U.S. Army's 1st Brigade Combat Team (1-BCT) "The Ready First" which consisted of the largest armor and infantry alignment in modern warfare. I worked directly for Task Force 1-9 Infantry Battalion (TF 1-9 IN) "Manchu" under the command of Lieutenant Colonel Chuck Ferry, U.S. Army.

During this nearly nine-month deployment (our mission: kill or capture Anti-Iraqi Forces [AIF]), Echo Company stood in the line of fire daily in Ramadi—the most dangerous and most densely populated area of insurgent activity in 2006. It would test us and would take the best of us.

I do not want to boast Echo Company was the most badass company of Marines ever to walk a battlefield, or that we endured the most pain. Many other units were plenty tough and endured an equal level of pain and loss, if not more than we did.

What Echo Company and our U.S. Army brothers accomplished in such a short amount of time made a difference in the most dangerous area in Iraq, and it certainly made a difference to the Marines who fought.

Echo in Ramadi is not a story about my time as a Marine or an infantry company commander, or the job I did when I was privileged to lead some of the best men I have ever known. I think I will admit more than most that I am quite sure I had more than my share of fuck-ups and tough decisions to make.

This story is about—and for—the warriors of Echo Company, 2d Battalion, 4th Marines, and their families. It is their voices that tell of the battles we fought, the relationships we shared, and the pain we still bear today. It is a tribute to them—to those that are gone, those who served, and those who continue the fight today.

During our time in Iraq, we didn't think about war movies, parades, and shiny medals.

All I thought about was bringing my Marines home alive.

CHAPTER 1

Phone Call

When I lost my first Marine in Echo Company, I was thirty-six years old. We'd been battling in Ramadi, Iraq, in support of Operation Iraqi Freedom in 2006. Echo Company was made up of 248 men. But they were my men. Each of them was my watch, my responsibility. I trained them hard hoping that it would protect each and every one of them from the dangers of combat. I knew it was impossible in reality. I knew in my head that Ramadi was a dangerous place. I had prepared myself for the inevitability of losing Marines—or at least I thought I had. Now one had died, and it felt like a part of me had gone missing.

Corporal Dustin Libby—twenty-two years old from Maine—had taken a fatal bullet during a grueling four-hour firefight in Ramadi. He had died fighting to protect his platoon. Our Company. My Company.

■　　■　　■

Libby's death hit me hard. It was almost incomprehensible to me to think about it. There was so much chaos that night. His death stunned us all, and when we heard the official report—the blur of fighting throughout the dark hours had distracted us from expressing any real emotions. But as the morning came, so did the reality that Libby was gone.

■　　■　　■

I was stationed at Camp Pendleton in Oceanside, California, when I met Libby before shoving off to Iraq. I was living in my office at the battalion command post and Libby, like the rest of the single Marines, was at the Bachelor Enlisted Quarters.

They tell us from day one as an officer that we should never have favorites, or at least not show that we have preferences in our unit. But I would be lying if I said Corporal Libby wasn't one of my favorites. He was one of many, I suppose.

He had a cool, nonchalant attitude about him, yet he exuded confidence well above his years. Libby was as even-tempered as they came. He wasn't timid in any endeavor—this included engaging his superiors in conversation.

I showed up at the barracks late one evening. Libby stood on the catwalk leaning against the metal railing. He was a good-looking kid with blonde hair—wiry 160 pounds at five-ten. He was shirtless. I read the Old English style letters "USMC" tattooed across his stomach, about four inches and centered above his belly button. Tattoos were badges of pride that many Marines wore.

I had none.

I'd come close on a couple of occasions as a lance corporal—drunk and waving a fistful of cash at a local tattoo artist in Oceanside and both times denied service.

Libby politely struck up a conversation as I approached his room. Like British royalty asking me to sit down for tea, he had a beer at the ready and asked if I would care for one. I didn't decline.

It was times like those that my relationship with Libby developed. From then on, I always counted on his honesty, opinions, and loyalty to the Marines he led. His force of personality was something that made Libby indispensable to the men of his squad and made his leaders depend on him. When rounds are flying, they don't distinguish between rank, age, color, or religion—Libby understood this intrinsically. We were all brothers thrust into the chasm, and we took care of each other better than anyone else we've ever known.

■   ■   ■

On that fateful night, Lance Corporals Jonathan Neris, Christopher Muscle, Jonathan Yenglin, and Hospitalman Nate "Doc" Dicks, sat with Corporal Libby in their room at Entry Control Point (ECP) 8, their battle position in the heart of central Ramadi. They were bullshitting and cracking jokes at each other's expense like most Marines do to kill time. Libby regaled his men with excerpts and quotes from his favorite movies, *Hang 'Em High* and *The Boondock Saints*. They were interrupted when gunfire snapped against the walls. Their adrenaline surged.

Fourth Platoon was completely engaged in one of the most complex attacks we'd faced to date. They raced to the rooftop. A blaze of intense small arms fire lit the air. Deafening bursts from machine guns made it impossible to communicate. The battle raged on, and the Marines fought side by side. Neris caught Libby out of the corner of his eye. He heard Libby say, "I'm reloading my M-203." But then Libby didn't come back up. He looked down and saw that Libby had fallen.

With rounds still smacking the walls of ECP 8, Neris took a knee in the middle of the roof. Tears came down his face, his chest heaved, and he tried to stifle the short audible gasps. He didn't want his squad to see him cry.

As the firefight wound down in the early morning hours, every Marine in 4th Platoon found out about the loss of Libby and began to feel it. The next day, I carried their pain and mine, and I moved about numb and willing myself to not break down. I couldn't because my Marines were looking to me for strength.

■   ■   ■

There is a formal process in the Marine Corps called the Casualty Assistance Calls Program (CACP). Select Marines—Casualty Assistance

Calls Officers (CACOs)—have the unenviable job and the immense responsibility of being the first to officially notify family members of Marines killed in action (KIA). They arrive in formal blue dress uniforms and knock on front doors of family members, bearing the worst news anyone could ever get—or ever give. The CACO process had already been completed for Corporal Libby when I began to put pen to paper and started writing my letters of condolence to his mother, Geni, and his father, Judd.

Marine Corps officers get a minuscule amount of training on how to properly approach family members about the loss of their son or daughter. Normally, "training" involves a class or two with a homework assignment of writing a fictional letter. I've got a news flash—no class can teach the right protocol. To find the right words in real life is near impossible. Emotions run rampant at the death of a Marine who, hours before, stood next to you, fought beside you, was someone you knew at a personal level—someone who became your brother—someone who would have died for you.

But I knew I couldn't just write Libby's parents a canned letter of condolence.

He deserved better. His parents deserved a phone call.

■　　■　　■

In terms of time, Ramadi is eight hours ahead of Castle Hill, Maine, so it wasn't until late that night that I was able to call Libby's family via an Iridium satellite cell phone.

Everyone from the Echo Company headquarters staff was in the Tactical Operations Center (TOC) in our little corner of the battalion command center planning space. I told First Sergeant Thom Foster that I had to step out to make a phone call.

He looked at me with a face lined with deep wrinkles. Those around his mouth were set and grim. In a quiet voice, he said, "Take all the time you need, sir. I have everything covered for a while."

Outside the TOC, darkness engulfed the area. Within the confines of Camp Corregidor, AM General High Mobility Multi-Purpose Wheeled Vehicles (HMMWVs—also known as Humvees), generators, and pallets of supplies were laid out in no particular fashion. The M1-A1 tanks, however, were lined up in a nice neat row, twenty deep.

I found a place out of view from the soldiers and Marines. A Humvee sat parked in the shadows behind the TOC, so I set my helmet on the hood then placed my satellite phone next to it. Despite the cool night air, when I ripped open the Velcro closure on my body armor, musty steam instantly escaped. I rifled through my breast pocket. The dialing instructions for the phone and my CACO sheet with family notification phone numbers sat tucked inside.

I turned on the small red-lens Petzl helmet light strapped to my Kevlar so I could read the information. The papers were damp from my sweat, and I pushed the tiny power button of the phone on. The keypad and screen lit up with a greenish glow. My stomach began to knot tight as I dialed the number for Libby's mom.

As the phone rang, my throat tightened from nerves as a hundred thoughts of how this speech was going to sound ran through my head. I thought for sure she wouldn't even want to talk to me. I had no idea what to say to a mother who had lost her son. I thought that surely everything I had to say would sound so canned and insincere as if I was reading off a pre-written government script.

On the fifth ring, a frail-sounding, sweet voice came on the line. "Hello."

Geni Libby. Corporal Dustin Libby's mother.

I introduced myself. "Mrs. Libby, this is Captain Scott Huesing, your son's company commander and…"

My voice began to crack. I had to take a moment and find the words.

"…I can't tell you how truly sorry I am at the loss of Dustin."

Tears came quickly to my eyes, and a lump rose in my throat as I uttered that first sentence. I had not felt that afraid to speak since I was a child and endured that uncontrollable terror of having to tell the truth after something bad happened—I struggled with it.

I tried to imagine what Geni looked like as I spoke. I wondered what she was doing and if her family was around her at the time. I didn't expect it to be so hard, and I tried to hold back the pain, but I couldn't seem to get a grasp of my emotions. I knew she could hear it in my voice.

As the conversation continued, I tried evading some of her questions, but she pressed me for specific details about that night. She already knew that he had died from a single gunshot wound to the neck, having been told this by the CACO.

I gently tried to explain the events, including how I was in the Tactical Operations Center at Camp Corregidor when the call for the casualty evacuation (CASEVAC) came across the radio as we raced to her son's aid.

I told her that Dustin had fought bravely in the face of a tough, well-organized enemy, and that his actions saved the lives of countless Marines in his platoon before he was wounded. I told her how we rushed Dustin to the battalion aid station at the Combat Outpost in my Humvee.

"Thank you for telling me the truth," she said.

"Dustin meant a lot to me," I said. "He was truly one of my favorites in Echo Company. I know there isn't anything he wouldn't do for his Marines."

Geni was silent for a moment. "Dustin loved being a Marine more than anything. I'll pray for your continued safety. Please continue fighting."

I told her we'd stay safe and that Dustin would be with us in spirit as we continued our mission. "He won't be forgotten. He didn't give his life in vain."

We spoke for several minutes more, and she kept telling me how proud she was of all of us and they'd be thinking of us and praying for us.

She thanked me for calling.

She was thanking me?

Tears spilled freely down my face, through the layers of dust, as I listened to Geni's soothing voice speak to me not as a Marine or Commander, but as a mother would to any son. It was humbling beyond words. I felt cared for so much by this lady whom I'd never even met. A sense of relief, compassion, and forgiveness came over me all at once. My breath began to come back to me as I felt the love she had for her son and for all of us fighting in that miserable place.

She passed the phone to Chris, Dustin's older brother. I told him that his brother was a warrior who took it to the enemy that night and how all of the Marines in Echo Company were proud at how fiercely Dustin fought.

After we spoke, Geni came back to the phone. "If there's anything that you and the boys need, you just let us know. We love all of you, and we're proud of all of you back here."

Geni, in all of her pain, and as only a mother can, knew how hard it was for me to make that phone call. In her compassionate way, she thanked me again.

Where do people like this come from?

They're not ordinary people—they're extraordinary.

They lose so much, yet can still care so deeply for others like me and the hundreds of others that Libby died protecting that night. I was—and remain—in awe of the strength she possessed.

It wasn't any easier when I spoke to his father who lived apart from Libby's mother. When I finished, I pressed the red button on the Iridium and the phone shut off.

I felt as if someone had rammed a stake through the middle of my chest. My heart was straining to beat. I took short, painful breaths, exhaling through my nose as I folded up the papers and shoved them back into my left breast pocket.

As I fastened my body armor back together, I scanned the area to make sure no one had been watching or eavesdropping on my conversation during my brief moment of weakness. I always wanted to be emotionally steady in front of the Marines.

I wiped my hands down the front of my cargo pants to clean them off and then pressed the heels of both palms hard into my eyes to repress the swelling from the tears that had been pooling there for the past half hour.

As I gathered myself back up, I walked back toward the entrance of the TOC, to the Echo Company office. It was almost pitch black. Only a few streams of artificial light peeked out of the buildings around me to illuminate the area. Even though I carefully navigated the darkened pathway, I tripped and ripped open my shin on a sharp metal tent stake jammed into the ground for no apparent reason.

"Great! Being fucked up like this isn't enough; this is just what I need!" I wanted to yell. At least, for an instant, the bleeding gash in my leg took my mind off the emotional hole in my heart.

I walked back into the Company Operations Center and put the satellite phone into its case and tucked it away. As I did, the eyes of every soldier and Marine in the TOC were on me. Everyone in that room knew where I had been. No one wished they had been in my boots.

I told Foster the call was the toughest thing I ever had to do. He pursed his lips and nodded—silently expressing a sober understanding of what I had just endured. Unfortunately, it wouldn't be the last time I'd go through that experience during our deployment.

19 December 2006

Geni mailed me a letter. It wasn't until late January 2007 that I received it. The words she wrote eased my heavy heart and at the same time reaffirmed my resolve to keep fighting. To keep the boys together. To win.

Cpt. Scott Heusing,

I am Cpl Dustin Libby's mother

Thank-you very much for calling me. It must be very hard making those calls. Dustin told me how bad it is there.

The Marines helped us give him a funeral with full millitary honors. We had Dustin cremated (it was what he wanted) and we are going to sprinkle his ashes on a little mountain he grew up climbing and playing on, next spring. The Marines are coming back then and have a little ceremony on the mountain. May God bless you and keep you safe.

Sincerely,

Geni Libby

CHAPTER 2

Lieutenants

The story of Echo Company in Ramadi is a series of instances of collective discipline, life-saving vigilance, ceaseless patience, depthless love, and steady resolve demonstrated daily by young men of the strongest character.

Among those young men were the lieutenants in my company. It was their leadership that was the difference between life and death on most days. They were lucky, though. They had some of the best and most seasoned senior enlisted Marines by their sides to guide them along the way.

■ ■ ■

Within the Marine Corps—and across all branches of the military—the Infantry Officer Course in Quantico, Virginia, is acknowledged as one of the toughest schools.

It is a grueling thirteen weeks of patrolling, offensive and defensive tactics, marksmanship, hiking, and drilling designed to push students past their physical and mental limits. The lieutenants going through IOC will never be as hot or as cold, as tired or as hungry, or as fatigued in combat as they are in training. Only select few make it into IOC, and not everyone makes it out. That is by design. The Marine Corps entrusts only the very best to command our nation's finest.

■   ■   ■

I was a captain in Twentynine Palms, California, when I got the first chance to meet the lieutenants who had orders to Echo Company—they'd been flown to Twentynine Palms to conduct desert training. My good friend, Major Martin "Crawdad" Wetterauer, was the director of the Infantry Officer's Course. I called him up to let him know that I'd be stopping by the training area—our old stomping grounds—to meet them.

Marty was a "mustang," like me—we'd been enlisted Marines before receiving our commissions. I served as his company executive officer in Lima Company, 3d Battalion, 4th Marines, in 2001 at the Marine Corps Air-Ground Combat Center in the high desert. Marty taught me a lot about leadership, even though I had to decipher his teachings through his thick, Louisiana drawl—his relentless methods shaped how I led and pushed my lieutenants.

My lieutenants were in their final stages of IOC when I was introduced to them. Their squad advisor, Captain Brian Chontosh, escorted John McLaughlin, Jay Grillo, Pete Somerville, and Seth Nicholson over and introduced them to me. They looked beat up. From the looks of their tired, gaunt, sweaty, and begrimed faces as they stood in front of me, the Infantry Officer Course was obviously still the unrelenting bastion it had always been.

But behind the grime and sweat that covered their faces, there was excitement in their eyes. They had that fire that all new lieutenants have. They were ready to lead. They had spent a year of their lives in Quantico, preparing for the chance to step in front of a rifle platoon as its commander.

During IOC or under my command, I made them train as if it were the last day.

They undoubtedly had heard a lot about being an officer at The Basic School—that training period that all Marine officers go through at the start of their careers—and IOC. But I was their commander; I had my own philosophy, and I made them listen.

I told them, "There is no such thing as combat leadership—just leadership."

I never subscribed to the idea that because one had been in combat, shot at, or injured it made them a better leader. Leaders lead in any condition, although some shine a little brighter under chaotic conditions—real leaders control the situation even in the absence of chaos. Training for restlessness and boredom is not a mission-essential task, but something a good leader has to deal with to keep Marines sharp when the madness begins.

All infantry lieutenants have received phenomenal training and gone through rigorous mental preparation before they enter the operational forces. What they tend to lack is a fundamental understanding of the magnitude of their responsibilities that only combat can prove to cure.

My lieutenants were keenly aware they lacked experience, but tried to make up for it by bulldozing through the friction when presented with tough decisions. I doubt any of them would admit it, but this amateurish mindset was wholly absent from the essence of what it meant to lead Marines. It is a lesson that I like to think I set by example.

My lieutenants were young, around twenty-four years old when they came to Echo Company. It was evident to them that I had a passion for the Marine Corps. I had a visceral excitement about being a Marine and I never tried to mask my enthusiasm, and it probably intimidated them a bit.

I required more of my lieutenants than anyone else because that is what's needed to be a Marine officer. I never let them forget that. Like most young Marines, they enjoyed their time off. But I infringed on it on occasion. They would have rather been on the beach in southern California, or out romancing the girls, or spending time with their families. Yet they knew that it was a necessity within our shared vocation.

Like most things in the Marine Corps, our timeline was very compressed, especially within a Marine Expeditionary Unit (MEU). It wasn't uncommon for me to call my lieutenants on their days off to talk about the Marines, or have them come in on a Sunday to work on our standard operating procedures as a helicopter-borne company.

I insisted they visit the Marines at the barracks on the weekends to see how they lived—those who stayed around and who didn't go on liberty—and try to connect with them. As a former enlisted Marine, I knew that officers who really cared, or at least made an effort to care, were the ones you could trust.

During their training period, I impressed upon them the importance of what good officers do. There were a few bad examples of what "*wrong*" looked like throughout my career insofar as leadership went. I never wanted to be "*that guy*" to my lieutenants or my Marines.

It was always the little things that mattered the most, and I wanted my officers to understand what a difference they could make. Never intending to portray myself in the image of a Marine poster boy, I'm the first to admit that I was no Boy Scout, but I tried to lead by example.

I was usually at the barracks on the weekends and at night (probably much to the chagrin of the boys at times) to check on them. In training or combat, I was always right there with them. If there were sandbags to fill, I had a shovel in my hand. If there was shit to move, I moved it, and shoveled it on occasion, right alongside the Marines.

If there was a patrol, I was on it.

If there was a firefight, I was in it.

I never subscribed to the notion or adage that, "*Officers need to know their place*," suggesting that officers shouldn't be seen doing menial tasks only enlisted Marines would have to do. I was part of a team—my place was always with my Marines doing what they were doing.

Period.

I explained to my lieutenants, "Every infantry officer is expected to know how to lead a platoon. I know you can lead a platoon. That's what IOC produced. My job is not to train you how to be platoon commanders. My job is to teach you how to be company commanders."

They were probably shocked to hear this, and some may have falsely assumed that IOC gave them their learner's permit and I would be the one handing them the keys to the car along the way. That wasn't the case. I expected them to be able to drive in the fast lane when they showed up.

They all had different personalities, but all had one thing in common. They were so enamored with the guts and glory aspects of what being an infantry officer should be—they shunned the other mundane but essential tasks of being officers.

Like most, they did not enjoy tasks like writing fitness reports, preparing page after page of operations orders, creating PowerPoint briefs, the relentless bureaucracy of the awards system, and all the other administrative headaches they neither understood nor appreciated.

I was proud of my ability to excel, not just in spite of the minutiae we all coped with, but also because of it. I learned early on from my mentors that it is easy to be good at your main job, but excelling at the collateral duties young officers are assigned is what sets you apart from the pack.

Honing communication skills, learning to write with clarity, serving as something like the voting officer, recognizing a Marine's accomplishments through awards and acknowledgment—these were the sort of "little things" that made the difference.

Put another way, they saw the bureaucratic aspect of the Marine Corps as a nuisance. I saw it as a channel through which I properly took care of my Marines.

An example of this came in late December 2006 in western Ramadi.

■   ■   ■

We had just ended a long clearance operation during which we didn't sleep or eat much, even by Marine Corps standards. We were under a tight timeline to clear a part of the city, and we pushed hard, at times working twenty hours a day straight. It was mentally draining and physically exhausting work.

After a long push, I'd pull my Kevlar helmet off and could feel the top of my head throbbing from its weight that had dug into my skull. I scratched my hair for some relief.

I cursed my helmet often.

At the conclusion of this and similar operations, the immediate reflex is to take care of yourself—get some sleep, take a shower, find food, or just decompress at the firm base.

We weren't back for more than an hour or so when I called for all of the lieutenants to come to the company office. It was a metal cargo box on the back of a dilapidated U.S. Army 7-ton truck parked outside of the Task Force 1-77 Armor Battalion (TF-1-77 AR) command post at Camp Ramadi.

When they arrived, I told them that the commander of the task force had given us the opportunity to recognize our Marines who had been fighting in his unit's battlespace for weeks by awarding them medals—called "impact awards" that are presented for actions during specific time periods of meritorious action and valor. The catch was that we—that is to say, they—needed to write the award citations. Furthermore, they had to be done immediately so the task force could approve them the next day. I did not want to miss any chance to recognize the Marines.

They were tired, hungry, and filthy, but I ordered them to sit down at the computers and start writing out the citations for deserving Marines.

For the next few hours, I made them work on the citations until they delivered acceptable products.

I returned draft after draft to them saying, "These need to be better, cleaner. These are *your* Marines. Don't give anyone a reason to deny your Marines the recognition they earned."

I sensed the resentment for being so strict about something the lieutenants thought others should have to do. I'm quite sure they were under the impression that there were little award fairies who typed these things up and sent them to some magical place from which shiny medals and colorful ribbons and proper award citations then appeared.

I am quite sure they were thinking, "Why the fuck are we doing this? Isn't this what administration Marines do? We're warfighters. Admin is bullshit!"

The fact is, good officers do the right things for their Marines. Making sure Marines were recognized for their actions was the right thing to do. In the end, their hard work paid off and we got the citations in on time, and my lieutenants and I pinned Army Achievement and Commendation Medals on fourteen Marines in our company. My officers saw how their jobs as leaders were not limited to leading their men on the battlefield.

Each lieutenant had his strengths, but each still had a lot to learn about the gravity of his responsibilities. Their leadership development was vital to the success of the company.

■　　■　　■

Ever since Second Lieutenant John McLaughlin was a child, he fantasized about the military. He didn't know that he would be a Marine, but he did know that he would serve the military in some capacity.

The advertised culture of the Marine Corps is what drew him to it. The more he learned about the Corps, the more he desired to earn the title of U.S. Marine. The more closely he followed the news of the burgeoning stages of the wars in Iraq and Afghanistan, the more he realized he had to contribute as much as the Marines who were serving.

McLaughlin was oblivious as he watched the Middle East conflicts unfold, not realizing that many of the young men whom he admired and wanted to emulate would soon be under his charge.

McLaughlin imagined that his first platoon would be an experienced group of guys. Subordinates, yes, but only in rank and billet. Trusting the guys who had been in for a while was a tenet of leadership that would be unchallenged. For the Marines of Echo Company, the term *"experienced"* was never thrown around loosely.

About fifty of the Marines in the company had experienced a grueling deployment to Ramadi in 2004. During that mission, Echo Company and the battalion as a whole sadly amassed a casualty count that would be rivaled by few other units during the War on Terror.

When he received his commission as an officer in the Marine Corps from the U.S. Naval Academy, the war in Iraq was already more than two years old. McLaughlin didn't know what to expect, but by the way the news portrayed the war, he anticipated an incessantly kinetic environment in which both he and his Marines would perform superhuman acts in the face of certain death on a daily basis.

Certainly, the combat that Echo Company experienced was frequent, intense, and probably quite similar to what thousands of other operators on the ground experienced during their time in Iraq. Nonetheless, it was not a constant. In fact, the experience of Ramadi could be best described as periods of extreme boredom punctuated by episodes of inexplicable chaos.

McLaughlin was twenty-four years old. He stood six-two, physically fit, with broad shoulders. His short, cropped hair was dark brown and he wore a smile on his face even when things were at their worst. He spoke with a thick, muddled New York accent, like a cab driver from Long Island. His voice was deep and fitting for his size, but I could always hear traces of the innocuous kid within it. He was confident about everything but humble. He knew he had as much to learn about following as he did about leading—it was one of his most admirable qualities.

While he never diminished the sacrifice, diligence, and courageousness of the Marines of Echo Company, McLaughlin never boasted that his platoon or the company had experienced more combat than any other unit. His accomplishments in Ramadi gave him a professional education like no other, and rid him of any inaccurate preconceptions of service in the Marines, and helped him grow as an officer. He found quickly that being boisterous about what Marines endured in war was reckless and it was immature to make trite comparisons of death, destruction, and wildness.

■   ■   ■

Most Marine units are given definitive timelines and are assigned to specific areas of operation well before they deploy to a combat zone. This deployment was one plagued by uncertainty and continual extensions. Living aboard the USS *Boxer*, it seemed as if we floated around aimlessly. We didn't find out where we'd end up. We didn't know how long we would be there. We didn't know when we would go. We were only told to "Be Prepared."

The USS *Boxer* (LHD-4) was a 40,000-ton Wasp Class amphibious assault ship—an eight-hundred-foot-long mini-aircraft carrier with more than forty helicopters and airplanes from which the Marines launched operations. Nearly two thousand Marines and sailors lived inside the large vessel. It was one of the several ships in the Expeditionary Strike Group (ESG) that sailed together out of San Diego to the Middle East.

Platoon commanders had to get to know the Marines. Beyond their likes and dislikes, they became intimately acquainted with who they were, the commonalities shared, and the differences they had. The tight confines of the ship made becoming familiar much easier.

Over the course of several months, McLaughlin came to understand that the Marines who had been in combat before were different than the rest of the men in his platoon. They had an intangible grit to them, and something that exacted respect. It wasn't necessarily synonymous with maturity. He couldn't exactly put his finger on it, but he believed it was something that could only be possessed by young people who have both lived amongst—and caused—unnatural death for an extended period.

After McLaughlin had received official word from me that we were getting called forward to reinforce a U.S. Army unit in Ramadi, he experienced what he later described as "a scared giddiness" to share the news with his platoon.

McLaughlin got his platoon together in the berthing spaces and told them everything I had briefed him on. Knowing the system by then, McLaughlin would never take full credit for breaking the news to them. The ubiquitous *"Lance Corporal Underground,"* a rumor mill that spread faster than wildfire, tended to beat anyone to the punch every time, and it certainly did in this case.

They still talked about it, though, as a platoon. As vividly as anything else that had ever happened in McLaughlin's life, he quickly learned that the area that Echo Company would be operating in was the same exact place where his combat-experienced Marines had deployed two years prior. He listened intently to his platoon's Ramadi veterans.

Some appeared detached from the discussion. Others spoke with a level of detail he'd never heard before. It wasn't their eloquence but the palpable emotion behind every fact they stated that made everything seem more real.

McLaughlin, like many other lieutenants, would lose Marines during his time in combat. He thought about the Marines who paid the ultimate sacrifice. He thought about the other Marines in the platoon and how much those incredible young men meant to each other.

Combat is a very real thing, but the severity of it has a tendency to escape you if you are not being shot at, and mortared, or whatever else. The repetitiveness and the boredom, the chaos and the horror seemingly don't exist. But they do—and they are never more real than at those moments when you look the parents of a young Marine in the eye and express your sympathies for the death of their son, the young man who was ultimately your responsibility.

■　　■　　■

McLaughlin braced for the shock of what he imagined his first war would be like as we drew nearer to Ramadi—many of the other Marines did as well. Their training was sound, but even the most demanding training can never fully prepare anyone for the full force of war's impact or teach how to react to it.

Echo Company's seven-month deployment would ultimately turn into almost nine—extended twice by our higher command—a psychological kick in the sack for all of us. But we endured for over two hundred fifty days.

For most, they would be the most important months they ever lived.

CHAPTER 3

Movement

It is not easy to kill another human being. Not for anyone—no matter how it is portrayed in fiction, on television, or in movies. There is nothing romantic or cavalier about it. It is horrific. Life-changing. Killing is what happens, and Marines are trained to kill. But in war, destruction is everywhere. It eats everything around you. Sometimes it eats at you.

Killing is an unnatural act.

It starts with the enemy fixed in the scope. The breathing is controlled, but the heart races, muscles tense, and eyes adjust sharply. Slowly, deliberately, the finger slips onto the trigger of the rifle and then presses smoothly. A piercing crack. The gentle recoil. The small bullet, no bigger than the tip of a pencil, crosses space in an instant. It penetrates flesh and tears through the body. As the small projectile searches for the path of least resistance to exit the body, it shatters bone, explodes organs, severs veins and arteries. Crushed and mangled inside, the enemy falls. With a small, seemingly simple movement, executing one conscious decision—it is then you know you have killed.

Marines are masters of their art—but they do it not only with lethality, but also with honor, knowing that they are fighting for a greater purpose.

8 November 2006

When the USS *Boxer* Expeditionary Strike Group moved into the Arabian Sea, it 'chopped'—that is, it came under the control of—the U.S. Navy's 5th Fleet, headquartered in Bahrain. The amphibious warships then pushed north through the Straits of Hormuz and into the Persian Gulf. Two days later, on the 231st birthday of the Marine Corps, the 15th MEU Commanding Officer, Colonel Brian Beaudreault, stood on the *Boxer's* flight deck and announced to the hundreds of Marines and sailors gathered there that we'd be going into Iraq.

They responded to the news exuberantly.

I sensed an excitement from the new Marines, the ones who had never been in combat before. Many, I suppose, still harbored romantic notions of how combat was going to be—running into the blaze of battle, firing their M-16s, and annihilating an untrained, inferior enemy.

If that's what they were thinking, they'd know better soon enough. They were about to experience the intensity of combat and see death on a scale like they'd never imagined.

15 November 2006

Captain John Smith, the commander of Fox Company, 2d Battalion, 4th Marines, and I flew into Iraq after the colonel's announcement to get an idea of the environment in which we'd be operating. We landed at Camp Ramadi, and we waited for a ride from the brigade headquarters to Camp Corregidor to where we'd meet Lieutenant Colonel Chuck Ferry, U.S. Army, the commander of Task Force 1-9 Infantry.

At Camp Ramadi, a television was tuned to Fox News—hammering away with coverage of the war. A breaking story came across the air. The correspondent informed the viewers that the Marine Corps was deploying twenty-five hundred specially-trained warriors of the 15th Marine Expeditionary Unit to Al Anbar Province as part of the broader "surge strategy."

Smith and I looked at each other in disbelief. We had been told that our plans to flood the battlefield in places like Al-Anbar Province were secret.

"So much for Op-Sec," Smith said.

"Op-Sec" meant "operational security" steps taken to keep the enemy from knowing your force's composition, movements, and intentions.

I replied with appropriate eloquence, "Holy shit!"

The gall of the news media. Did they have any regard for the fact that what they announced to the world might affect our mission and our safety?

A surly, older-looking U.S. Army second lieutenant walked into the lobby. He was dressed out in full battle gear: helmet, body armor, and Army-style issued digital battle dress uniform. His M4 carbine rifle, covered in dust, dangled from his right shoulder from a D-Ring clip. His uniform's nametape read, "Peterson."

He spotted us and came over. "Excuse me, gentlemen. I am Lieutenant Peterson, and I'm supposed to be picking up some Marine, some Jack Ryan character. I'm expected to take him over to meet Lieutenant Colonel Ferry. Is that you?"

The derisive reference to the Tom Clancy novel series didn't strike me as funny.

I only responded, "Yeah, that's us. You ready to roll?"

He was.

Outside, a four-Humvee convoy awaited us with the engines running.

These were not like the Humvees Marines had. They were outfitted with the most up-to-date gear—high-powered radios, Raytheon GPS systems, Blue Force Tracker—small computer monitors that displayed high-speed digital moving maps that showed all of the friendly unit positions at all times, and electronic counter-measure devices meant to thwart remotely detonated roadside bombs or improvised explosive devices (IEDs). Armed with M240B 7.62mm and M2 .50 caliber machine guns, they were combat ready.

We drove what we would come to know as Route Trans Am, moving slowly, maybe five miles per hour, on the left-hand side of the road which had been cleared of IEDs. The vehicles bounced and rattled as we moved down the unimproved roads that were gutted with potholes and craters from mortar strikes and IEDs.

On the right-hand side of our Humvee's windshield, someone taped casualty evacuation (CASEVAC) procedures and call-for-fire (templated methods for calling in artillery and air strikes) like cheat-sheets for a pop-quiz, to the bulletproof glass, ready for immediate use. Additional tactical notes, written in black grease pencil, were scrawled on the glass. The radios chirped and beeped before and after the transmissions as they broadcast across the net.

It was a crisp, clear day. We could see that during its years of being the site of some of the most kinetic fighting in Iraq, Ramadi had been torn to shreds. Everywhere, there were piles of concrete rubble and garbage, bullet-pocked houses, and shattered remains of houses that barely stood. Some structures literally looked like "half-houses," as if someone had taken a giant sword and sliced diagonally from the top corner to the bottom corner—one part left standing, the other reduced to a pile of wreckage on the side of the yard.

Concrete barriers that were once used for counter-mobility were reduced into mounds of rubble on the roadsides from constant attacks—Ramadi looked like a vast wasteland from some post-apocalyptic fantasy novel.

The only intact structures were the mosques. I counted at least a dozen. Their minarets accented the cityscape which towered between thirty to fifty feet high—blue domes stood in stark contrast to a sea of gray and tan wreckage that was the capital city of Al Anbar Province.

The infrastructure was flattened. Telephone and electric wires dangled from bent poles that jutted from the ground at strange angles.

Nothing was green. Even the few surviving palm trees were covered with a film of gray dust kicked up by explosions and dust storms.

Peterson pointed out the Army checkpoints as we drove past. They were nothing more than dilapidated buildings reinforced with sandbags, concrete dividers, and HESCO barriers—square, collapsible, metal cages lined with cloth and filled to the top with sand that when interlinked, made an impenetrable wall. I could see the barrels of rifles and machine guns poking out of sandbagged windows.

As we pressed close to Camp Corregidor, our vehicles zigzagged through a maze of four-feet-high concrete barriers that were arrayed to slow down traffic as it approached checkpoints.

Our driver slammed on the brakes.

I said, "What's up? IED?" I thought the worst.

Peterson quickly looked over his shoulder at us. "No, sorry, just a dog."

I watched as a small brown dog padded past the truck and zipped into a house on the other side of the road, immune to the surrounding madness.

"Random," I thought.

■ ■ ■

We flew out of Ramadi the next day to Camp Al Asad. The Regimental Combat Team commander, Colonel W. Blake Crowe, welcomed me with a big handshake and bear hug. He had commanded my battalion when I was a first lieutenant stationed in Twentynine Palms in 2002. He then took me back to his office to examine a wall-sized map of the entire area of operations for which he was responsible.

After an hour with Colonel Crowe, he sent me to his intelligence section for more imagery (maps and satellite photos). Afterward, Smith and I went on our way to Al Taqqadum (*Tah Kay Dum* or TQ), where most of our unit already had been marshaled.

Smith and I boarded an Army UH-60 Blackhawk helicopter out of TQ and were joined by our battalion sergeant major, Joe Ellis.

Sergeant Major Ellis was the senior enlisted leader of 2d Battalion, 4th Marines. A consummate professional, he had dedicated twenty-three years of his life to one thing—the best interests of the Marines.

Ellis was a strack, clean-cut, model picture of a Marine. Lean and fit, he could outrun, out-hike, and out-smart most half his age, without question. He offered his opinions to commanders in a manner that was so goddamned honest and utterly unvarnished but never made you feel that he was talking down his nose to you.

I landed late that afternoon at TQ and linked up with my company staff who had set up a makeshift headquarters in one of the temporary staging tents. It was a large domed space. Cheap bunk beds lined the walls with no bedding. The thin mattresses still covered in plastic looked as though they'd never been slept on. We taped maps of Ramadi onto dry erase boards so that we could study them together.

Meanwhile, a good share of Echo Company had begun cleaning weapons and prepping their gear.

Others made their way to the Post Exchange to buy additional gear. There always is a small segment of Marines in any unit who can never have enough "Gucci Gear" that seemed to have a mental effect on their performance in the field. They love it—some are willing to spend almost half a paycheck on the stuff they think makes them more productive and comfortable than the Marines who stick with basic issue field gear from the battalion supply section. They bought extra kit to make their lives a little better for the upcoming months—small, finger-sized flashlights, custom Wiley-X eye protection, Storm Safe waterproof notebooks, beef jerky, Wet Ones baby wipes, permanent marker map pens, and whatever else caught their eye.

I wanted to speak to my Marines. On my orders, First Sergeant Foster, Echo Company's most senior NCO, gathered the entire company in formation on the sandy face of an old Iraqi Army ammunition bunker that stood forty feet high, arched with large steel doors for re-supply trucks to drive through to deliver ordnance. Most likely it had been filled for decades at some point with Soviet and Iraqi arsenals—small arms, artillery munitions, mortars, and rocket-propelled grenades.

Unsurprisingly, I overheard a high degree of bitching and moaning about the photo-op from the Marines. "What the fuck are we doing this for?" started it off, and the usual "You've got to be kidding me" rounded it out.

Despite the soliloquies of gripes and groans, every Marine wanted a copy of that photo the minute the camera clicked. They swarmed the photographer and handed their email addresses to him to get a copy.

It would be the last photo we all took together.

After the picture, they were restless but quieted down as I walked in front of them. Some took a seat and placed their rifles between their legs. I looked out into the sea of sturdy faces fixed on me. The majority of the Marines had shaved their hair down to the scalp—some ritualistic way of preparing for battle.

As my Marines fought in Al Anbar Province, I wanted the physical movement associated with killing to be instinctual. I never wanted them to hesitate when it mattered most or have them feel remorse for doing their duty. To do so, they needed to know that, in the end, I would bear the burden, the inescapable burden of command. I spoke in a forceful, confident tone and encompassed much of the advice I had accumulated over the years from my mentors.

"This is the first time in combat for most of you. You will have to fire your weapon at the enemy. You will have to kill. I don't expect that this will be easy for anyone. It shouldn't be. But know this. I am ordering you to kill. You will kill, and when this is all over it will be my responsibility. It will be my burden to carry because I am ordering you to do it. We are Marines, and we follow orders. You'll kill the enemy but you will leave this place without regret, and we will win. Is that understood?"

The senior NCOs nodded their heads in approval during my address. They knew everything I said to be true—having walked the same streets of Ramadi only twenty-four months ago.

■   ■   ■

22 November 2006

It was late in the evening when Echo Company, laden with gear, lined up and readied to fly into Camp Corregidor on a flight of the Army's big, twin-rotor Boeing CH-47 Chinook helicopters.

As we staged in our sticks and serials, neat rows of twelve and twenty-four Marines all lined up, First Sergeant Foster took special care to ensure complete accountability before embarkation on the impressive flight of Chinooks that landed in front of us.

Most Marines decide to enlist when they are in their late teens or early twenties. Foster was twenty-seven. He went to college and then bounced around from job to job. He worked construction, did a little pest extermination, and even managed a ski lodge in western Colorado. He never found his niche. He wanted something bigger. He wanted a purpose.

Foster's younger brother, Steve, was a U.S. Marine on recruiting duty in their hometown of Grand Junction, Colorado. Foster called and told him he was interested in joining.

His brother hung up on him.

Foster persisted. Eventually, like any good recruiter, Sergeant Steve Foster signed him up to enlist.

Foster spent his twenty-eighth birthday at Marine Corps Recruit Depot, San Diego, as a recruit with the aspirations of becoming a heavy equipment operator. Right before his graduation in July 1990, his drill instructor went down the roll call of their platoon and rattled off the Military Occupational Specialties (MOSs) to the new Marines.

When he came to Foster's name, he barked out, "Foster, 4421, legal specialist."

Since Foster shipped out for boot camp early, his brother had to fill a quota and re-assigned him while he was in training. Like many Marines, Foster now had a "How-My-Recruiter-Fucked-Me-Over" story. Unlike most of them, however, his recruiter was his brother—a tough story to beat.

Foster spent the next fifteen years as a legal clerk and legal chief before he was promoted to the rank of first sergeant. When promoted to first sergeant, a Marine is given a new MOS—8999—that makes him or her assignable to any unit, regardless of previous experience. This policy is designed to provide diversity based on seniority.

Foster was assigned to the infantry community. Aside from serving on a mobile training team in Iraq training soldiers for the Iraqi Army, Foster had no real experience with Marine Corps infantry.

He was given orders to 2d Battalion, 4th Marines, in 2006 and became my senior enlisted advisor. I had no bias to the fact he was new to the infantry—on the contrary, I loved it, because everything was new to him. He hadn't been burnt out after years in the infantry.

I instantly liked him because I could tell he'd found a place where he wanted to be. He was fascinated and excited by the new challenge and the fact that he was on the 'cutting edge' at last—finally getting the opportunity to live out the excitement he'd only seen in the movies and glamorized on recruiting posters. He was totally dedicated to his duties. An added benefit for me was that, since Foster joined the Marines at twenty-seven, he had a few years on me in age. I was no longer "the old man." He was. Most constantly reminded him of this fact—not me, of course.

I was grateful to have him next to me throughout everything Echo endured. I couldn't have done it without him.

After checking in, Sergeant Major Ellis briefed Foster on how Echo Company was the rowdiest company in the battalion, with a mixture of a few dozen combat-hardened Marines that had all been through hell in 2004, and a bunch of young kids with personality and attitude. Every squad and platoon was filled with Marines with character larger than life.

Foster found this to be true. He knew that Echo Company was inescapably not an elite unit, but undeniably an extraordinary team of Marines with remarkable chemistry.

■   ■   ■

We moved inside the Chinook helicopters. I was impressed by the sheer size of the aircraft when we boarded. The interior blushed with a fluorescent, greenish-blue glow of the lighting in the fuselage. The hydraulic fluid that dripped from the pressure lines smelled sweet as it speckled our packs and uniforms as we readied for take-off.

The flight crew took special care in handling our gear and baggage. There was no random tossing of our kit inside the plane. All packs were stacked and strapped down to ensure safe transport. Echo had done this type of thing before in training. We were meant to be inserted into combat by helicopter. While it was familiar, it also was different. This was the real thing.

We landed at Camp Corregidor around 0100 hours and began to disembark the flight of Chinooks. We trotted along in column, through mucky dirt—it was winter in Iraq, and it had been raining. At a slow pace, we moved toward the reception area. It was only a couple hundred meters of walking from the HLZ to the camp, but, as soon as I started, I already knew I had over-packed.

The pack on my back drove down hard into my shoulders despite the thick body armor I wore. The two additional over-stuffed kit bags I carried cut deep into my fingers as I strained to hold onto the handles. All the while the muzzle of my M4 carbine jabbed me in my right thigh with every step.

"Yep, definitely over-packed," I kept thinking to myself, as my shoulders ached and my swollen fingers burned, turning shades of bright pink and white. I laughed at myself as I thought about the clumsiness of it all—making me regret bringing so much unwanted gear.

■   ■   ■

The day after we arrived was Thanksgiving. The staff and officers served a turkey dinner in what had once been a building that many of those who had fought in Ramadi in 2004 remembered. We wore white paper side caps as we slung chow on their trays, like those worn by countermen in 1950-style diners, with our cammies. That gave the boys a good laugh.

As we settled into our living spaces, I wasted no time getting together with my Army counterparts to familiarize myself with the battlespace firsthand.

Captain John Tate, TF 1-9 IN's Able Company commander, was eager to show me around. Tate was five-nine and lean. He wore yellow-lensed ballistic glasses that made him stand out from the other soldiers. His company occupied the Sina'a (*Sihn Eye*)—or Industrial District as it was commonly called, an area of demolished factories and warehouses that was part of the area we were going to take over.

Tate walked me around Camp Corregidor and the headquarters compound. Camp Corregidor had been part of the College of Agriculture in Al Anbar Province. It took up one square kilometer of what had been a large campus, and the TF 1-9 Infantry headquarters was the largest building on it.

Palm trees had been hacked down all around the camp—soldiers and Marines sat on the odd-looking two-foot stumps as makeshift stools as they prepped their gear. There was an improvised hundred-meter target range carved out in the dirt at the back of the camp where we zeroed our rifles. The firing line was nothing more than a big sheet of six-by-six-foot aluminum siding. It served its purpose.

We walked north across Main Supply Route (MSR) Michigan to the Combat Outpost (COP) to the Battalion Aid Station (BAS) and then to Able Company headquarters. The COP also served as the maintenance shop for all of the mechanics who repaired the vehicles damaged by IEDs or those shot up in firefights.

All of the camps were dusty scrapyards of military refuge. There seemed to be no rhyme or reason as to how the camps were set up. They were cluttered with blown-up Humvees, wooden pallets of gear, concrete barriers, sandbags, and fighting positions. Shot-up buildings served as both homes and offices and were draped in desert camouflage netting more to provide shade than concealment from enemy observation—since there was no aerial threat whatsoever from the insurgency. The only evidence of military-style order were the columns of General Dynamics M1-A1 tanks—and rows of three to four blue port-a-john shitters perfectly aligned.

Tate had his convoy staged out front of the HQ. A couple of my lieutenants and NCOs and I hopped on board.

We drove slowly, which was still new to me. During my previous combat tours, the usual tactic had been to drive as fast as possible past any suspected roadside bombs or IEDs since most were command-detonated, meaning there was a "trigger man" at the other end of the wire or cell phone who detonated them. Now, the insurgents were using pressure-plate devices. When a vehicle rolled them, its weight would press two metal plates together, completing the circuit and detonating the device. That was bad enough. Making things even more dangerous was the fact that the explosives they used were often 155mm artillery rounds buried underground.

The damage they could cause was catastrophic.

The new tactic was to drive slowly and look for signs of anything out of place. If we found an IED buried in the road before we popped it, we'd mark it with a flag, go around it, and then call for the Explosive Ordnance Disposal (EOD) teams to reduce it.

■   ■   ■

The first post we stopped at was "7 West," located at the "Y" intersection of Sufia Road and MSR Michigan. It was nothing more than one single armored Humvee with a .50 caliber machine gun tucked behind several four-foot high concrete barriers. Hanging out there alone, it received fire frequently and was arguably one of the most dangerous positions to be at. But it was in a key spot to provide almost 360-degree observation and covered two of the main avenues that led to Camp Corregidor.

The next stop, Observation Post (OP) Hotel, was a thousand meters west.

Tate turned to me and said, "OK. So, when we get out of the truck, don't fuck around, run fast, and get inside. We've had a lot of sniper fire in the area. Cool?"

"Cool."

It was good advice too. No sooner had we gotten into the building when we heard small arms fire and the snap of rounds hitting the building and random gunfire in the distance.

Living conditions at OP Hotel were abysmal. At four stories, OP Hotel was one of the taller structures in Ramadi. It was solid concrete, but it was in extremely rough shape. Almost every support column had been eaten down to the steel rebar from small arms fire as if some giant dog had chewed on them. It had large, open windows draped with chain link fencing to detonate RPGs before they sailed through. The walls and corridors inside were pockmarked by incoming rounds. These marks served as a helpful visual reminder to minimize your exposure even inside the building.

There was no functioning plumbing at OP Hotel (or at any of the posts). To relieve themselves, the men who manned the observation post pissed in plastic water bottles and then tossed them outside—a mountain of urine-filled piss bottles amassed in front of the post. The bottles often broke, and the urine saturated the ground outside. It was nauseating, but there was no real way to rectify the situation. It might sound crude pissing in a Gatorade bottle, but it was a necessity and not worth going outside to take a leak and getting shot by a sniper.

OP Hotel had eight fighting positions: one at the entrance, one on the stairwell entering the third floor where the Marines slept, and six more on the fourth floor and roof. From the top, we could see for miles. It gave perfect observation of the surrounding rooftops, MSR Michigan, and the streets below, and we had a front-row view of the red and green tracers that would light up the night sky.

There was a .50 caliber machine gun position on the southwest corner of the fourth floor. It was set back in the room to hide its muzzle flash and to give the Marines the ability to fire in multiple directions. The surrounding concrete walls echoed the blasts when the Marines opened fire with the heavy machine gun that was deafening. The sound it made was impressive, its effects deadly: it unequivocally contributed to the hearing loss of its operators.

After the tour of OP Hotel, we pushed back down MSR Michigan and hung a left northwest on Sufia Road to OP South House. The OP resembled a dungeon right out of medieval times. The shoddy brick and mortar that once constituted the walls of someone's house were barely intact. The floors were made entirely of fine dirt, or what we called "moon-dust," which refused to let go of anything it touched.

The first floor had a few rooms for storage of engineer gear, ammunition, and an assortment of medical supplies. The common area was where the Marines staged for missions and slept in between manning their posts and patrolling. It defied any western standard of living, but as always, the Marines made it work.

I had assigned OP South House to 1st Platoon.

Shortly after taking over the position, 1st Platoon decided it was too small and asked to move into a larger house a dozen meters away. I agreed.

If they were anywhere other than Ramadi, the move would have been easy, but the deadly operating environment demanded that they move at night.

The next day, Echo Company relieved all the Army units from their new positions.

Within hours, the calls started coming across the radios that Marines were engaging the enemy. Scanning the battlespace with rifle sights, scopes, binoculars, thermal devices, and infrared optics, the Marines started picking up the insurgents' every move. More than two hundred sets of fresh eyes watched every detail.

We never stayed static at these positions, what we called "firm bases." We would move continually and patrol aggressively as combat hunters to do what we had come here to do—kill and capture the enemy.

From day one at boot camp Marines are trained to kill. Punctuating their sentences in the affirmative with the word "kill." They are indoctrinated and imbued with a warrior mentality—it's an accepted form of behavior.

Training was about to be set into action.

CHAPTER 4

Pressure

In Iraq, I faced two pressing responsibilities. The first was to bring all my boys home safely. There were times when I told myself not to give a fuck about anything else but that. But I couldn't do that because we were sent to Iraq to kill the enemy. It meant I had to put my men into dangerous situations—despite the admirable love I had for my Marines, I knew they'd have to fight, and possibly die. My only goal was that by killing more insurgents, we'd suffer fewer casualties—like an insurance policy that we'd have to pay for every day.

■　　■　　■

I also couldn't stop thinking about another responsibility that I had.

I received an email from my wife containing a short video clip of my two-year-old daughter, Bailey. This precocious little redhead stood on top of a chair in our kitchen in Yorktown, Virginia. She wore a red-and-white checkered chef's hat and apron that were two sizes too big and was icing a sheet cake with a rubber spatula.

In the background, I heard my wife faintly prompting my daughter what to say.

Bailey announced in a singsong voice, "Daddy, we're making you a cake."

My wife asked, "What kind is it?"

Bailey replied in her delicate, high-pitched voice, "It's pink!"

She could not have been more pleased with herself. But it made me think of how much I had to lose as well if I didn't make it home alive.

■   ■   ■

29 November 2006

Major Jared Norrell called me into his office. He was the Task Force 1-9 Infantry operations officer, and asked if I felt comfortable taking on some more battlespace in Ramadi to help some of the other Army units in the task force south of MSR Michigan. He wanted to establish more combat positions in southern Ramadi.

From Dallas, Texas, Norrell already had six combat deployments as an Army Ranger. He'd enlisted out of high school and then received his commission after attending North Georgia College. Norrell was never happy to just wait out his time in Ramadi. As the task force operations officer, he was aggressive in how he orchestrated units on the battlefield, and his methods made them more lethal—and he made Ramadi a safer place.

At the time, the U.S. Army and the Iraqi Army (IA) soldiers had been taking heavy casualties in the Ma'laab (*Mah Lob*) District located south of the Industrial District, our principal areas of operation.

The area between the Industrial District, Quatana (*Kah Tana*) and Ma'laab districts formed a three-by-three-kilometer area of the battlespace. They were known to be crawling with insurgents. Phrases like "The Heart of Darkness" and "Hotbed of Insurgent Activity" were commonly thrown around to describe them.

At this time, Army infantry companies could put only about eighty to a hundred soldiers into the zones because of the casualties they had taken during the more than a year they battled it out in Ramadi before we arrived. The unit, call sign "Manchu," would spend nineteen months in-country during its deployment.

Echo Company with all our attached personnel—combat camera photographers, military working dog (MWD) handlers, interpreters, combat engineers—boosted our top strength to more than 250. In the eyes of the Army, we looked like rock stars by our sheer numbers alone. The Army units had been crushing the shit out of the insurgency, but our manpower provided the task force leverage needed to go after the enemy like never before.

After Norrell and I had talked a bit, he handed me a black grease pencil and gestured at the Plexiglas-covered map.

"Just show me how much more you think you can take on in the Ma'laab, Scotty."

I drew an odd-shaped triangle and carved out a new zone that stretched from MSR Michigan south to Market Street that lay between the Grand Mosque to the west, and the Al-Haq Mosque to the east. I also estimated that the Echo Company Marines at OP Hotel could patrol another five-hundred-by-one-thousand-meter section of real estate to the south of MSR Michigan.

The area was not much bigger than our original area, but it was densely populated—crawling with insurgents, comprised of two- to three-story residential houses. A mix of light and dark brown structures looked as if they had all been standing at point blank at the barrel of a shotgun blast on multiple occasions. They were riddled with bullet holes the diameter of a human thumb from the .50 caliber machine guns that pounded them during past attacks. No glass stood in the panes of the windows; most had been smashed or blown out from attacks and the overpressure of explosions.

That same day, the commander of 2nd Platoon, Second Lieutenant Jonathan "Jay" Grillo, who was in charge at OP Hotel, decided to start getting into it in the Ma'laab right away and submitted a plan for a patrol to the TOC at Camp Corregidor. His patrol request was approved.

He and his Marines had no way of knowing the bloody day that lay in store for them.

■   ■   ■

Grillo studied engineering at Clarkson University. He never intended to put his degree to practical use. After 9/11, he knew he wanted to join the Marines and fight. He grew up in Arkport, a one-stoplight town in western New York surrounded by fifty miles of alfalfa and cornfields. As a kid, he learned to shoot at a young age and always filled his quota of woodchucks, and then counted the days until deer season. It made him a quintessential outdoorsman, and made the infantry seem like a natural fit to him.

It was. He was a natural.

He was almost six feet tall and weighed 180 pounds; he was trim and solidly built. His brown eyes always seemed to squint with a bit of mischief. Always full of energy, he was eager to take on the world. I loved lieutenants like Grillo. I would rather have one lieutenant like Grillo, whose leash I might have to yank now and then, than one hundred that I had to kick in the ass to get moving.

Knowing that Grillo sent out a patrol, I went to monitor the unmanned drone feeds of the area. I stood there watching intently when word came in that there was a casualty, shot by a sniper.

Shortly afterward, the radio operator came across the radio with the wounded Marine's "battle number." Every Marine had one; it consisted of the letter "E" for Echo Company, the initial of his last name, and the last four digits of his Social Security number. Most Marines morbidly referred to them as "Kill Numbers."

Quickly reaching into my left breast pocket, I fished out my personnel roster and scanned the column with all the battle numbers listed on it to make a match.

"Fuck! It's Espinoza," I thought.

Sergeant Jonathan Espinoza was 1st Squad Leader in 2nd Platoon, Echo Company.

I was incensed. "They shot one of my squad leaders!" I thought. "Motherfuckers!"

I immediately ordered First Lieutenant Pete Somerville to jock up a convoy and get ready to move. Within minutes, he had Humvees staged out front ready to roll, and I climbed aboard.

Before we left the gates of Camp Corregidor, we tried to raise 2nd Platoon on the net, but couldn't get through on the radio.

There is a simple term that I use when, because of chaos, weather, equipment breakdowns, or simple human error, things don't work the way they're supposed to or were planned—Friction. We know it happens—and we train to deal with it. It doesn't make it any less frustrating. We had communication with other supporting and adjacent units.

We pressed on.

■   ■   ■

Espinoza had joined the Marine Corps out of El Paso, Texas, at the age of seventeen. He had one brother and two sisters. Like every young recruit, he envisioned serving his country gallantly and experiencing the romance of what he'd bought into the day he stepped out of his recruiter's office.

He had been to Ramadi in 2004 as a lance corporal with 2d Battalion, 4th Marines—his first test in combat. He was in direct contact with the enemy daily on the city's streets. One day, during that deployment, a 120mm mortar round sailed through the window of the fighting position he and his fellow Marines occupied. When the round, roughly the size of an NFL football, exploded, it destroyed the post.

"Espo," as many of his friends called him, survived, but received shrapnel wounds to his head and a large portion of his back. He was CASEVAC'd—and received his first Purple Heart Medal at the age of eighteen.

29 November 2006

Espo's day started by putting together a patrol request and a map overlay that detailed his plan of action and the route his patrol would take into the Ma'laab, on Grillo's orders. By 2200 hours, Espo submitted his plan and reviewed it with Grillo. The initial plan included taking a squad of Iraqi soldiers with them on patrol. The IA soldiers shared space at OP Hotel with the units that occupied it, and it was common to incorporate them into the plans. Espo felt uneasy taking the IA soldiers with them in an unknown area. He felt rushed. He also wasn't comfortable with the fact that the U.S. Army never went south into the patrol area—which meant it had not been cleared for quite some time.

Around 2300 hours, the IA captain bailed out of the patrol, saying his men had been tasked to support another unit. Espo was skeptical. He didn't completely trust the Iraqi soldiers, thinking that they might be collecting information on them and providing it to the insurgents.

He felt as if they were being set up for a trap.

He told his theory to Grillo, but Grillo said that the patrol would go ahead regardless of Espo's uneasiness of any unconfirmed suspicions. The squad was scheduled to step off from OP Hotel at 0500 hours, but modifications had to be made to the patrol route, and the start time slid back to 1000 hours.

Friction.

Espo woke up his squad of twelve Marines at 0800 hours and began to prep for combat and conducted their pre-combat checks and inspections for the daytime patrol.

Patrolling during the day in Ramadi was something we eventually learned not to do.

We learned the hard way.

The step-off time came and went as the number of Marines on the patrol increased by one—Grillo.

Espo called the personnel roster into the platoon sergeant, Staff Sergeant Wayne Nugent. He wasn't a fan of last-minute changes, or of officers sticking their noses in what he considered enlisted business.

Nugent had a harsh deportment most of the time. He was direct and had a distinct, monosyllabic tone when he addressed the Marines. He was aggressive and confident to a fault. The boys fed off that. They liked their leaders to be assertive—Nugent fit that to a T.

Espo checked his kit and realized he'd forgotten to take his pyro—signaling flares and smoke grenades—with him. He made a mad dash back to get it. When Espo did his final communications check, the cryptographic fill—a secret code which scrambled the radio signals so the enemy could not intercept them—had been erased. Espo had to return to the COC again to get the radio working.

It was around 1100 hours when the squad finally stepped off on their patrol. One of their first objectives was to check out and conduct a raid on a suspected sniper position or "hide-site" on Front Door Alley.

They crossed south on MSR Michigan and grabbed some loose plywood and tossed it onto the triple-strand concertina wire (C-wire) so they could walk across it. C-wire has sharp razor-barbed blades on heavy gauge wire that comes in fifty-meter rolls like a giant Slinky Toy that will cut the shit out of anyone trying to walk through or over it. The Army had thrown up a lot of it around its positions in Ramadi. It certainly kept out the enemy, but it kept us out too.

Espo planned for overwatch and supporting fires from the rooftop of OP Hotel to cover their movement into the zone to the sniper hideout—there would be a team of Marines with high-powered, long-range rifles and observers watching their every movement. As the patrol approached the objective, Espo directed Corporal Jeremy Ramirez and Lance Corporal Joshua Bradford to take their four-man fire team into the building while the third fire team would isolate the area. One team would gain a foothold at the entrances while the other, led by Lance Corporal David Quetglas cleared the building.

Bradford was a lanky twenty-year-old from Duncanville, Texas; Ramirez was a twenty-three-year-old grunt from Erie, Illinois. They both enlisted to fight.

The raid went off in a textbook manner. The squad found it empty, save for a few shell casings. They also found some spider holes—spots knocked through the walls that snipers used to target the Marines and soldiers.

Espo's patrol moved west along their route clearing the houses in their zone—taking weapons out of homes that had been staged inside, awaiting employment at the discretion of the insurgents.

It was never black and white when we found Iraqis with weapons in their homes. We never knew if they were victims of the insurgency or part of it. But unless they were pointing and shooting the weapons at us, we were not allowed to engage them. If there was an overwhelming amount of contraband in a house, we'd detain them and move them back to Camp Corregidor for questioning by the Army's Tactical Human Intelligence Team (THT). It was a daunting challenge for us to know who the good guys were and who the bad guys were—insurgents didn't wear uniforms and blended in with the locals all too well.

When the squad pushed to the corner house on the block on Little-A Street, they began to take machine gunfire. Bradford's fire team ran past Espo, and the other Marines raced for cover, scrambling in multiple directions to escape the hail of bullets.

Quickly scanning the area, Espo saw a large, two-story house with a big, black gate on it. Bradford grabbed a Benelli 12-gauge tactical shotgun, blasted three rounds into the door latch, and kicked it open. Espo told Quetglas to get his fire team inside and directed his other teams to cover them as they did so. As Bradford set security, Espo saw Ramirez's team bounding up the street.

Espo went into the street to see what was going on, yelling to Ramirez to get his men into the courtyard behind the black gates. As he did, a string of automatic weapons fire snapped between them—they felt the heat and heard the cracking as the bullets laced the ground.

Ramirez instinctively took cover—in the wrong house.

Espo tried to wave them over. As he did, he got a report that two of his Marines—Lance Corporals Shaughnessy and Acosta—were nowhere to be found.

Exposing himself to enemy fire and determined to locate the missing Marines, he stepped past the gates and dropped to one knee.

Espo felt a sharp whack to his chest as if someone had struck him with a baseball bat at full swing. Shaking it off, he stood to go back in the house and get a report. As he did, one of his legs began wobbling and buckled slightly. But he managed to get inside the gates.

Espo made his way in and found Grillo. "Hey, sir. I think I just got hit."

Grillo sharply replied, "Espo, this is no time to be fucking around!"

Then Grillo took a good look at his squad leader and read the intensity on his face. He saw a tear in the top of Espo's body armor, on the front of his chest.

Grillo ripped open the body armor and saw an 8mm armor-piercing sniper round the size and shape of a tip of a crayon, lodged in the vest material. It had grazed the top of the bulletproof ceramic plate protecting Espo's chest, which had slowed it down. Still, the round had torn through the flesh and muscle—gashing his chest severely. Blood seeped from the wound.

Grillo called, "Doc! Get over here! Espo's hit!"

The platoon's "Doc"—the Navy corpsman attached to it, the equivalent of an Army medic—moved quickly to Espo and started first aid. His wound was critical. Within minutes, Doc administered morphine for pain and bandaged the wound with a pressure dressing.

Admittedly not a religious man, Espo began praying out loud. "Dear God, please let me make it home. Let me see my unborn son and hear him cry."

Lying there with his blood pouring out of the gash on his chest, Espo could hear the Marines frantically yelling as they fought—still, his only concern was for the safety of his men. He tried to get back up.

As he lay in the courtyard, Espo could see Bradford jumping from rooftop to rooftop trying to get his radio to a good spot to raise communications. He could see the top edges of the house burst into dust as the machine gun fire grated into the stone, trying to kill Bradford's team.

Doc pushed Espo back. "Lie down, Sergeant! Just lie down!"

Espo would later say he was proud of how his squad reacted under fire. Everyone did their jobs, just like he'd trained them to do. The irony was in training he'd always been the one to get shot so the junior Marines could learn to step up to the next level and lead, as Quetglas did that day.

Espo had a half-smile of pride on his face with morphine kicking in. He didn't have long to wait as two Marines escorted him to an armored personnel carrier waiting outside the house to take him to the battalion aid station at the Combat Outpost.

Within minutes of arrival, Espo was being rushed into the battalion aid station.

As Espo lay in the trauma room, the Task Force 1-9 Infantry Command Sergeant Major, Dennis "Birdog" Bergmann, bellowed out in his abrasive, southern Georgia drawl, "Hey, soldier. Take a look at that Marine! Now that—that's a wound!"

Espo smiled quietly, as he always did, and drifted into a morphine-induced trance.

■   ■   ■

When we arrived at OP Hotel, I grabbed Somerville and a few others from the convoy, raced into the building, and met up with Staff Sergeant Nugent. I told him we couldn't raise the squad on the radio, and I had no idea what building they had gone into for cover.

Nugent plastered his finger to the map. "Sir, Espo was shot here, and we think that the other guys have gone firm in one of these buildings." Going firm meant a unit held a building for an indefinite amount of time but didn't intend to stay there permanently.

I told Nugent that we were going to relay our communications through him until we reached Grillo and the squad.

"Make sure you keep someone on this radio and monitor it at all times. This situation is going to get worse before it gets better for the boys."

We mounted up in Somerville's convoy after giving all the drivers and team leaders a quick brief on what we'd be doing and where we were going. Although the Ma'laab District was right across the street from OP Hotel, we didn't know how long the mission was going to take.

We swung the vehicles around and headed south. One block or ten miles didn't matter. We always wanted to be ready for the worst situation.

As we tried to gain access to the street, we were stopped by the C-Wire obstacle that Espo's squad had encountered earlier that day. We now faced the same dilemma—the Army had effectively wired itself into the zone, and we couldn't drive over the wire. Regardless of how it's portrayed in the movies, C-Wire is tough and will do what it is designed to do: stop dismounted personnel and vehicles, including us.

More friction.

We quickly tried to formulate a plan to get around the wire, but we didn't have any engineer tools in the trucks and no bolt cutters on hand. The only thing we had were handheld multi-tools that had a small pair of pliers that folded out with a wire-cutting tool in the jaws of it. Most self-respecting infantrymen carried one, or something similar, on their belt wherever they went.

Realizing the danger of being exposed in the open for so long during broad daylight, we had to work quickly. We started bending the wire and snapping it so we could breach the wire to get to the distressed squad. We broke through a section of the C-wire, jammed the buttstocks of our rifles into the mess and started pulling it apart, creating a gap twenty feet wide—just enough to allow the Humvees to drive through.

As we feverishly mangled the C-wire into submission, we heard the distinctive reports of AK-47 fire. Someone was in a fight close by, maybe a block or two away—maybe our boys. Still trying to raise 1st Squad on the radio, we moved about a block into the zone and scanned to find any signs of the Marines.

Nugent called us on the net and said, "Longhorn Six, be advised they have gone firm in the vicinity of Building 14...they're on the north side and have popped red smoke." This was a canister, about the size of a soda can, with a grenade firing pin assembly on the top. When you pulled the pin, it would provide three-to-five minutes of thick colored smoke that could obscure your position or mark it.

I passed the word to start looking for red smoke. No one saw any.

Still unable to get direct communication with the patrol, I ordered the convoy to press forward to the area where I suspected they were located. Then, one of the Marines in the turrets caught sight of a burnt-out smoke grenade on the street by the curb. We halted and began to dismount.

There was still no radio communication with the Marines, but I now heard people yelling.

I looked up to see Marines on the top of a roof, positioned in overwatch for security.

We'd found them.

I made my way into the house. Most of the squad stood huddled in one room on the first floor. They all looked a little rattled, but were glad to see us. They had been pinned down and getting shot up from every direction when Espo was hit.

I got a head count of all the Marines—Shaughnessy and Acosta had been found—and I formulated a plan for our exit back to OP Hotel in the most expeditious manner.

As we moved to the awaiting convoy, we started taking heavy fire from the south part of the Ma'laab. A few rounds smacked into the tops of the buildings and a couple of the trucks got pinged too. It wasn't well-aimed gunfire, but it motivated us to get the fuck out of there.

Suddenly, the volume of fire intensified. The enemy engaged—firing automatic weapons, and it appeared that another dozen insurgents had joined the party.

Two M1-A1 tanks arrived to support us. One of them sat at the intersection of Little-A Street and Cinema Street, twenty-five meters from my position.

I had no radio communication with the tanks. Also, the Army version of the M1-A1 lacked something the Marine version had: the "Grunt Phone." It was an old-school, black, military-grade telephone handset affixed to the outside of the tank in a protective metal box at the right rear of the machine. It allowed grunts to talk directly to the tank crew, while the latter remained safely buttoned up inside with their hatches secured. I would need to communicate in an even more old-school way.

I moved at a fast trot toward one of the massive tanks and took cover on the right side of it, by the tracks—the steel, linked caterpillar-like treads that it rolled on.

Yelling was futile as the high-pitched whine of the M1-A1's turbine engine tended to drown out most sound. Added to that, the cacophony of the ensuing firefight made it impossible to communicate through the shell of the tank.

I made the risky decision to jump up onto the tank and began to bang on the tank commander's hatch with the butt of my M4 carbine. I banged and banged.

"Fuck me," I thought. "Open the fuck up."

Finally, the lieutenant cracked the hatch.

Lying flat on my stomach on the tank with my head craning to get a look inside the hatch, I saw the lieutenant with his helmet on. Rounds began to snap and ping off the tank. Dust kicked up from the street as automatic fire walked in around our position. Since shooting at an M1-A1 with an AK-47 or a machine gun is as futile as trying to extinguish a forest fire by pissing on it, I figured the enemy was aiming at me as a clearly visible target now.

I yelled with impotent frustration at the lieutenant. Neither of us could hear each other. Finally, I yelled at the top of my lungs, "Lieutenant, open the fucking hatch! Now!"

His eyes widened as if he'd had an awakening. He cracked the hatch open slightly and cocked his helmet to one side, exposing his right ear but he still stayed tucked down inside the vehicle, like a rabbit in his hole.

A couple of rounds cracked sharply on the tank, and I heard the ricochets distinctively. "Hey! They're down there—to the south. Do you see the muzzle flashes?"

He replied, "Roger that, sir."

I said, "No, not roger that. Get that 'coax' in gear and start giving us some suppression on that shit while we move out."

Again, he replied, "Roger that, sir."

I was still uncertain if the urgency of my request sank in with him to use the coaxial 7.62 caliber machine gun aligned with the tank's 120mm smooth-bore cannon against the enemy to the south.

I began to slide backward on my belly to the rear edge of the tank— my Marines shouted at me as I slid off the side and jumped down. Yelling, Marines waved me over to the convoy. As I prepared to make the dash, a string of automatic enemy fire laced the tank from front to back. I crouched down by the tracks trying to reduce my silhouette as much as I could. I wanted to be small. I heard the enemy rounds ping in rapid succession off of the tank. Seconds later, the M1-A1 blasted out several long bursts of fire from its machine gun. Music to my ears.

Pushing off the track with my right foot, like a sprinter out of the starting blocks, I raced toward the convoy and hopped in the back of my vehicle.

The assistant driver with the radio handset tucked between his helmet and one ear turned to me and said, "Sir, we can't go! We don't have Lieutenant Somerville!"

My first thought was, "How the fuck did they lose Somerville?"

My second thought was, "What a fucking awesome team of Marines." In the midst of chaos, they had maintained the situational awareness not to leave a fellow Marine behind.

I called over the radio to the vehicles to find Somerville. From the building to our front at the end of Little-A Street, enemy fighters began to shoot at our Humvee. Some sprayed small arms fire at us from the rooftops.

The man who deserved to be most concerned about this development was Lance Corporal Drew "Tex" Sturrock, who was sitting in the gunner's turret, partially exposed as enemy gunfire beat down on us. In a random moment, I looked at his feet and noticed he didn't have his boots tied.

Tex yelled down at me, "Sir! Sir! They're hitting us from that building right there in front of us. What do you want me to do?"

"Tex, get back on that .50 cal and start engaging those fuckers!"

Tex replied in his southern drawl, "Roger that, sir!"

I shook my head and thought with some contempt, "Really? Enough of the 'Roger that' shit. Just start shooting for fuck sake!"

Tex unleashed the .50 cal, and hot, brass cartridge casings the size of small cigars sprinkled into the Humvee. The rounds ripped into the stone face of the building, completely suppressing the enemy position.

In combat, Tex was a Marine to the core—a trained killer who did his job effectively when shooting the enemy. As he felt the pressure around him, being with me that day granted him some semblance of VIP access. Some Marines become more efficient under pressure in combat, and Tex was one of them. He went from just posturing as a tough guy to understanding the reality of what was happening to him. The intensity of the firefight was as real as it got for him.

We had spent so much time together training there was implicit trust and a complete release when I looked up and told him to shoot.

He felt the pressure, but I was making it OK to kill.

No placebo could imitate the type of fear, anxiety, love, and bond formed under those conditions—the core of brotherhood. For Tex, it created a superstition with the guys he rode with that day—men that he relied on for his safety.

Much to Foster's frustration, Tex didn't lace up his boots again for the rest of the deployment. His way of relieving some of the pressure, I suppose.

■   ■   ■

We were clearly in what was shaping up to be a classic "L"-shaped ambush in the alley.

The A-Driver turned back around to me and said, "Sir, we got him! Somerville! He's in the last vehicle! We've got everyone. We're ready to go, sir!"

I gave him a quick thumbs-up and, with Tex still on the .50 cal engaging targets around us, we pushed to the west end of Little-A Street and made our way back out to the wire we had snaked through an hour before.

It was as Theodore Roosevelt called it during the battle of San Juan Hill, "A Crowded Hour." We had successfully extracted a pinned-down patrol, moved them back to OP Hotel, and made our way back to Camp Corregidor.

Espo was already on his way to Balad.

As we drove back, beads of sweat stung my eyes. So I could wipe my face clean, I took off my Kevlar helmet, setting it in the center of the Humvee.

When I reached for it to put it back on, the Marine sitting next to me was fiddling around with it and examining it.

He looked up at me. "Fuck, sir. You just get this? You're lucky as shit, sir."

I saw the tan digital camouflage fabric helmet cover had a long shred in it. When I peeled it back, there was a fresh scar of bristling Kevlar fibers in the skin of the helmet. A round had grazed the top of my helmet and engraved its signature across the top.

I cursed that piece of gear and the weight of it on my head on a daily basis.

Not that day.

CHAPTER 4.1

Phrogs

Espo was never over the top—he was what I referred to as a cool professional. His actions always spoke louder than his words. He didn't talk
much, but he said a lot. The Marines he led always followed him, trusted
him completely, and knew that he'd do anything for them.

On the twenty-ninth of November, he'd proved it again.

■   ■   ■

First Sergeant was by Espo's side as the medics rushed him to the
trauma room. There, the medical staff prepped the wound, cleaned it
out, and put a big, clear plastic bandage on it. Espo looked down at the
dressing as it began to fill with yellow puss and blood.

His blood.

Fiddling with the morphine-laced, intravenous drip that dangled
from his arm, he leaned over to Foster and asked with some guilt, "Hey,
First Sergeant, who was in charge of the CASEVAC? Please tell me it
wasn't Gunny."

Foster replied, "Don't worry about it. I'm in charge of it from here, Marine."

"Sorry, First Sergeant," Espo murmured. "It's probably the drugs talking."

Espo was moved to the helicopter landing zone and placed on a waiting CH-53E Super Stallion and flown to Al Taqquadum (TQ) Air Base for additional treatment.

When he arrived at TQ, a good-looking Asian nurse spoke calmly to Espo. "Hi Sergeant, we're going to put you into this little 'Hot Pocket' to keep you warm." The medical warming bag she referred to ensured patients didn't go into shock from body temperature shifts.

Espo was still lucid when the nurse unzipped the bag and rolled him to his side. She reached down his backside and performed a check for any internal bleeding with her lubricated, latex covered finger.

She said, "All right, looks good, Sergeant. No problems."

All Espo could think was, "Man, I get shot in the chest. Now, this?"

The TQ medical staff rushed Espo onto a Marine Corps CH-46 Sea Knight, affectionately referred to as a "Battle Phrog" helicopter for a flight to Balad Air Base for surgery.

Moments after takeoff, Espo lost consciousness.

The next thing he knew, Espo was coming to in the back of the helicopter. The distinctive whopping of the Phrog's dual rotors beat the air into submission, and the sound filled his ears. The in-flight medic stood directly over him holding a defibrillator pad in each hand.

Espo blurted, "Hey, what the *fuck* are you doing?"

The Doc replied, "Damn, that's good. You were out for like two minutes, Sergeant. We couldn't get a pulse."

The helo landed at Balad, and the ramp of the Phrog lowered. Espo felt the force of the cold air pushing into the fuselage over his body. He was placed on the back of a John Deere Gator utility vehicle that took him to the surgical center.

The medical staff hovered over him in the operating room and removed the bandage on his chest and stuck him with another IV.

The anesthesiologist said, "OK, Marine. I want you to count back from one hundred." Espo counted out loud. "One hundred. Ninety-nine. Ninety-eight. Ninety-seven…"

■　　■　　■

Espo woke up in a comfortable hospital bed, still groggy from the anesthesia. He rolled gingerly around in his soft bed, trying to make out his surroundings. As he turned his head from left to right, he noticed that the pillow was covered in a Superman pillowcase, the kind found in a child's bedroom.

His five-star-like accommodations at the hospital were now significantly more luxurious compared to how he'd lived throughout the entirety of his infantry career.

Another attractive Air Force nurse approached his bed. She smiled pleasantly as she looked him in the eyes. "Good. You're awake."

"Yeah, I'm good. What's up with this pillowcase, by the way?"

The nurse checked his vitals. "Well, you're the first gunshot-wound-to-the-chest survivor we have ever had, so we put that Superman pillowcase on since we figured you could stop bullets with your chest."

Again, Espo drew a collected, humble smile across his face and laid his head deep into the plush pillow to rest.

Espo awoke hours later and rolled his head to the right. He could see that there was an Iraqi Army general in the bed directly next to him. He felt very uneasy. The IA general kept glancing over at him, staring intently, as if to elicit a conversation.

Finally, Espo, a little freaked out, said in exasperation, "What?"

The Iraqi general, wounded by shrapnel from an IED explosion, leaned up from his bed and turned to Espo.

"Thank you for coming to our country," he said.

Someone else might have accepted the general's thanks warmly. But Espo harbored a lot of animosity toward the Iraqi Army and didn't take it as the intended compliment. Instead, it enraged him. He dismissed the accolade and turned his back to the general, snubbing him with indifference and contempt.

■   ■   ■

Espo spent the next four days recovering at Balad Air Base, and his family had already been notified by our command headquarters that he would most likely be returning stateside as a result of his wounds. Espo wasn't read in on that plan, however. His only thought was to get back to Ramadi and his unit.

Espo was on the mend, and was now ambulatory. The doctors discharged him from Balad with no orders or guidance. By his volition, he decided to get moving. First, he hopped on a CH-46 and made his way from Balad to Baghdad. He caught a flight out of Baghdad the same day to Fallujah and then made another connecting flight into Camp Ramadi.

Camp Ramadi, one of the largest U.S. Camps in the city, was roughly on the other side of town, five miles west of Camp Corregidor. He managed to hop one more helicopter ride from Camp Ramadi that landed him back at the Combat Outpost, where he'd initially been CASEVAC'd.

Espo made his way across MSR Michigan to Camp Corregidor. It was 0300 hours. Dressed in a civilian blue pullover shirt, and sweatpants from his stay in Balad, he carried a clear, plastic bag of his own bloody cammies. He walked up to the back of an armored personnel carrier that was parked at the entrance of the camp and banged on the steel hatch.

A U.S. Army soldier, looking half asleep, opened the hatch and greeted Espo with a nonchalant "What's up?"

Espo thought to himself, "How about some fucking security and situational awareness, motherfuckers? That's what's up. How about challenging some weirdo walking down Michigan in a blue sweater? Fuckers."

Instead, he said nothing, knowing it didn't make a difference either way. He dismissed the lackadaisical soldiers and made his way inside toward the Echo Company workspace.

Lance Corporal Andrew Marrari, an infantryman and one of the Echo Company clerks, was on radio watch when Espo stepped into the COC.

Espo got right to business, "Hey, Marrari, can you get Two Bravo on the net for me?"

Marrari turned in his chair and looked as if he'd seen a ghost. "Yes, Sergeant." Then he spun around to the stack of radios and called over to OP Hotel for Staff Sergeant Nugent.

Marrari keyed the handset, "Two Bravo, Two Bravo, this is Longhorn COC, over."

He extended the handset to Espo. When Espo heard Nugent's voice on the other end, he felt like he'd made it home. He felt safe again. Espo told Nugent he was back and ready to go.

Espo's sense of comfort was short-lived by the time Foster made it back into the COC and saw him standing there. Usually not a "yeller," this time he erupted. "Sergeant Espinoza! What the hell are you doing here? You're supposed to be on your way stateside! Holy shit!"

He then gave Espo a thorough "welcome home" ass chewing for not staying in the hospital. He then finished by telling Espo that he was "benched." Until he healed up, he'd be part of Headquarters Platoon.

Espo stood there and took the whitewashing from Foster. Again, he forced back a cool smile he wanted to display, thinking about the round that went through his chest days before. He thought of the hospital, the pretty nurses, the fucking Iraqi general, and the travels he endured to get back. His collarbone still throbbed as a result of the hairline fracture in it. A new scar on the center of his chest was four inches wide. A couple dozen staples held the wound closed for now.

But, fuck it, he'd made it back.

CHAPTER 5

Sixth

6 December 2006

That cold December night in Ramadi was one the Marines of Echo Company would never forget. Sporadic machine gun and AK-47 fire rained on Army and Marine positions in zone—it was the beginning of one of the most complex, coordinated attacks from Anti-Iraqi Forces. Echo Company had been out patrolling the entire day when the fighting began.

It was impossible for them to know that they were about to be in one of the longest fights of their lives.

I was in the TOC at Camp Corregidor with the Task Force 1-9 Infantry commander, Lieutenant Colonel Ferry, and the entire battle staff—their eyes all fixed on the feeds coming in from drones flying overhead. The four-million-dollar drones loitered at ten thousand feet and gave us all a bird's-eye view of every single movement on the battle-field.

A call came across the radio. One of Echo Company's positions—ECP 8—was in direct contact with the enemy—and it was taking a beating.

ECP 8 was a jagged three-story structure and had the familiar exterior of most buildings in Ramadi—embossed with bullet holes on every side. Its height made it ideal for observing the areas Echo Company covered—and also an easily identifiable target for the insurgents. From its roof, it was possible to see Ramadi General Hospital—a massive, white seven-story building about two kilometers to the east. More importantly, ECP 8 covered two main avenues of approach that insurgents used to filter into the city, avenues that we were determined to seal off. There was an adjacent Iraqi Army compound located directly across the street. Both compounds formed a makeshift cul-de-sac partitioned by numerous ten-foot-high concrete barriers laid around them.

Ferry's reaction was immediate. "Scott, get down there!"

I was to take the Quick Reaction Force (QRF)—four Humvees mounted with .50 caliber and 7.62mm machine guns and packed with Marines—to the rescue.

"I'm gone, sir!"

I ran down the stairs from the second floor of the TOC and burst through the front door into the spiraling cloud of dust kicked up by the QRF vehicles when they had come to a screeching halt in front of the TOC.

I was about ten feet from the Humvee when small arms whizzed above and cracked into the stone-faced buildings and the dirt around our feet blistered with every strike. The entire compound at Camp Corregidor seemed to sizzle. The rounds weren't just from the enemy. Some of them were "spillover" from friendly positions—rounds that missed the enemy targets and landed in our locations.

After a quick communications check, our convoy pulled out of Camp Corregidor, veered left onto MSR Michigan, and headed west toward ECP 8. The distance from Camp Corregidor to ECP 8 was no more than a couple of kilometers.

The fighting had become even more intense. At 7-Bravo, Marines in a Humvee were taking fire from the "Mushroom House," so named because of its odd mushroom-shaped roof, and were giving it as good as they got, furiously returning fire with their vehicle's .50 cal. As we drove past, we could see the tracer rounds from the machine gun ripping into the target.

As we moved toward ECP-8, the southern skyline lit up with red and green tracer rounds from all the firefights. I realized that these attacks weren't spontaneous—they were all part of a well-coordinated enemy attack. The sound of explosions, machine gun fire, and the crackling of AK-47s surrounded us.

Some insurgents had taken cover in the Al Haq Mosque, one of the main mosques on MSR Michigan. They fired furiously from the compound and the minaret into the sky like a phalanx—a shielded wall of protection, but now enemy rounds jutted out instead of those like ancient spearheads. It wasn't the first or last suspicion we had that the insurgents were using mosques as safe havens, exploiting the fact that they were off limits to the MNF due to political and cultural sensitivity issues.

As we continued our race to ECP 8, tracers streamed in front of and over us, and I heard the snapping and zinging of rounds hitting and ricocheting off the heavily armored Humvees as we moved closer to our destination. Two rocket-propelled grenades hit near us, adding to the chaos.

Our turret gunners crouched in their semi-exposed positions and returned blazing fire—short, three- to six-round bursts cut into enemy positions. They were vulnerable in doing so because, under the circumstances, it was difficult for them to get positive identification (PID) of the enemy—adding to the uncertainty, they were constantly afraid of hitting friendly positions.

The radio blasted that ECP 8 and all of the other positions were completely engaged. We were in the middle of the most dangerous and complex firefight we'd ever faced. The QRF, comprised of Echo's 3rd Platoon led by First Lieutenant "Sneaky" Pete Somerville, had its work cut out for it.

A mild-mannered twenty-six-year-old from Edina, Minnesota, a suburb of Minneapolis, Somerville stood out from other officers in that he was a Yale graduate, and had a philosophy degree no less. To his credit, he never flaunted his Ivy League education or came across as an intellectual elitist, although he may have been mistaken for one on occasion by those who didn't know him. On the contrary, he seemed to relish any opportunity to listen to and learn from those around him. He'd ultimately learn as much in the Marines as he ever did in college.

Somerville struggled with "the mask" he wanted to wear in front of his Marines and peers. He wanted to appear professional and acute at all times, and so he didn't engage in the normal sophomoric antics others did—I respected that about him, and I knew that it was tough for a young lieutenant under those circumstances. He took more than his share of ribbing from his peers and the senior NCOs who cracked "New Lieutenant" jokes at his expense. He always rose above the jabs or ignored them entirely.

Some might have taken his quiet nature as shyness or a lack of assertiveness—but I didn't see that in any of his actions. Somerville was sturdy, dependable, and trustworthy. His calm nature made him the diplomat of any squabbling that went on between the other young lieutenants in the company. His easygoing style never stopped him from leading his Marines with aggressiveness, tempered by his keen intellectual abilities—with his nose frequently buried in Thucydides or the kind.

His nickname came from his knack for silently walking up on the fringes of a conversation already in progress. First Lieutenant Bobby Lee, my executive officer, the self-appointed ringleader of wisecrackers, said, "We'd all stop mid-sentence blathering, turn our heads, and find Somerville standing there, taking it all in, and I'd think, 'Sneaky.'"

■　　■　　　■

Lance Corporal Jonathan Neris, a fire team leader in 4th Platoon's 1st squad, raced to the rooftop of ECP 8. He could see the muzzle flashes of the insurgents' weapons coming out of windows as close as fifty meters away. Neris and the other Marines drew down on the insurgents, aiming their sights on the enemy fighters running back and forth between buildings. As Marines spotted them, they opened up with their weapons. The firing was intense. Deafening bursts rang out from the M-249 Squad Automatic Weapons (SAWs), and the M-240B 7.62mm medium machine guns—making it almost impossible to communicate to each other as they fought. Neris could see the bodies of the insurgents drop to the ground as the Marines tore them apart.

Neris was twenty-one years old and good-natured. He was a big kid at six-feet even and 190 pounds. He had a dense brush of thick black hair on top of his head. It was long, unlike most Marines who kept their hair buzzed short. He had wide black eyebrows, cheerful brown eyes, and a big, bright, toothy smile. You could see his smile in his eyes.

His father had left his family's Chicago home when he was two years old. His mother taught him everything she could, but learning to be a man was something he'd had to do on his own. Neris wanted a challenge—the chance to push past his limits—to his breaking point. The Marine Corps gave him that—and he was grateful for it.

Neris caught sight of Libby out of the corner of his eye and then heard him say, "I'm reloading my M-203." Libby then took a knee to slide open the breach of the grenade launcher mounted under his rifle.

Moments later, Neris looked for Libby to come back up. When he didn't, Neris looked down and saw that Libby had fallen.

He immediately dropped down to his squad leader's side and saw a bulge in his neck. Libby's eyes stared directly back at him. Neris' heart dropped. The other Marines quickly gathered around illuminating Libby with their flashlights to assess the damage.

Neris couldn't believe it was happening. He stood frozen in shock. It didn't seem real. All he could say to Libby was, "I'm sorry."

Still not realizing the full gravity of the situation, Neris instinctually tuned back into the fight and resupplied his Marines with ammunition. He had to think about the men who were still alive. They were now his responsibility.

Hospitalman Nate "Doc" Dicks and Staff Sergeant Miller crouched low as they moved over to where Libby had fallen and lifted him carefully. Precariously they moved him down a rickety ladder to the safety of the COC.

■   ■   ■

My convoy rolled up to the position. Enemy rounds were cracking all around us.

Fourth Platoon, which held ECP 8, was commanded by Second Lieutenant Seth Nicholson and his platoon sergeant, Staff Sergeant Brent Miller.

Nicholson was a twenty-three-year-old from Charlotte, North Carolina. Earning an English Literature degree from Appalachian State University had sharpened his wit and provided him with plenty of snappy comebacks when needed. He was confident and stood over six feet tall at 195 pounds and often flashed a clever, bright smile. His brown hair was cropped short and came to a sharp widow's peak in the center of his forehead.

Miller was a twenty-nine-year-old infantryman from Houston, Texas. He was quiet, never excitable, and he always took care of business.

When I walked into ECP 8, I immediately witnessed Doc Dicks and Lance Corporal Christopher Muscle performing first aid on Libby, who lay on a green military cot that had soft digital poncho liners strewn on top of it—padding the bed their brother now rested on.

Nicholson told me that Libby had suffered a gunshot wound to the back of the neck—the bullet struck him just above his protective ballistic plate.

We didn't have time to wait.

I asked Nicholson, "Is Libby the only casualty that needs to be CASEVAC'd?"

He answered, "Yes!"

I went back outside and told Somerville, "Get the trucks turned around. We don't have time to wait for a CASEVAC. We are the CASEVAC."

I ordered the Marines to get Libby into my Humvee. Four Marines carried him to the back of my vehicle. As they did, they yelled at each other.

"Be careful with him! Be careful! Easy! Easy with him!"

The convoy roared back home with Somerville's vehicle in the lead. We pressed past the enemy positions and rushed past OP South House, which was occupied by 1st Platoon.

Firefights engulfed the city, and our vehicles got caught in the crossfire.

Lance Corporal John Fillbach drove my Humvee. I rode shotgun. Lance Corporal Jared Flanagan was in back, holding Libby tightly while Corporal Jeremy Vandegriffe manned the turret-mounted machine gun. At fifty miles per hour, we barreled down Sufia Road, past the Al Haq Mosque, and left onto MSR Michigan, heading to the COP.

Lance Corporal Trenton Drew "Tex" Sturrock was in the turret of Somerville's lead vehicle, manning the .50 caliber machine gun. Tex was a machine gunner by trade—the .50 cal was his favorite gun, and he knew it inside and out. He was from Woodlands, Texas. There was nothing original about his nickname other than the fact he acquired it after getting the state flag of Texas tattooed on his left shoulder. He was nineteen when he enlisted in the Marines and would celebrate his twentieth birthday in Iraq that year on his first deployment.

Tex spoke with a smooth, southern drawl, exuded confidence, and had a gregarious personality that allowed him to bond with the men in Echo Company. He was undeniably one of Echo's many "large personalities."

Tonight, Tex struggled to return effective fire at the enemy—but not from a lack of desire. His night vision goggles (NVGs) dangled clumsily around his face, obscuring his sight.

An older model of the Harris AN/PVS-7 NVGs, they had come loose from brackets that were supposed to hold them in place. He still could see, however, tracer rounds whizzing close past his face, their glow accentuated by the NVGs.

Tex held his breath and tensed his body and thought, "This is where I get hit."

He didn't flinch, though. It was not in his nature. Enemy gunfire just seemed to piss him off, and never scared him. No names, no faces, just the enemy.

He pressed his thumbs down hard on the butterfly-shaped trigger of the Browning machine gun, blazing ten- to fifteen-round bursts into the enemy positions as we raced to the COP.

I heard Flanagan in the back of the truck yelling, "Hang on, man! Hang on! Come on, Libby, hang in there!"

Flanagan leaned over the front seat and yelled at me. "Sir, I can't get a fucking pulse! There's no pulse. There's blood everywhere!"

"Keep talking to him!" I said.

We had already radioed ahead to let the COP and BAS know we were headed in with a casualty. The Combat Outpost's gates were wide open, and the way to the aid station's front door was marked with glowing light sticks, looking all the world like an airport's runway lights.

The U.S. Army medical staff who ran the BAS had already seen so many casualties they had their procedures down to the last detail. Marking the entrance to the trauma room with chemlights was an indication of their professionalism.

The Marines got Libby out as carefully as possible. There was no time to put him on a stretcher. Doc had put a cervical collar on him and inserted an emergency tracheotomy tube in his mouth to clear the airway.

I stared down at Libby. I thought to myself, "God, he looks so young. He's so fucking young. Please! Please hang in there, brother."

I couldn't believe this was the first casualty the battalion was suffering and it was happening to us, Echo Company.

I tried to press inside the BAS. First Sergeant Foster, who met me as I exited the vehicle, grabbed my shoulder. "Sir, I've got him. We've got it from here. We'll take care of him."

Deep down, I wanted to stop everything I was doing and stay with Libby. But the BAS had a top-notch crew of medics, and Foster had things under control. He was right. There was nothing more I could do.

I had to focus on the other two hundred Marines that were still out there in direct contact.

The chaos and bloodshed were not over—we had a long night ahead of us. It was just the beginning of the longest night of fighting we would encounter.

CHAPTER 6

Terps

A few days after I arrived at Camp Corregidor, I heard about an incident involving an Iraqi named Mohammed who worked for contractors collecting garbage from the Multi-National Force (MNF). He decided to work for the MNF to earn money for his family as well as support the cause of a free Iraq. His choice branded him as a traitor to the insurgents.

One day, soldiers spotted a trash truck parked on the side of a road east of Camp Corregidor on MSR Michigan. They cautiously inspected the truck for vehicle-borne improvised explosive devices (VBIEDs). The VBIED was a common tactic employed by insurgents. They'd pack a car or truck full of explosives, park it on a street, and, when a patrol walked or drove by, they'd detonate the device. It was a cheap but effective tactic that yielded tremendous shock effect if done right.

Instead of a bomb, the task force soldiers were shocked to find a dismembered body stuffed in the cab of the truck. For his dissidence, after a hard day of work, he had been murdered by the insurgents. My thoughts were consumed of how this unassuming man who was willing to pick up our trash could suffer such a horrible death.

Mohammed's story is similar to that of many other courageous Iraqis who sacrificed so much—in some cases, their lives—to help us accomplish our mission.

■   ■   ■

The Iraqis we dealt with the most, the ones who became closest to us and vice versa, were the interpreters, or as we called them "Terps."

Terps were essential for our success on the battlefield. Few soldiers or Marines spoke fluent Arabic. We had some basic classes before deployment and used what we called "pointy-talkie" cards, laminated papers with key phrases and pictures on them to help us get by, but that was about it. If we needed to talk to the locals—and we did—we needed Terps.

To become a Terp, Iraqis first had to take and pass written and verbal tests administered by the contract companies that recruited Terps for the MNF. These were designed to check the candidates' English proficiency level. Depending on how well they spoke, read, and wrote determined what category of Terp they would be. The best went to the high-level commands and special forces—others were farmed out to the regiment level and below.

But that wasn't all. The results of security screening and background checks played a large part in the decisions about where to place Terps. Again, the better the security clearance they received, the better the job they got.

By 2006, Terps were in such high demand across Iraq that some contractors cut corners on the language requirements and focused on the security screening. It made sense from a business perspective. The more Terps the contractors placed with the MNF, the more money they made. For those of us in the field, it meant that the quality and skill of the Terps could vary considerably.

Many of the Terps were drawn to the job's relatively high pay. At a time when the average Iraqi salary was $500 a month, Terps pulled in three times that. It was a lot of money by Iraqi standards, and it apparently was enough to balance out the risks they'd encounter on the battlefield and at home.

They never got any formal training on how to be effective as Terps— the best experience was on the job. Their successfulness depended greatly on their relationships with the Marines.

Insurgents commonly targeted Terps during combat operations. It wasn't too hard to do. The Terps stood out like a sore thumb. They looked different, they sometimes wore different uniforms, and the vast majority sported beards, something that only special-operations forces usually got away with. At home, if they were exposed while working for the MNF, they and their families became targets of threats, kidnappings, and murder. Some Terps were killed when they went back home to spend time with their families. Often, it was enough to drive them to quit. Terps would leave for home—and never come back.

The news of murders and kidnappings of Terps spread even before the surge strategy was underway. When the MNF withdrew from an area, it became even more dangerous for Terps. They were left alone and afraid, without their military protectors to shield them from the violence.

Within the MNF, especially the U.S. military, there were two unofficial categories when it came to interpreters. Terp lovers—those who valued the immense contributions they made to our cause and respected them for the sacrifices they made to serve with us—and Terp haters— those who felt they were nothing more than embedded spies forced into their ranks by higher command, and not to be trusted.

I was a Terp lover for more reasons than I can explain, mostly because I owe my life, the lives of my Marines, and the success of our operations and the hundreds of patrols we conducted to the bravery of these citizen-warriors. As a commander, I'd often think how lucky I was to have these brave young men, who gave up everything, by my side.

To this day, I am eternally grateful to the Terps that made a difference to Echo Company—we were total strangers to them, yet these patriots, no more than twenty years old, sacrificed so much to help us fight and win.

Happily, my Marines shared my view of Terps. They treated them as part of the team because they *were* a part of the team. They ate, slept, and worked with the Marines every day. They contributed to our success on the ground. The Marines bonded with them—to the point that they often subjected them to the same rough humor and curt language they used amongst themselves.

First Sergeant Foster, who took care of everyone, was as concerned about the Terps as he was any Marine. He knew that if the Marines pushed them too far, they might quit and leave us in a lurch. One day, Foster gathered the NCOs and platoon sergeants together. "Look, you have to take it easy on the Terps. They're not Marines. They're not used to being fucked with like you guys. You got it?"

Terps usually were known by their call signs, another way to protect their identity. One of ours, Big Sam, was one of Echo Company's most skilled interpreters.

Big Sam was not that big really. He was tall, six feet even, and weighed around 150 skinny pounds. He was eighteen, with olive skin and dark black hair. His face was gaunt but clean-shaven, unlike most Iraqi men.

Forced to grow up fast surrounded by Baghdad's violence and hatred, Big Sam had a serious and mature look about him. He had every right to it.

He had been forced to leave his home in Baghdad, and he missed his family keenly. He felt depressed about that and the fact he couldn't confide in even his lifelong friends.

He knew, too, that many of his countrymen regarded anyone who worked for the MNF as "*Kha'en*"—a traitor—or "*Jasoos*"—a spy. The labels haunted him.

To ease his anxieties, whenever Big Sam went to sleep—normally for only three or four hours a day—he would try to remember the faces of his family. Small things, like the memories of his family, helped him keep his sanity.

Our other Terp, Ford, was baby faced, six-two, and slim. He was the quieter of the two, and his English was not as advanced as Big Sam's.

But, whatever Ford lacked in language ability, he made up ten-fold in effort. Ford had another link with Big Sam: they had been best friends in Baghdad.

Born in 1987, they were in high school when Saddam Hussein's regime fell. Big Sam planned to pursue a degree in computer engineering—a skill that was in great demand in Iraq, as the war-torn country was on the brink of rebuilding itself.

In 2005, while still in high school, Ford and Big Sam spent time talking with American troops in Baghdad. They were curious about Americans and bullshitting with the troops allowed them to improve their English.

By 2005, even casual conversations with MNF troops were risky. Even the thinnest rumor floating around a neighborhood could put their entire family at risk for retribution—cozying up with the American troops was something that just wasn't done.

One day, Big Sam and Ford went to the International Zone (or Green Zone, a place designated as a safe zone by military doctrine) in Baghdad to talk with a representative from one of the interpreter contract companies and test for the job. At the time, Big Sam had no intention of actually doing it. He just thought the experience of taking the test would be fun.

Both of them passed the tests, and the company offered them positions.

Ford smiled and said they should try it out.

Big Sam was categorically against the idea. "No way, brother. I don't need the money. I want to stay focused on school. Plus, I'm seventeen. They won't even hire me."

Big Sam was a sharp intellectual. He wanted a university degree and knew working for the coalition forces would surely derail his plans.

The boys returned home and evaded questions from friends and family as to where they had been. They didn't want anyone to find out they'd been in the Green Zone associating with the Americans.

One day in mid-June 2006, when Big Sam arrived home, he spied an envelope sitting inside the high, steel gate outside his home. He picked it up carefully. As he did so, he felt a small lump inside the package.

When he opened the flap, he found a long shiny 7.62mm bullet and a short, handwritten note:

"*Leave your houses, or we'll behead you and your family, Shia infidels.*"

The insurgents had targeted Big Sam and his family and had now made that abundantly clear.

Before receiving this sinister package, Big Sam and Ford had enjoyed pleasant lives.

They grew up in stable neighborhoods, had plenty of friends, lived in beautiful homes, and had hardworking parents who provided for them. They were like other Iraqi teenagers who enjoyed talking on the phone, playing soccer, and just plain hanging out.

They had known about the insurgency and its effects and had heard of the increase in sectarian violence throughout Iraq—bombings, murders, and intimidation. But it had never carved its way into their lives.

Now, it had.

Big Sam and Ford were forced to abandon their homes and relocate to a Shia area. They hastily gathered up everything they could, but had to leave behind most of their clothes, furniture, and personal belongings and mementos—including irreplaceable photos that defined their childhood.

Big Sam felt utterly helpless as if someone were kicking him as he lay face down in the dirt, and he couldn't get up to fight back. Things seemed hopeless.

It often pained him to look at his mother's and sister's eyes so often filled with tears at times and saw the despair painted on their faces.

Despite his pain and frustration, Big Sam's indomitable spirit gave him the optimism that somehow, he'd find a way to get back everything that his family had lost, especially their sense of safety.

Ford continued to encourage Big Sam to become an interpreter. "Brother," he said, "we've lost our homes, our stuff, and our respect. We've got to go to work as interpreters. Fuck those insurgents! It's our only way to strike back at those assholes."

Big Sam now embraced the idea. "All right, *sadiq*. Let's do this. I can't stay here any longer, and it's killing me to see my family like this."

It was a difficult and risky decision for both young men.

Big Sam broke the news to his father as they drove through Baghdad days before his departure. He told him he'd already gone through the entire process to be an interpreter and that he and Ford had already signed their contracts.

Big Sam's father was shocked. "Son, I can't let you go work for the coalition forces. They're occupiers, and it's too dangerous for everyone. I won't let you do it."

His father was a loyal Iraqi who truly loved his country.

Big Sam appealed to his father's patriotism. "Dad, the U.S. troops aren't occupiers. The real occupiers are the insurgents who have taken everything away from us, who took our homes and destroyed our lives and what you built your whole life."

His father continued to try to make Big Sam change his mind and stay. He tried to assure him that he'd make a better living for them with the help of the family—together. Allah would help them do it.

Big Sam pleaded, "I have to do this, Dad. I can't stand staying here seeing Mom and the girls in so much pain and living day in and day out with the grief."

Reluctantly, but with a father's pride, he acquiesced and agreed that no one from the family would know specifically what job Big Sam would be doing. More importantly, they wouldn't mention where he'd be doing it—in one of the most highly contested and dangerous areas of Iraq.

Both agreed to tell Big Sam's mother that he'd be working for an oil company in northern Iraq, a relatively safe area at the time. Ford contrived a similar cover story to tell his family.

Together, they stood ready to begin an adventure that would change the course of their lives.

The next day, Big Sam and Ford went back to the Green Zone. The company asked where they wanted to work. Big Sam said without hesitation, "I want to work in Al Anbar Province and serve with the Marines."

Big Sam was enamored and impressed with the Marine Corps from the images they portrayed in the movies. He had interacted with them on the streets of Baghdad and knew they were special—he wanted to be a part of that.

Big Sam and Ford were scheduled to fly out on a U.S. helicopter a few days later, hundreds of miles away from their families and homes. Before they left everything behind, Big Sam wanted to spend his last night in his old home in Baghdad.

Ford didn't want to stay—it was just too risky. He'd already said his goodbyes to his family. He was sure insurgents would kill them if they knew they had returned.

Big Sam insisted. He needed the connection one last time, and later that night they sat in Big Sam's childhood bedroom and played video games. Through the darkness, they heard strange men on the street chanting loudly.

"*Al Moot LeKofar*!" It meant, "*Die, Infidels!*"

Ford turned to Big Sam with panic written on his face, "Great. Thanks. We're going to get killed because of your stupid idea of spending one last night at your house."

Big Sam ran into his parents' bedroom and found the AK-47 rifle that his father had kept. Neither knew how to use it, and they fumbled with it clumsily, trying to figure out how to load it and shoot it.

The shouting stopped, but the boys spent the night wide awake, crouched in the corner of the bedroom, holding the rifle—it felt like an eternity to them.

When morning finally came, Big Sam's brother picked them up. They quickly snuck out of the house, got into his car, and hunkered down out of sight.

Big Sam's brother drove them straight to the MNF staging base. Later that day, Big Sam and Ford and a handful of other interpreters boarded an Army UH-60 Blackhawk helicopter and headed from Baghdad to Camp Al Asad for assignment to the units they'd be supporting.

It was their first time on a helicopter—excitement and fear flooded their senses.

Flying a thousand feet above the ground, Big Sam looked down at the harsh landscape—the place he once called home. He pulled out his cell phone and typed out a text message to his girlfriend.

Big Sam and his girlfriend were happy to be just that, friends, and they pragmatically scoffed at the idea of true love at such a young age. Big Sam let her know he'd be gone for a while and asked her to keep him in her prayers. He concluded his message, "I'll miss you a lot."

Big Sam swelled with emotion, hurting inside, as his hometown passed out of sight.

He thought, "Baghdad, do you believe I'll see you again alive?"

His sense of unease was heightened when, miles outside the city, the door gunner of the Blackhawk opened fire from the aircraft's .50 caliber GAU-19 machine gun and the helicopter banked and rocked violently—it scared the shit out of Big Sam.

He thought, "What the fuck have I gotten into if this is just the beginning?"

One hour later, they reached Camp Al Asad and were put through the paces of getting outfitted with all the gear they'd need: helmets, camouflage uniforms, boots, backpacks, and twenty-pound armored vests they'd have to get used to wearing daily on their already slender frames.

Neither knew anything about the military. Both were plucked from civilian life and planted right into the Marine Corps—the most hardcore branch of warriors in the world. They got no training. It was a complete culture shock. While they lacked military experience and were now in an utterly unfamiliar world, both Ford and Big Sam pressed on.

What they didn't know is how indispensable they would become to Echo Company as we continued to fight.

CHAPTER 7

Seventh

I moved from the Naval Weapons Station in Yorktown, Virginia, where I was serving with 2nd Fleet Anti-Terrorism Security Team (FAST) Company, to take command of Echo Company at Camp San Mateo at Camp Pendleton, California. I traveled unaccompanied, that is, without my wife and daughter, who stayed in Virginia. I drove cross-country. I checked in on a Tuesday, parked my Jeep in the battalion parking lot, and took command that Friday.

The next week the battalion was at Twentynine Palms, California, in the heat of the Mojave Desert participating in the Enhanced Mojave Viper training program that was designed to prepare Marines specifically for urban combat scenarios they were facing in Iraq at the time.

With less than five months until my new battalion deployed, I decided to forgo renting an apartment and live in my office in the battalion command post.

The command post was a dilapidated, two-story building that smelled like a musty cellar. Mice infested the ceilings. At night, I would hear them scurrying above the white, flaky, industrial ceiling tiles. There was no air-conditioning, and the windows were always open. The ledges made an ideal perch for birds who defecated on the well-worn carpet—and occasionally my uniform that I regularly hung on the back of my office chair.

If only one unit used the building, it might have been in better condition. As it was, because units rotated through it constantly, no one had taken ownership of it—I viewed it as equivalent to a beat-up mobile home rental in a trailer park.

When the Marines found out that their CO was residing in the command post, they most likely thought, "Oh, hell. Here we go. This guy has no life, and we are never going to get off work early."

Some would say that might have been the case, but in retrospect, I think I was rather even-keeled about the arrangement. We worked and trained hard because I knew what was on the horizon for all of us.

One of the perks of "office living" was the fact that I could swing by the Bachelor Enlisted Quarters (BEQ), or barracks, and check on my Marines whenever I felt like it. I knew firsthand that the best way to find out what was going on in a unit was to hang around the enlisted barracks on a Thursday night. It was "field day" in the Marine Corps—the day when enlisted Marines cleaned their rooms to be inspection-ready when the company first sergeant examined them on Friday morning. The smell of Pine Sol multi-purpose cleaner when walking in the rooms was strong enough to bring the toughest Marine to his knees.

My closeness to my Marines produced many benefits. The most important of which was that I got to know the Marines that I would ultimately be putting my confidence in, while they got to know the man they'd be entrusting their lives with as we fought in Ramadi.

■   ■   ■

7 December 2006

I exited the BAS feeling empty after leaving Libby behind—the image of his face was still fresh in my mind, but I pushed back the thought. I had to get back out into the fight and position myself where I thought the most friction was.

It was past midnight when the Quick Reaction Force headed back to ECP 8.

While 4th platoon was fighting hard at ECP 8, two of my other platoons also were battling hard against the enemy. First Platoon was slugging it out at OP South House, a couple of hundred meters south of ECP 8. Second Platoon was equally engaged north of MSR Michigan at the four-story complex of OP Hotel.

OP Hotel came by that name naturally. It actually had been a hotel, The Ramadi Inn. I was quite certain it lost its five-star rating after a suicide bomber detonated a dump truck filled with explosives directly in front of it in 2004. Since then, it had been peppered with so many bullets and RPGs that it looked like a massive chunk of Swiss cheese. Frankly, I was astonished that the building was still standing.

Once inside ECP 8, I saw the radio operator, Lance Corporal Christopher Muscle, monitoring the tactical radio nets. He told me that OP South House and OP Hotel were getting into it hard and the Marines would need an ammunition resupply soon.

Also in the COC was Staff Sergeant Miller who sat on top of a green, folding military cot with one boot off. He told me that he thought he had busted his ankle coming down from the roof with Libby on the makeshift ladder made of two-by-four lumber.

I asked him where Second Lieutenant Nicholson was.

"He's up on top. He's on the roof, sir."

I scaled the busted wooden ladder. I was instantly exposed to fire as I crossed an open gap between the two buildings that joined ECP 8 to the house next door.

It was pitch black, but I could tell that ECP 8 was standing engaged from every side by small arms and medium machine-gun fire from enemy fighters who were trying to get close enough to our position to throw grenades into the compound. Green, blue, and red tracers streaked into the air, bright against the blackness of the sky. Everywhere was the rattle of small arms fire, the deeper thud of machine guns, and the sound of loud explosions from every direction.

I started yelling, "Where's Lieutenant Nicholson?"

He called out to me, "I'm over here, sir! I'm right over here!"

I crouched low to the ground and duck-walked toward his location only a few meters away. Spent brass ammunition casings rolled under my boots as I shuffled closer.

The air was thick with smoke that had the distinctive spicy chemical smell of rifle fire which always reminded me of lighting off a brick of firecrackers.

"Nicholson, what's going on, man?"

"They're all over, sir! They're all around us—you'd better stay low!"

I'd been in situations like this more times than I cared to remember, and I heeded Nicholson's advice.

Nicholson told me that there were at least five teams of enemy close by who had maneuvered into a series of buildings to our west. I looked across the street and watched an enemy squad trying to engage us with machine guns.

He pointed out that the enemy was also engaging the Iraqi Army (IA) position across the cul-de-sac, and one of his squads was trying to support it with fire from their M249 squad automatic weapons (SAWs) and rifles. The enemy was trying to advance south on Route Apple toward the IA compound.

I thought to myself, "The IA better hold their fucking ground tonight and fight back."

I asked Nicholson what he thought was the biggest threat. He said the building east of ECP 8. There, the enemy was getting ready to engage us with hand grenades and RPG fire.

I told him, "I'm on it."

The rooftops of the complex at ECP 8, like most Ramadi homes, were built with traditional, flat, concrete roofs, similar to sundecks on certain American-style homes. I made my way across the roof and down the rickety, makeshift ladder into the COC to get in contact with the task force headquarters back at Camp Corregidor.

Less than halfway down, I was knocked off the ladder by the jolting blast of an RPG that smacked into one of the walls. Flailing and skipping several rungs, I fell hard on top of all my gear.

My helmet crashed into the side of the wall. I felt a sharp "snap" in my neck and pain in my back. I shook it off. Gathering up all my gear from the 'yard sale' the blast had just made of my stuff, I made my way back inside the COC.

One of the Marines looked at me and could see I was a bit disheveled as I shook myself off, trying to sort out my gear. Like a turtle snapping back into its shell, he reared his head and neck back with a concerned look on his face. "What was that, sir? You alright?"

"Yeah, I'm good, brother." I tried to compose myself after having the shit knocked out of me seconds earlier.

I picked up the handset of the radio and called the task force's operations officer, Major Jared Norrell. I requested that he send the tank QRF to my position.

Norrell responded, "They're on their way."

The tank crews kept their hatches buttoned up in their Abrams as they drove. Rounds bounced off like gnats. Echo Company Marines tried to talk them onto the targets over the radio. The tank crews had limited situational awareness and observation from inside the vehicles. They relied on our radio communications to paint them a picture.

When the tank QRF, consisting of two M1-A1 Abrams, rolled up, they checked onto Echo's tactical radio channel (TAC): "Longhorn Six, this is Blue One and Blue Two. Over." ("*Longhorn*" was Echo Company's call sign, and, as Echo's commander, my call sign was "*Longhorn Six*." The commander of every unit is called the "*Six*").

"We're outside on Sufia Road. Ready for tasking. Over."

The two Abrams, armed with their 120mm main gun and 7.62 caliber coaxial machine gun, were ready to get in the fight.

Coordinating their support was complicated. The radio I needed to talk to the tankers and the map I referenced—an alphanumeric map that is a gridded reference graphic that had every single building plotted out—was in the Command Operations Center.

But, with us being in a close-quarters battle in a built-up area, I needed to confirm the targets with my own eyes. I had no choice then but to shuttle back and forth—using the goddamned ladder—forced into a dance between the COC and the rooftop each time we wanted to clear the fires of the tanks. I ran up and down the ladder until I sorted them out.

To help the tankers see where they needed to shoot, I told the boys to mark the buildings where the enemy was holed up and to go heavy on the orange-tipped tracer rounds. To the tankers looking through the thermal-imaging equipment in the M1's, the tracers would look like streams of light heading into the target. As they did, some of the Marines poured machine gun fire onto enemy positions to suppress them from shooting back.

I yelled up to Nicholson, "Once you mark those buildings, get everyone down flat on that roof when the tanks blast those buildings."

The blast of the tanks' 120mm gun was loud, huge, and powerful in any case. In a built-up area with narrow streets and high walls, the force would not dissipate, but be channeled upwards, and off the walls acting like an invisible bulldozer.

The Marines laid down more tracer fire, and the tanks confirmed they had the target.

I yelled back up to Nicholson, "Get the boys down! I'm about to clear the tanks to engage with main tank rounds! Tell me when you're all down!"

Nicholson responded, "We're down, sir! We're all down."

I called the tanks. "Blue Two. This is Longhorn Six. Cleared to engage."

No more than thirty seconds later, Blue Two fired one 120mm tank round into its target. The effects were devastating—shattering the walls of the insurgent stronghold and killing those foolish enough to think they were safe inside. The Marines on the roof popped back up and immediately re-engaged the enemy with a heavy volume of fire.

The tank's crew apparently were unaware the Marines on the roof were back up and firing, manning the walls.

The barrel of the tank sat wedged in between two of the buildings, tucked in between the large pockets of concrete formed by the adjacent structures. The soldiers inside the tank assumed that each section was cleared to engage two rounds each.

Blue Two pumped a second main gun round into the same building it had just hit next door to ECP 8. The overpressure from the muzzle break of the barrel had nowhere to go but up.

Lance Corporals Jonathan Yenglin and Ryan Downing stood back up, continuing to mark targets. As the second round blasted from the tank, the resulting overpressure knocked both Marines flat on their backs.

Yenglin was a twenty-one-year-old from Las Vegas, Nevada. He stood five-eleven at 195 pounds, with brown hair and brown eyes that his amber-tinted safety glasses made barely visible. He'd been swayed at an early age by all of the Marines' fantastic recruiting commercials when he was fourteen. He wanted to slay dragons.

The Marines dragged Yenglin to the safety of one of the rooftop bunkers. Doc Dicks came to his aid. Knowing that he'd need to get Yenglin down the ladder somehow, he tried to duct tape him to a stretcher.

Yenglin, still dazed, looked back at Doc Dicks with all of the contempt he could muster. "Doc, there is no fucking way I'm going down that ladder duct taped to this stretcher! I'll walk." And, with another Marine helping him, he did just that.

Yenglin writhed in pain from the jarring blast as his brothers moved him to the COC. His insides burned, and his ears rang. His head throbbed and stung more than any hangover he'd ever felt. Worse, his vision was dark and blurry. He could barely see.

Lying on a cot, Downing looked like a rag doll. His arms and legs dangled over the edges. His face was pale and bore a blank expression. Downing was short and weighed about a buck-forty with bricks in his pockets. This was not his first Purple Heart—he'd been wounded in combat already. He was a 2004 Ramadi veteran with 2d Battalion, 4th Marines.

When the litter teams brought Yenglin and Downing into the platoon COC and laid them out on the cots, I immediately called on Company TAC to Blue Two and ordered them to cease fire. I radioed the TOC back at Camp Corregidor to advise them that we had two more priority casualties who needed to get to the aid station.

Somerville's QRF had managed to get his convoy back to the position accompanied by an M113 armored personnel carrier (APC) which would act as an ambulance.

Yenglin vomited as they hefted him into the vehicle. Both Marines were concussed badly.

As soon as they left, I ordered the tanks to continue to fire on Sufia Road and south on Route Apple. Using the muzzle flashes of the enemy weapons and the Marines' tracers to direct their fire, they drilled main-gun rounds into target after target with amazing precision.

■　　■　　■

Nicholson stayed on the rooftop the entire time and did an astounding job leading his Marines in a hellish combat environment. He had been in the operating forces for only five months, but he performed as if he'd been doing it for twenty years. For his actions that night, he was awarded the Navy Commendation Medal with Valor Device (known as the "Combat V").

■　　■　　■

In the midst of fighting, Neris asked Nicholson how Libby was. Nicholson walked away.

He asked again.

Nicholson replied, "He's stable."

Corporal Tom Welsh overheard the exchange. He was the 3rd Squad Leader in 4th Platoon.

Welsh never drank soda. The Marines nicknamed him "Juice Box" because of it. He was a twenty-year-old fitness junkie from Decatur, Illinois. He had black hair and brown eyes and, at five-ten and lean—almost skinny at 140 pounds—he looked even younger. His looks belied his manner. Welsh was as dependable and as trustworthy as they came.

As enemy rounds still thrashed the walls of ECP 8, Welsh walked up to Neris and told him in a sullen tone, "Man, I can't lie to you. He didn't make it."

For the second time that night, Neris took a knee in the middle of the roof. Tears again streamed down his face, and his chest heaved as short gasps escaped his lungs. He tried to stifle any audible crying because, again, he didn't want the other Marines to see him cry.

Welsh reached down and grabbed Neris by the six-inch, nylon strap on the back of his body armor, shook him from side to side and said, "Come on, man. We can't do this now."

The attack continued relentlessly.

Nicholson called down to me that he was taking a high volume of fire from the west side of the building. I was talking to Norrell at the time, and I told him I needed more fire support.

"Manchu Three," I said. "Manchu" was the task force's call sign. "Three" was the designation for the operations officer. "What type of aviation do we have on station now?"

Norrell replied that we could have a section of fixed-wing aircraft—two Marine fast-movers, McDonnell Douglas AV-8B Harrier attack jets—to be precise. I immediately generated a close air support (CAS) request and passed the information to the TOC. It was going to be a Type III control, meaning that I could provide only observation and information on the targets to the TOC—they would have to approve the mission and then relay it to the pilots.

The Harriers would be checking in armed with 500-pound MK-82 bombs—ordnance normally used against medium to large structures and minimize collateral damage.

I told Norrell that it was going to be "danger-close" for what the Harriers were packing since our position was only one hundred meters from the target. Although the effects of the bombs would be safely mitigated by intervening concrete structures, the bombs' devastating effects would still put us within the danger radius.

There was a mad scramble to get everyone off the rooftop—we had only minutes to get the bombs dropped on the target.

Nicholson confirmed that everyone was down. I called back to Manchu Three and told him that we were safe, and he could approve the mission.

"Two minutes until impact," Norrell said.

I heard the roar of the jets and braced for the shockwave of the bombs, hunkering underneath the plywood table. I tucked the radio handset between my helmet and ear, freeing my hands and allowing me to jam a big dip of Copenhagen in my bottom lip.

Lance Corporal Brian Dickinson leaned near me. "That's not a bad idea, sir. If that bomb misses the mark, I want to go out with a fat one in [referring to the dip of Cope]. This shit is getting pretty hairy."

The flight passed overhead.

Norrell got back on the radio. "Longhorn Six, this is Manchu Three. No drop. No drop. Over." The bomb had failed to release from the wing, what aviators call "hung ordnance."

The flight was advised to conduct a re-attack since the jets had enough gas.

Nicholson called down. He wasn't able to positively identify the mark made by the forward air controller-airborne on the target. He couldn't see it, even with night vision goggles.

The mark wasn't easy to see in the first place as it looked like an infrared flashing strobe light—only visible through NVGs. It wasn't like a huge floodlight shining at a used car extravaganza sale, beaming down from the sky.

I did a quick stubby-pencil drill on my map—re-checking the geometry. Suddenly, I had visions of the bomb missing the target—and hitting us. The hairs on my neck stood up—it was going to be too close. Without hesitating, I called the TOC. "Abort, abort, abort!" There went our air strike.

Norrell called back, "The only thing I have left for you is GMLRS." We pronounced the acronym as a word in slang: "*Gimlars.*" The Army's Guided Multiple Launcher Rocket System (GMLRS) fires a rocket that resembles a twenty-foot telephone pole, carries a 200-pound warhead, and is guided by GPS. Even at its maximum range of more than twenty miles, it can hit its targets with surgical precision. In fact, the Army GMLRS Battery that was firing in support of us was located outside of Fallujah.

I looked on the wall in the COC and saw an MRE carton taped to the wall on which was written the GMLRS call-for-fire instructions. I quickly called back to the TOC with the following transmission:

"Manchu Three, this is Longhorn Six. Request GMLRS, one rocket each. Sector two-six-five, buildings six-six and six-seven. Immediate Suppression, Over."

The voice from the TOC read back, "Distance 165 meters from friendlies to target."

■　　■　　■

My company executive officer, First Lieutenant Bobby Lee, was inside the TOC when I called in the GMLRS mission, watching the video feeds from the drones buzzing over our zone. He heard my call for fire support come across the radio, as did the Air Naval Gunfire Liaison Company (ANGLICO) representative, and the Army "battle captain" who stood watch over the TOC staff.

Lieutenant Colonel Ferry was standing beside Lee when the battle captain turned to Ferry and said, "Sir. You do know that each one of those rockets cost like $100,000?"

Ferry's response affirmed the unwavering loyalty he had for the Marines he commanded in his task force.

"I don't give a fuck if they cost one-hundred *million* dollars!" Ferry replied with certainty. "They killed a U.S. Marine tonight. Approve the mission."

■　　■　　■

The Marines cleared the roof only minutes before the rockets struck their targets.

We called in more rockets. Having seen what happened to Downing and Yenglin, the Marines on the roof were anxious to be under shelter when the rockets arrived.

There was a small room on the roof of ECP 8, no more than four by four feet in size. As the rockets launched, Muscle called to the Marines on the roof, "Get the fuck in here." As clowns seem to do in a circus car, ten Marines, laden with gear and weapons, piled into the room for protection. After a few minutes passed, the absurdity of the situation spurred their laughter. Pressed tightly against one another, one by one they started laughing.

From the middle of the dog pile, squished by the other Marines piled on top of him, Muscle chuckled. He asked the group, "Does the CO know what *"danger close"* is?"

Another Marine from the pile chimed in jokingly, "I want to say, I love you guys. Just in case we're about to get fucked up."

The rocket unit in Fallujah fired five missions within roughly one hour's time, starting at 0017 and ending at 0119 that night.

When the rockets hit, their warheads detonated with a sharp, but somewhat muffled explosion. We barely felt any shockwaves even though we were less than two football fields away. It was sort of underwhelming—that is until we saw the massive damage they inflicted.

I would use the GMLRS throughout my time in Ramadi. I discovered that one rocket on a target would suck the life right out of the building and paint the walls red; two in the same building would bring it to the ground, and there'd be no need for a search afterward. Nothing would survive such devastating impacts.

After the last rocket struck, the enemy fire ceased. Keyed up, the Marines were still blazing away at whatever targets they still had in their sights. I heard screaming from the rooftop. It was the squad leaders yelling, "Cease fire! Cease fire! Cease fire! Fucking cease fire!"

They did.

Crickets.

The rockets killed the insurgents and sent any remaining for the closest avenue of escape from the destruction that had just rained down on them.

In the quiet, the Marines scanned the area with their thermal imaging scopes—the dead, but still warm, bodies lay waiting to be counted—a massive number of enemy killed in action.

Reports began to come in as the Marines and soldiers started identifying the enemy that littered the streets.

There were dead insurgents in the doorways of the houses. In the middle of the streets. Behind abandoned cars.

Some asked permission to go out on patrol to search the enemy dead for intelligence. I refused. In all our time in Ramadi, I never allowed it. I always told them, "Fuck 'em. Count them up and then let the fucking dogs have 'em for dinner."

Comments like that motivated the hell out of the boys. In reality, I knew that the risk of trying to recover the bodies far outweighed the value of any intelligence they'd provide. Plus, the insurgents fighting in the area had their own highly effective means of conducting casualty collection. They forced civilians to bring the dead and wounded to safe houses and mosques; the latter of which were off-limits to the MNF.

I remained focused on controlling the battle at ECP 8, but 2nd Platoon at OP Hotel and 1st Platoon at OP South House had been heavily engaged as well. Several other Echo Company Marines were wounded that night, but none of their injuries were life-threatening. I was amazed that we suffered so few casualties considering that we'd been in contact for almost five hours.

■   ■   ■

It was past 0300 hours.

Nicholson looked at me as we sat in the COC. "Hey, sir, I'm glad you were here tonight."

"Glad I could make it. I wouldn't have missed this shit for the world."

I rubbed my head and looked around surveying the green plastic containers full of chow sitting at their position. The boys had just started eating dinner when the fighting began. MRE boxes sat on the floor as makeshift dining tables with a few plates of ice-cold spaghetti sitting on them. Grease coagulated around the edges of the misshapen meatballs.

Nicholson picked up one of the plates. I knew he was about to devour it, but I still asked, "Are you really going to eat that shit?"

Sure as anything, he wolfed down the plate of spaghetti. "I'm fucking starving, sir. I think this spaghetti just saved my life!"

"Now that's bravery—eating that shit."

Muscle dug into a dirt-covered can of Maxwell House and started a pot of coffee. He knew everyone in the platoon would need it.

The other Marines gave Muscle a hard time. They referred to him as my little brother since he had a brush of red hair on his head, and we were both about the same size. He was five-eleven, 190 pounds and athletic. He was a twenty-year-old rifleman from Lewisville, Texas, north of Dallas. His accent was not as thick as some of the other Texans', which was why he was possibly one of the best radio operators in the company.

Muscle was bright. He was always studying books on field medicine, tactics, and patrolling. He read whatever he could find about war and combat. His maturity, aptitude, and collected nature set him above his peers.

We sat and waited for the mobile QRF to come pick us up as we sipped the strong, hot, black coffee from little tan paper cups that Muscle made.

Staff Sergeant James "Mac" Mackenzie, Somerville's platoon sergeant, walked into the COC and briefed me that all the casualties from the night were back safely at the COP. With great foresight, he and Somerville had mustered a couple of rough squads of men from 3rd Platoon to start relieving the boys at ECP 8 who were worn out from fighting all night. These Marines stood post in place of their exhausted brothers for several hours, even though they'd all been driving from post to post, conducting ammo resupply all night.

■   ■   ■

Mac was a drill instructor, and it showed in the self-confident way he carried himself. He was a stocky thirty-year-old and stood five-seven and 180 pounds. He had been the quarterback and captain of the football team at Bristol-Plymouth Vocational-Tech High School in Taunton, Massachusetts, where he grew up—forty miles due south of Boston.

Mac was a military brat. His dad served in the Air Force and raised him and his two siblings alone. He knew he wanted to follow his dad into the military, but he wanted nothing to do with the Marines. Being a crazed killer, like the Marines he saw in every movie, was not for him. He was much more attracted to the relatively cushy lifestyle of the Air Force.

A year after high school he sat in the Armed Forces Recruiting Office, waiting patiently for the Air Force recruiter to show up.

A Marine staff sergeant walked through the door instead, glared at Mac, and growled, "What the fuck are you doing here?"

Mac was taken aback but intrigued by the man's audacity. In no time at all, he was practically shamed into leaving the Air Force office and sitting in front of the staff sergeant's desk that was draped in camouflage netting. There he signed his enlistment papers guaranteeing him infantry duty in the Marines.

Mac was proud of what he had done, but he was nervous about the reaction he would get from his father.

His dad was surprised but smiled big, then chuckled. "Well, good luck with that."

■   ■   ■

I made one last sweep on the rooftop to talk to all of the boys and tell them how proud I was of them. The roof of ECP 8 looked like a god-damned brass factory, scattered with spent cartridges from all of the ammo they'd shot over the past five hours; literally, thousands of shell casings covered the roof. Random gunfire cracked in the distance of the city like the last few kernels in a bag of microwave popcorn after the timer had shut off.

Physically banged up from the events, I was exhausted and emotionally drained—running off pure adrenaline.

I kept my motivation high. I wanted to make sure all the boys knew I was there for them. It was important for me to look collected and confident, even though I may have felt beat to shit personally.

With the fighting over for the day, Neris lay down and slept. He dreamed that night about Libby, but not as the tough Marine. He appeared in a white suit, strolled toward Neris, and thanked him. In his dream, Neris thanked him back. Libby gave him a cool, approving head-nod.

Neris woke up. It was all very real to him.

Muscle, too, was spent. He looked like a zombie. Nicholson knew that he hadn't slept in days and said, "Muscle, go use my room and rack out for a few hours."

Muscle made his way into his lieutenant's room to crash out. Before he could get settled in, he noticed Libby's body armor and gear were staged neatly against the wall of the tiny room, a painfully visible reminder to Muscle of the loss his platoon suffered that night.

Before he lay down, Muscle walked over to Libby's gear and gently draped his soft, digital camouflaged poncho liner over it. He couldn't rest knowing that if he woke up, someone had disrupted Libby's gear. I don't know if he did it for his peace of mind that morning before he slept, or as a final gesture to his fallen comrade.

By mid-morning, all of the Marines found out that Libby had died.

My one regret that night was calling back to the TOC at Camp Corregidor to ask the status of my Urgent CASEVAC (Libby) during the fight over the radio. I had the sense to turn off the volume on the radio speaker box before I made the call.

Norrell called back, "Do you really want to know?"

I said, "No, disregard. I got it."

It was a tough lesson for me to learn. There are some things you don't talk about on the radio.

We'd conducted plenty of patrols and had multiple contacts with the enemy before 6 December. But the intense, grueling five-hour firefight that night set a new standard for all of Echo Company of what it meant to fight in Ramadi.

CHAPTER 8

Angels

I never knew what exactly happened to my dead and wounded Marines once they left the battlefield from the point of injury. The injured—well, I figured they went from the aid station and then to some hospital that was unknown to me.

As for the dead, I had a few ideas, based on what I had seen in films and books about World War II and the Vietnam War. The dead stacked up like cordwood in the back of a truck or stuffed into black plastic body bags with heavy metal zippers, scattered randomly in a rice paddy and then unceremoniously chucked onto the back of a Huey helicopter. Eventually, they'd make their way to some cemetery for a military funeral, complete with a flag-draped coffin, three volleys, and Taps.

Even as an officer with more than fifteen years of service at the time in 2006, I never really knew how the whole process unfolded. I had no classes on the matter. I couldn't describe the chain of custody for a Marine who died on the battlefield. I had a simple faith that they'd be taken care of—or hoped they would.

Libby died shortly after arriving at the Combat Outpost, despite all possible efforts to save him. After he died, I left him in the capable hands of Foster and the medical staff. That was the last time I saw him.

■　　■　　■

First Lieutenant Mike Perkins was twenty-six years old and from Sunrise, Florida. A KC-130 pilot, his call sign was "Dolby," which he'd gotten from his squadron mates due to the uncontrolled volume of his voice every time he spoke. Dolby was loud. He was six feet tall, with brown hair and matching brown eyes. He was making the third flight of his first combat deployment to Iraq when he learned that he would be handling fallen Marines, flying them to Kuwait. From there, an Air Force C-17 would fly them and others to Dover Air Force Base, where all fallen U.S. military personnel first come home.

As he stood by the side of his plane before he boarded, a mortuary affairs soldier handed him a piece of paper. It was the manifest, listing the fallen Marines he'd be taking to Kuwait that night. There were three names on it. Dolby was perplexed. He distinctly remembered seeing only two caskets being fastened down in the plane's cargo bay.

He summoned the soldier back over. "Excuse me, but you've got three names on this, and I only have two caskets on board."

The soldier stood quietly for a moment before responding. "Well, it's unfortunate, but sometimes there isn't much left, and we have to put what we can together and send them home in one casket."

Dolby's stomach tightened. He exhaled sharply through his nose. His first thought was contempt toward the government for trying to spare a minuscule expense of using one casket for two fallen warriors. But as he thought longer, he imagined the two Marines were flying home together—and the "who" became critically important to him.

He climbed into the flight deck of the plane and pulled out a three-by-five-inch green U.S. government issue notebook with the word "*Memoranda*" stamped diagonally in cursive writing across the cover. Dolby copied the names of the three Marines into his book, the names of his first three Angels. The term "Angels" is not something Dolby came up with; it is how Marines refer to fallen warriors once they are aboard an aircraft.

Five months later, the pages of Dolby's notebook bore the names of dozens of Angels—and his plane was in the air, headed to Al Asad airbase in Iraq on a cargo mission when he received a tasking for an Angel Flight. He turned the plane around immediately—Angels took priority over everything else—landed, and offloaded the Humvees and pallets loaded with supplies that it had been carrying.

A white van made a trip to and from the back of his plane for each casket. When it had made its last run, the cargo bay was entirely filled with fifteen caskets. A soldier again handed him a manifest. Seventeen names.

The plane took off to Kuwait and carried the Marines and soldiers— a gut-wrenching feeling fell over the flight crew carrying the seventeen heroes killed in action.

They flew back to Al Asad—the cargo mission still had to be completed. Dolby took out his notebook and began to count up the names in it. Page after page, he counted.

There were ninety-four.

A wave of guilt washed over him. He felt as if he had done something wrong by keeping this horrific list. He also found himself wondering why the United States was even in Iraq. What did their sacrifices add up to?

In retrospect, it is not surprising he felt this way. He never saw what men like those in Echo Company were doing on the battlefield, the fights we were winning, and the defeats we were inflicting on the insurgents. All he ever saw were the dead we had lost.

Now, as he stared down at the page, the hand in which he held his GI black Skilcraft pen began to shake. Four flights later Dolby wrote the one-hundredth name in his notebook.

It was then he decided that he was done writing names down. "Why one hundred? What is so significant about that number?" he thought. "Why not twenty-three, or fifty, or seventy-five? Wasn't that enough?"

Whatever the reason, he couldn't do it anymore. Dolby stowed the notebook neatly in a footlocker—out of sight, out of mind. He wanted to become ignorant of the names, and the notebook had become a constant, physical reminder to him.

Later, he mustered the will to bring the notebook back out. He carried it carefully in the zippered pocket that ran diagonally across the chest of his tan flight suit. A few days later, when he reached into the pocket, it was gone.

His heart sank—broke, really. He had wanted to keep it, knowing that he'd want it so that, in the years to come, he wouldn't forget what he had done—as if anyone who experienced that ever could.

Dolby recalled, "It's one of those things that gives you goosebumps even to think about it. Regardless of whoever was transporting the Angel, the Marines treated the fallen warriors with so much respect."

"The first time I ever saw a fallen Marine moved from the air station to the plane, I couldn't help but be emotional. I remember thinking that if anything happened to me; they [the Marines] would take care of me. Watching the ceremony, you knew that no matter who it was, they were one of your brothers. I knew every single person on that flight wanted to do everything possible to make sure that the fallen Marine was absolutely one hundred percent taken care of."

Even in the midst of demanding combat operations, the Marines at the air bases in Iraq took special care whenever a fallen Marine started the journey back home.

The engines of the massive Lockheed Martin KC-130 Hercules were shut down for this solemn movement. A white civilian van carrying the Angel's remains drove from the holding area directly to the awaiting airplane. Personnel from the on-duty squadron marched slowly onto the flight line, instinctively gravitating toward the aircraft and formed up to pay respect to the fallen Marine.

Once the Angel was ready, a group of Marines formed a traditional pallbearer detail and moved him ever so delicately onto the plane. The flag-draped caskets always went aboard headfirst with the flag's field of stars over the Marine's heart. Nothing was allowed to denigrate the importance given to these flights. There was a strict rule—absolutely no other cargo was allowed on the plane. No luggage, pallets, chow, vehicles—nothing besides the fallen warrior. The only exception was the transportation of personnel, and they were usually flying with their comrades to ensure their safe transit home.

As the casket was carried aboard, the Marines formed on the tarmac near the rear of the aircraft to salute their departing brother. As the ramp began to rise slowly, the Marines dropped their salutes, but remained standing sharply in formation until the ramp closed. It was—and is—one of the most moving moments to witness.

The aluminum caskets were strapped down onto the deck of the plane as the flight crew respectfully adjusted the American flags covering the caskets, smoothing any persistent wrinkles.

No one was allowed to walk past the caskets once all were strapped down to the bed of the aircraft. The passengers had to enter from the side of the plane and sit at the front of the troop compartment on the red canvas seats with cargo netting to their backs. They made the two-hour ride to Kuwait International Airport in silence with nothing to look at besides their humbling cargo.

■　　■　　■

The crew chief signaled the aircraft commander that the rear of the plane was all set and ready for takeoff.

The pilot radioed, "Tower, this is Hercules 76 ready for takeoff."

The personnel in the air traffic control tower purposefully changed the flights' call sign by adding the word "Angel."

"Roger. This is Tower, over. Angel Flight 76, you have taxi priority. Taxi to runway three-zero via alpha, over."

The Hercules sped down the runway, reaching its takeoff speed of 150 knots, just over 175 miles per hour, and gracefully lifted off the runway. The loud, deep, bass-like rumbling of the four massive turbo-prop engines hummed and reverberated through the entire aircraft.

The flight crew didn't engage in the usual acts of humor and grab-ass with which Marines routinely pass the time. There was no idle chitchat. No one used the onboard microwave to cook a burrito. No one brewed coffee. Everyone onboard was fixed on the responsibility of delivering their precious cargo.

When the plane landed in Kuwait, the process repeated itself albeit in reverse.

The airport terminal ramp closed. The plane's engines shut down. The ramp lowered.

A detail of Marines came up the ramp to retrieve their fellow warrior. First, they slowly turned the casket so that the Marine would come headfirst off the plane. Then, slowly, reverently, they moved the fallen hero from the plane. They turned their fallen comrade over to the crew of a U.S. Air Force C-17 Globemaster, which then flew him to Dover, Delaware. From Dover, the CACO personnel escorted the fallen Marine on the last part of his journey: to his home, to be laid to rest.

Marines love each other deeply—even if they don't know each other. Almost certainly, the Marine in the back of the plane was unknown to the crew. But they are fellow Marines. Brothers. Sisters. Deserving all the respect and honor that they can give them.

■   ■   ■

While serving as a young captain with 2nd Fleet Anti-Terrorism Security Team (FAST) Company in Virginia, I was talking to some good friends of mine who were Navy SEALs on a close-quarters battle range. One of them told me with complete, unsolicited sincerity why he thought the Marines were the best. "They're disciplined to a fault. They're great shooters. They're physically fit, and they're aggressive like no one's business."

He added, "I think the reason we (SEALs) enjoy our level of success is that we are a smaller unit. We've got a shitload of money, and we get a lot more specialized training—but I would never have a second thought about fighting alongside the Marines."

He was right, but he had left something out—what truly underlies the greatness of the Marine Corps. I have to admit that, early on in my career, I didn't have the wisdom or experience to understand it. Later on, I did.

What makes us good, what makes us great, is the brotherhood.

It's not that the individual Marines are the most lethal weapons on the battlefield, nor how straight they shoot, nor how they attack and kill the enemy with an unbridled ferocity that makes them so great. They're not just warriors—they're artisans, musicians, poets, comedians, and yes, sometimes writers.

When we lose one of our own, we understand that the entire Marine Corps has lost someone special. Being part of that brotherhood, that tradition, is nothing short of amazing, and seeing it in action, we understand that the world has lost one of its best.

CHAPTER 9

Livestock

It was bitterly cold in Ramadi during December 2006. I grew up in the Chicago area, enduring many winters of bone-chilling lake-effect winds. I had spent plenty of time in the mountains at high altitude in training as well. I had known my share of cold. Without question, I had never felt or endured the cold as I did in Ramadi that year.

I'm quite sure the sleep deprivation, the regular malnourishment of my diet, dehydration, and persistent fatigue played a large part in it. The human body doesn't want to function the way you want it to under those conditions—it has to be forced through individual will.

We constantly sweated through our body armor that weighed over fifty pounds with all of the ammunition, water, and gear strapped to it. After hours of patrolling at night, our uniforms would be soaked with sweat. When we came to a stop and went firm at the day's target house, the moisture would interact with the cold air and set us all to shivering.

We'd beg the sun to shine hard and warm us as fast as it could.

■　　■　　■

One night, Echo Company prepared to root out what we called high-value individuals (HVIs) who were known to be in the Sufia District during a clearance operation, an area of the city that had largely gone untouched by the U.S. Army for some time. An HVI is a person who is essential to the enemy's operations, someone who is critical to their success. The primary goal is to capture them and turn them over to an intelligence unit for interrogation and exploitation—resisting capture usually turned out badly for those who chose that option.

The area was south of the Euphrates River and scattered with date palm trees, random cinder-block sheds, agricultural fields, garbage, and demolished vehicles.

Iraqi Army soldiers were mixed in with the patrol's lead elements. We also had military working dog (MWD) teams which were an essential part of any clearance operation to sniff out weapons caches. Most Iraqis hated dogs. They viewed them as foul creatures and wanted no part of them. It was extremely rare to find one kept as a pet. Most of the ones we encountered were strays, mangy and diseased. We had to put down more than a few that became aggressive toward our patrols.

The MWDs were different. They were Belgian Malinois, a ferocious, compact breed of shepherds—not cuddly, malleable little pets. They were a bold combination of attack and bomb-sniffing K-9s. The dog handlers were the only ones allowed to touch the dogs, but just having them around boosted our morale. Man's best friend and all that.

We staged our forces ready to execute Operation Kasserine located at a firm base called OP Crater. It was an Iraqi Army compound a few hundred meters northeast of ECP 8. OP Crater was worn down, lacking electricity, and it was gutted out—the house had no real function.

The platoon staged inside before we stepped off. We had a few hours to wait; the boys huddled together and tried to stay warm. Still wearing all of their battle gear, some of the boys were snuggled under a thick, red, satiny blanket with white trim around the border, trying to catch some sleep. The tan Malinois lay at the Marines' feet, curled up in a ball with his handler next to him. I smiled as I watched them.

My battle-hardened Marines looked somewhat innocent—resembling toy soldiers stuffed gently into a Christmas stocking—the soft, white, satin border of the red blanket tucked snugly underneath their arms.

When we stepped out on a six-hour operation, we did so under a starry sky through which moved a bright half-moon. In the greenish glow of our NVGs, this light highlighted the shapes around us.

As we moved forward, my nose began to pick up what smelled like a well-used horse paddock. Through the narrow, 20mm monocular optic, I scanned the area to try to make out the source of the smell. As I panned my gaze to the front I was dumbfounded to see a huge spotted cow. It was the first cow I had ever seen in Iraq.

The cow softly mooed as it grazed—or tried to. After staring at it for a few seconds, I looked behind me, where I knew my Forward Air Controller (FAC), Captain Richard "Bam-Bam" Rasmussen, was located whenever we patrolled. My gaze hit Bam-Bam directly, and I could make out his face clearly and the optic mounted on his helmet.

I said in a quiet whisper, "Bam-Bam, it's a cow."

Bam-Bam, a Wisconsin native, turned his view toward the direction of the beast and then slowly turned his gaze back to me. I saw his optic bobbing up and down in the affirmative, acknowledging that he saw it too.

Bam-Bam said in a low, calm tone, "Yeaaahhhh."

I guess that he seemed so unfazed by the sighting of what I thought to be—and what indeed might have been—the only cow in all of Iraq because so much of what we'd already seen in Iraq bordered on, and often crossed into, the surreal.

We always had so much kit strapped to our bodies, like the NVGs on our helmets. Optics and scopes and flashlights. Everything mounted to aluminum rails on our weapons and wherever else we could secure a high-tech gadget to gain the upper hand on our enemy. Only the Marine Corps could find a way to make the latest hi-tech, lightweight gear cumbersome. We must have looked like spacemen to the locals, with all of our high-speed gear strapped and fastened to our bodies.

Bam-Bam joined 2d Battalion, 4th Marines, as our FAC in February 2006. After three consecutive deployments to Iraq, flying CH-53E Super Stallions, huge single-rotor Sikorsky helicopters capable of hauling 24 loaded Marines or more than 30,000 pounds of cargo, he was ready for a change of pace and volunteered for a tour as an FAC. He insisted on being assigned to an infantry unit because he wanted to contribute to, support, and experience the Marine Corps at its most elemental. His job was to direct jets and attack helicopters as they delivered fire support for us.

The words "highly fortunate" don't begin to describe how I felt having Bam-Bam with me. He was the epitome of what an FAC should be. He worked fast, knew his stuff, and never faltered, even in the fiercest fighting. He also served as a sounding board for my ideas and provided a much-needed sanity check on most days.

Despite dragging him around the battlefield tethered to my hip by a radio cord, he was always there for me. I'll always be grateful for how he fought as a Marine—moreover to have him as my friend.

The way my patrols worked was that the company would go out as a whole. When the lead element, typically a platoon, came close to hitting the limits of its endurance or daylight drew close, whichever came first, I would choose a building on the map in which we would "go firm" and would make my decision on which building we would occupy based off of what is called a "map recon," which is a detailed study of the map of a certain area with special attention to its infrastructure and terrain.

Using preexisting buildings as firm bases made sense for many reasons. First, there were no pre-built fighting positions that we could use in the city. Second, we never stayed in one place long enough to justify digging in fighting positions as we would on a more open, traditional battlefield. Third, the buildings were made of solid concrete blocks, reinforced with stucco and mortar. The metal-framed windows had relatively small openings that limited observation from outside threats.

I always remember thinking that if I had to fight a war like this, Iraq was as good a place as you could get since the buildings were all made so damn well. The durability of the construction was far superior to what one would find in the United States. Insurgent 7.62mm bullets would cut through vinyl siding, standard two-by-four lumber, and drywall like a hot knife through butter if we were fighting in downtown San Diego.

The Marines would cordon off the building and set up perimeter security. They would post themselves on rooftops to allow for better observation and set up machine guns to cover avenues of approach, usually roads, that the enemy might use to advance against our position or drive a VBIED into our base. During the night, we would send out security patrols covered by marksmen posted on the top of the house. These patrols would ensure that no insurgent activity was brewing around us and no attack would occur without advanced warning. Those Marines not patrolling or manning positions would sleep or maintain their gear.

Procedurally, we'd knock on the door to determine if the house was occupied, not out of common decency alone, but also because we didn't want any surprises from the occupants. I had a Terp do the talking for us. The Terp would explain to the family that we'd be using their house as a position to hole up for the day, and if they had family living close by they should visit. We didn't want them to be in our way.

It was a necessity in this environment to use the local infrastructure to our advantage; living in the streets was not an option.

On this patrol, Jake was our Terp. He was one of our better ones, with remarkably good English. Like Big Sam and Ford, he was a young kid, certainly no more than twenty years old. He was five-ten, and as a soccer player growing up, he was athletic and physically fit. He was a good-looking kid with deep smile lines that cut from his nose to the corners of his mouth and into his neatly trimmed mustache and beard. Consistently cheerful, the only evidence of the toll that his job had taken on him were dark circles around his eyes.

His English was remarkable, and he loved to be in the middle of the action and out on patrols with the Marines.

Always "kitted-out" with the same gear the Marines wore, Jake loved to look the part, but he wasn't a poseur. He wore desert-striped cammies and a black balaclava ski mask to cover his face. On his right arm, Jake wore a Velcro patch of the American flag with great pride. Across his body armor, he sported a traditional Iraqi chest magazine pouch and carried an AK-47 with a metal, collapsible stock with the magazine inserted. He never had any ammunition.

In this case, the family of five who lived in the house we chose insisted that there was nowhere else they could go on such short notice. Still being relatively new to the game of how to be most effective while working in this part of Ramadi, I let the family stay. We isolated them in one of the house's larger rooms. We allowed them to use the bathroom, gave them food, and posted a guard to keep watch on them. We had searched the house for weapons and contraband upon our arrival.

We'd captured a few weapons during our movement that first night but never received any contact from the enemy.

Before I settled in for some rest, a Marine told me that Jake was not doing so well. I went to the living room where he was lying on the floor— sprawled out amongst a squad of exhausted Marines. I knelt down and asked him what was wrong. He told me he didn't know if he'd have enough energy to keep going the next day.

Jake's condition concerned me greatly because our Terps were one of our most valuable assets during any operation. I motioned to the squad leader to bring Jake's rucksack to me. I lifted its flap and started rummaging around inside to survey the contents. I rooted down to the bottom of the pack, I felt an odd shape—and then another, and another.

I turned on my helmet light to see if what I had in my hand was for real. To my shock and disbelief, it was Borden's eggnog. Not one, not two or three, but *six*, one-quart metal cans of eggnog. The standard conversion of one quart weighs a little more than two pounds. So, in addition to his normal combat load, Jake was carrying an extra fifteen pounds or more of thick, creamy eggnog, which he'd apparently snuck out of the dining facility.

"Jake!" I asked. "Son, why the fuck would you pack-out six cans of eggnog?"

In an exhausted voice and with a half-cocked and somewhat guilty grin on his face, he replied, "Sir, I love this *Egg-Nuug*." He placed a heavy emphasis on the hyphen and "*Nuug*" when endorsing his beverage of choice.

I ordered his squad leader, "Get rid of that shit. Only water for Jake from now on."

We had little activity that night—relatively uneventful. The Marines ate chow, slept, and cleaned their weapons. Small unit leaders inspected the boys' gear. Platoon sergeants made a note of any supply shortages, and we passed the information back to the operation center at Camp Corregidor. They'd coordinate a link-up position to get a re-supply to us before we'd kick off the next night's patrols and clearance operations.

As the morning unfolded, we heard a massive explosion nearby. Before we could contact the task force's TOC, we monitored a request for entry into friendly lines from Task Force 1-9 Infantry's command element. I agreed immediately, and soon we spotted a dust trail on a road to the south. Not long after that, a four-vehicle convoy rolled up to our position and posted in a herringbone-shaped formation in front of the house with their machine guns pointed outboard.

The Marines greeted the soldiers at the Humvees and began to brief them on where all of our positions were, and let them know the location of the friendly patrols we had out in the area.

The door on the lead Humvee opened up and the task force's command sergeant major, Dennis "Birdog" Bergmann, emerged. He looked like a human sugar cookie—covered from head to toe in fine, white, chalky dust. Evidently, the convoy had been blasted by a roadside bomb as Birdog and the other soldiers came out to visit us—just to check in and see if we needed anything.

Birdog was a professional soldier—a U.S. Army Ranger who had endured five combat tours already.

He had a clean-shaven head and was built well for a soldier in his early forties—five eleven and 195 pounds. He'd acquired his nickname in childhood because he had the knack for finding other people's misplaced stuff, a human Labrador of sorts.

At the pinnacle of his career as a command sergeant major, he had a cocky smile, and his bulgy eyes had a wild excitement in them as if he was eagerly anticipating the next fight. When he wasn't chewing soldiers' asses, he had a laid-back, familiar manner with everyone. Officers were no exception. He called most of those with whom he interacted, "Bubba," with an occasional, "Sir," thrown in. I loved it.

Birdog erupted. "Shit, that sucked! What a fucking way to start the day, brother."

He came over to me and began to give me the details of their short but harrowing drive from Camp Corregidor through the Sufia District. Luckily, the roadside bomb had caused only superficial damage to the convoy, and none of the soldiers were seriously injured—most just reeled from the blast with a definitive ringing in their ears.

I replied to Birdog, "You're right, my friend. One hell of a way to start the day."

We began to collect up all of our gear after Birdog's convoy departed. We let the family come out of the house. The kids were especially curious about what we were doing, and their fingers loved to explore all our gear.

The children also enjoyed getting candy from the Marines, and these were no exception. Several Marines emptied their pockets of candy into their tiny, wanting hands. Some were schmoozing and put their sunglasses on the younger children. "A risky gesture," I thought, because typically once kids get a liking for something, they want to keep it.

Jake translated my thanks to the family for the use of their home, and we gave them pamphlets with the phone numbers to the Civil-Military Operations Center (CMOC), a unit designated to deal specifically with the concerns of the local civilians—and take any reports of insurgent activity.

They rarely gave us any useful information unless it was to squeeze some cash out of the CMOC soldiers for "damages" that were supposedly caused to their homes while we stayed there.

We doled out the last of the candy to the kids at the house. Then, squad by squad, we moved out, continuing to clear the Sufia District as we struggled to stay warm and hunt down HVIs.

CHAPTER 10

Sacrifice

Kimberly Downing, a nurse in Norwalk, Iowa, never served a day in the military, but she made many sacrifices for her country. Over ten years, the three men in her life—her husband, Jeff, and her two sons, Ryan and Justen—served in Iraq. All of them were Marines. All of them served in the infantry. Ryan Downing was one of my Marines in Ramadi.

Only about a year apart in age, the Downing boys acted practically like twins growing up. Their mother had to have two of everything to keep them happy. They dressed alike. They played with the same kinds of toys—plastic guns, Tonka trucks. They built forts, and like many boys growing up, they loved to play soldier. If asked what they wanted to be when they grew up, they'd both say, "Army guys."

Kimberly thought they would eventually grow out of that phase, but they never did. In their high school years, they were introduced to the exciting new world of paintball guns, a step up from the toy cap guns that didn't have the same effect that being stung and splattered with paintballs provided. It was a new thrill.

Both boys came home from school and told their mom that a Marine Corps recruiter was going to be coming by the house that night—and both had decided to enlist. They wanted to join the infantry. Ryan had just turned eighteen. Justen was seventeen.

The recruiter came and talked with Mr. and Mrs. Downing and went over the details of the boys' enlistment contracts. Ryan sat in front of both of his parents and signed the enlistment papers without hesitation. He had joined on the Delayed Entry Program, which meant he'd still have a few months until he shipped off to boot camp.

Because Justen was still a minor at seventeen, he needed a parent's signature on the enlistment papers. Kimberly refused to sign. She couldn't bring herself to do it. But her husband Jeff, an infantry sergeant in the U.S. Marine Corps Reserve who had made two combat deployments, was not as reluctant and signed on Justen's behalf.

It wasn't that Kimberly was not proud of her sons' decision to join up. She was. But she was nervous about her boys being right on the front lines.

She thought, "What kind of career can you get from being trained killers? Why can't they be mechanics or something less dangerous?"

In most families, children leave home one at a time—usually off to some relaxed college, to fraternize and party and maybe get some education squeezed in at some point. Kimberly's boys were leaving at the same time, and heading, not to college, but off to the Marines and then to war—the toughest education in the world.

After the boys left, Kimberly packed up her kids' things and placed them into plastic storage totes. She was in tears as she put away the small mementos and items that defined their now-concluded childhood—wrestling equipment, baseball gloves, action figures, trophies, awards, and artwork.

Jeff came into the room and saw Kimberly sobbing and told her to leave the bedroom. "You go relax. I'll finish this up, honey."

Kimberly felt a pressure overcome her as she sat in the other room and knew that this was the hardest time in her life, knowing her boys were leaving—knowing they might never come home.

7 July 2003

The boys left for Marine Corps Recruit Depot, San Diego, California on the "Buddy System." Their plans to stay together in the Marines didn't work out. Justen went to 2d Battalion, 7th Marines, in Twentynine Palms, California. Ryan had orders to Echo Company, 2d Battalion, 4th Marines, which was scheduled to deploy to Ramadi in 2004.

6 April 2004

Ramadi, Iraq. Ryan fought in one of the deadliest battles in the history of 2d Battalion, 4th Marines—earning his first Purple Heart Medal at the age of eighteen. Ryan took shrapnel to his face, neck, arms, and legs from an enemy rocket-propelled grenade that exploded with devastating effects—his unit ambushed during a grueling firefight. In the aftermath, Ryan lost seven out of fourteen members of his squad. Despite his injuries and tremendous personal loss, he returned to his platoon and continued fighting.

7 April 2004

Kimberly and her husband were doing yard work when her phone rang on a warm spring day. She went into the house for the cordless phone and extended the antenna to answer.

It was the American Red Cross calling. The man on the other end seemed almost inaudible.

Kimberly thought, "What is this guy trying to tell me?"

She was in a daze as she tried to make sense of the voice on the other end of the line.

The stranger's voice asked, "Is this Ryan Downing's parent?"

She replied, "Yes." Her heart sank as the man continued.

He rattled on in a dry, scripted delivery, "Sir or Ma'am, I regret to tell you that your son, Ryan, has been shot during an ambush."

She shouted, "Where is Ryan? Is he alive? Where is he?"

He wasn't able to provide her any other information to abate her uncontrolled frustration.

She hung up the phone and frantically ran through the freshly mown grass, looking for her husband, Jeff, screaming for him.

When she reached him, all she could do was cry, "Ryan's been shot! He's been shot!"

■　　■　　■

Kimberly was there for Ryan's first homecoming at Camp Pendleton when the battalion came back from Ramadi in 2004. She was excited to see her son again, the young boy who had gone off to war.

The battalion marched in formation as proud warriors returning from battle. The families at the ceremony greeted the returning Marines with cheers. The ones whose sons had made it back shed tears of joy as they waited to wrap their arms around their sons—the ones who had made it home.

Thirty-five other families—those of the sailors and Marines who had died—were among the crowd as well.

The unit commanders dismissed their Marines. Friends and family members flooded onto the parade ground.

When Kimberly approached Ryan, he said solemnly, "Hold on, mom. I'll be right back."

Ryan then made his way over to a woman, who, she realized, was the mother of one of Ryan's fallen comrades. She observed reverently and with sadness, fully understanding what Ryan was doing.

Kimberly was proud of her son and stood in quiet veneration for showing such compassion to the family of his fellow Marine. But she also was concerned. "How is Ryan ever going to be the same after this?" she thought. "How does such a young man deal with something like this?"

■　　■　　■

The woman Ryan spoke to was Dianne Layfield from Fremont, California, a small town one hour outside of San Francisco. Her son, Lance Corporal Travis Layfield, was killed in action during the deadly ambush in which Ryan was wounded. Dianne and the other parents who mourned the loss of their sons now bore the title Gold Star Parents, which made them eternally connected to the extraordinary Marine Corps family.

Despite her unfathomable pain, she managed to share the happiness and pride for the others and show the immense love she had for all of the Marines.

Still, Dianne and her family struggled to suppress their emotions, trying to remain strong for the other families. The elation and excitement from the other families filled the air. There was laughter and joyous shouts. It was tough for Dianne, but she maintained a brave front as she courageously made her way to join the others—refusing to project any of her suffering onto those now in celebration.

After their reunion, many of the Marines and their friends gravitated toward the people who had lost a Marine, including Dianne. She was finally able to put faces to the names she had heard about for so long:

Sergeant Nate Apple, who honorably carried Travis's remains in a black body bag off of the battlefield.

David Swanson, the thirty-nine-year-old combat photographer from the *Philadelphia Inquirer* embedded with Echo Company, who had captured that act in a photo that horrific day.

Kimberly Downing, the mother of Lance Corporal Ryan Downing.

Ryan Downing, Travis's battle buddy and friend.

Dianne had been anxious to meet Ryan because Travis had told her that if anything should ever happen to him, he and Ryan had exchanged letters and would give them to their respective parents.

Ryan walked up to Dianne and her daughter, Tiffany. He hugged them both, and they cried as Ryan spoke to them. It's unimaginable that a nineteen-year-old boy stood there trying to be a pillar of strength for his friend's family. But he took on the job, took on that pain.

His childhood was a distant memory.

Ryan's presence soothed Dianne, and they made plans to meet the next day at a Mexican restaurant in San Clemente, California. She was certain Ryan was going to give her the letter Travis had written, and she wanted to have it because it was just about all she would have left of her son.

Dianne stood up as Ryan entered the restaurant and hugged him tightly. Releasing him reluctantly, smiling modestly, she slowly brought her arm from around Ryan's back and handed him a letter. It was Ryan's letter which had come home with Travis's personal effects.

Dianne had kept it in a black Sentry strongbox tucked safely in the closet of her bedroom so she could return it to Ryan when he came home. She never opened it.

Ryan reached out to take the letter back, and Dianne began to cry. She drew in short breaths and wiped the tears from her eyes. "Do you have Travis's letter for me?" she asked.

Dianne's heart sank deep into the pit of her stomach as he apologized to her that he didn't have it. She was devastated. Ryan explained that he was wounded, too, and that when all of his gear was shuffled around the battlefield, much of his stuff was lost. Ryan vowed that when he got his gear back he would deliver the letter to her in person.

■   ■   ■

Weeks turned into months with no news of the letter. Dianne tried a few times to contact Ryan but never heard back from him. Ryan was dealing with his own pain too—coping with his mental torment and the loss of his friend and the others that died in the deadly ambush.

In the fall, Lance Corporal Josh Laine, Travis's best friend when they joined the Marine Corps, lived in the Bay area. He called Dianne. Josh asked Dianne if she would take him to Travis's grave at the Golden Gate National Cemetery to visit his friend one last time.

Three days later, Josh, wearing his full blue dress uniform, young and handsome, arrived at Dianne's front door. Tears filled her eyes as she looked at Josh. Another living reminder of the son she had lost.

During the drive to and from the cemetery, Dianne told Josh how sad she was that she never received Travis's letter.

"I'll get the letter from Ryan. It may take some time, but I promise I'll get it for you," Josh said firmly.

■   ■   ■

Josh returned to Camp Pendleton and made his way to the command post of 2d Battalion, 4th Marines, to find Ryan. He searched the company area and found Ryan at the barracks and confronted him about Travis's letter. It was a tense conversation.

Ryan admitted that he had the letter. The unopened letter sat tucked inside a pocket of his cammies—the same ones that had been torn to shreds from the shrapnel that ripped through him on 6 April 2004. They rested at the bottom of his green nylon sea bag stowed in his wall locker in the barracks.

He'd buried the letter to hold on to the last physical piece of his best friend who died in front of him just months before, and to protect Dianne and her family from feeling the heartbreak of losing Travis all over again.

As time passed, he felt an ever-increasing guilt for neglecting to deliver the letter to the person to whom it rightfully belonged.

Now confronted by a fellow Marine, he did what he always knew he would have to do one day. He dug the letter out of his sea bag and handed it to Josh.

■   ■   ■

Not long after, Josh made the nine-hour drive from Camp Pendleton to Dianne's house. He exited his car dressed in civilian clothes holding the white envelope in his left hand.

When Dianne saw it, she raced to him, crying and shouting, "Is that it? Is that Travis's letter?"

She had been waiting nine months and two days to receive it.

Later that night, Dianne, her daughter Tiffany, and Tyler, Travis's younger brother, drove to El Burro restaurant.

They pulled into the parking lot. The glow from the amber street-lights peeked through the windows of her car as she pulled the envelope out and clicked on the dome light. She didn't want to read it alone.

The letter was hand-addressed to: "*John, Dianne & Tyler Layfield.*" When she turned it over to open it, she saw the letters "DL" in Travis's handwriting on the back flap—she instinctively knew what the letters meant. Death Letter.

She pulled it out, unfolded the two pieces of paper, and began to read her son's words aloud.

■   ■   ■

25 August 2004

Kimberly's phone rang. It was the American Red Cross calling again. She braced herself for the worst impact of the message on the other end of the line. Terror consumed her, having gone through this once before.

Again, the dry, canned delivery: Justen, her youngest son, had been wounded when a roadside bomb detonated near the Humvee in which he was riding. He was injured but would be alright. Justen received a Purple Heart Medal for wounds he received in the attack.

■   ■   ■

6 September 2004

Kimberly sat alone at the Kansas City International Airport at 0400 waiting for her flight. She had just sent her husband, Sergeant Jeff Down-ing, off on his third deployment with 2d Battalion, 24th Marines—a U.S. Marine Reserve unit.

Her cell phone rang. It was Ryan. Although elated to hear from her son, she could not stop sniffling back tears. A few minutes into the con-versation, she blurted out, "Ryan, I love you!"

Ryan tried to cheer her up, gently ribbing her for getting so emotional and making such a fuss. Suddenly, Kimberly heard the sound of gunfire and then a massive explosion. The line went dead.

Panic-stricken, she thought, "Oh my god, Ryan's dead! He just got killed!"

Minutes later, however, Ryan called back, and a wave of relief rolled over Kimberly.

That relief would be temporary. With only Megan, her seven-year-old daughter, for companionship and with all three of her men at war and in danger, Kimberly would never have a moment free of anxiety, fear, or frustration.

14 September 2004

Jeff and Justen crossed paths in Kuwait at the MNF's vast, intermediate staging base where coalition troops and equipment flowed in and out of the theater of operations. Jeff bounced from tent to tent, asking strange Marines where Fox Company, 2d Battalion, 7th Marines, was, trying to track down his son.

Jeff and Justen finally reunited, and they visited for a few hours as they ate pizza at the dining facility.

Against the natural order of things, the son now gave the father advice, raiding a can of his dad's Copenhagen snuff as he did. The other Marines from Jeff's squad sat at the table and listened intently to the conversation. Jeff paid close attention to his son's advice—rank and experience played little part in a wartime education in Iraq, since dynamics on the battlefield changed so quickly.

As Justen and Jeff parted, the son said to his father, "Keep your head down, Dad. It's a fucking shithole over there."

When Justen returned home a few months later, he told his mom how scared he was for his dad's safety. Justen knew firsthand how brutal things had become in Iraq. The situation was worsening, and every Marine was either fighting or preparing to fight. He said he was afraid that the all-too-quick meeting they shared was the last time he'd see his father alive.

■　　■　　■

March 2006

I graduated early from the Expeditionary Warfare School in Quantico, Virginia, an advanced school for Marine captains who were ready to assume command. Because of the deployment cycle, my unit wanted to ensure its rifle company commanders were in place. The battalion requested that I check in as soon as possible.

I was excited to get the news, but it left me short on time to get my personal matters in order. I knew my wife would be supportive—but was sure she'd also remind me of my most recent deployment in 2004. That year, I kissed her goodbye in the driveway of our rural Virginia home, as she stood there seven months pregnant, with tears in her eyes as I took off for Baghdad, Iraq, for close to nine months.

Within a week, I packed my Jeep and a trailer, and I left my family again, heading west. I drove straight through, stopping on the side of the road occasionally whenever I needed to rest.

April 2006

My first encounter with Ryan Downing occurred shortly after taking command of Echo Company. I led the company on a five-mile run. When we returned, First Sergeant Foster told me that two Marines had slipped out of formation just as the run started and didn't return.

I reflected on my days as a young enlisted Marine, and thought, "Man, that's a bold move. Stupid, but bold." Foster wanted me to punish the Marines for their disobedience. I agreed, but I decided I'd talk to both of them first. One of them was Ryan Downing.

When he came into my office, Ryan posted himself at the position of attention and centered in front of the desk I sat behind.

Ryan was thin and scrappy-looking and had a surly air about him. I could tell by looking at him that this probably wasn't his first run-in with his command, as he stood there confident and unwavering. Our discussion was brief.

I told him to stand at ease and look me in the eye. I then said that he wasn't being punished so much for what he had done, but in fairness to the other Marines who had done the right thing.

He understood. He almost seemed grateful for the opportunity to get a fresh start after his lapse in judgment.

Notwithstanding this act of blatant disregard for authority, Ryan was a battle-tested warrior who had already seen more action than most Marines ever would in combat. It was safe to say that I liked him. I always liked the challenging ones. Ryan reminded me of a Jack Russell Terrier, imbued with a ferocity and tenacity, and self-assured despite his small size, full of mischief, in need of a steady hand, but sturdy and loyal to a fault.

■　■　■

A friend gave Kimberly a service flag that she hung in the front window of her home with pride. On it were three blue stars, each representing one of her three brave Marines.

Those Marines and what they might be going through were never far from her mind. The television was constantly tuned to CNN or Fox News. She relentlessly surfed the Internet looking for stories and ways to stay in touch with other families from her men's unit. Unlike active-duty families who live on or near a base, Kimberly had no groups from whom she could draw support, no other wives she could lean on. She had only her parents and the boys' girlfriends.

She coped by staying busy.

She would get Megan ready and off to school every day. She worked. She'd mindlessly toil at mundane but much-needed yard work. She'd go to the gym to relieve stress. She took Megan to dinner, to the zoo, and to the park.

Nights and mornings were the most difficult parts of the day. There wasn't a night she didn't go to sleep crying. The mornings brought more tears, more thoughts about what her men were enduring, the dangers they faced. One day, as she sat on the porch of her house waiting for her daughter's school bus, she saw an ordinary-looking sedan drive slowly past her house.

Terror seized her as she saw two Marines in full blue dress uniforms in it—the same formal uniforms Marines on CACO duty wear.

She began to cry uncontrollably, dreading that the car might stop at her house.

It didn't.

She thought, "Thank God!"

She immediately felt a stab of guilt. She knew full well that those Marines could be delivering the worst possible news to another family.

She prayed she'd never see that car again.

■   ■   ■

4 December 2006

Ryan manned a medium machine gun on a Humvee that was protecting a convoy of Army water trucks that would pump water onto the streets in hopes of exposing any bombs or IEDs. The convoy received immediate contact from a small team of insurgents.

In the firefight, a bullet ricocheted off the vehicle's armor and cracked into his helmet. The bullet didn't penetrate the Kevlar, but it struck with such force that it gave him a concussion.

6 December 2006

During one of Echo Company's toughest battles at ECP 8, Ryan suffered his second concussion.

Kimberly should have received this information from the American Red Cross concerning Ryan's latest injury. Social media beat them to the punch.

She read a comment on Facebook from another family saying in part, "...[W]e're thinking of you Kimberly, and we're sorry to hear that Ryan was injured again..."

As she read the post, she nearly fell to the floor. The Red Cross then called with the news that Ryan was injured but OK. Ryan called her from an intermediate medical unit at Balad Air Base in Iraq days later.

She asked Ryan, "Are you OK? Are you in Germany? Can I come see you?"

In a steady voice, Ryan told his mom, "No, Mom, I'm OK, just got shaken up a bit. We got blasted by some friendly fire."

The irony wasn't lost on Kimberly.

She sharply replied, "What the hell is friendly fire?"

10 December 2006

I was in our Company Operations Center at Camp Corregidor planning our next mission when Foster told me he'd gotten an email regarding how screwed up the notification process had been for Kimberly.

I knew if I were in her place that I wouldn't have been too happy with it either. Reading about news on Facebook was another obstacle we faced. Often, we were out-cycled by social media or the news networks.

I told Foster I would take care of it and decided to call Kimberly myself on the sat phone. Outside, I scaled a ladder to the top of a single-story building so I could have the best possible reception.

When someone answered, I asked politely, "May I please speak to Mrs. Kimberly Downing?"

"This is Kimberly Downing." Steady and calm.

I introduced myself. "This is Captain Scott Huesing. I'm Ryan's company commander, and first of all, Ryan is OK." I then apologized for the way she had found out about Ryan's injury.

Kimberly said she understood. She knew how hard it was for us. I breathed a sigh of relief. I could tell that Ryan's mom was like so many of the other parents I had talked to in good times and bad. They had an immense amount of understanding of what we were going through and tremendous compassion for all of us.

Kimberly explained to me briefly that her youngest son and husband also were Marines serving in Iraq in the infantry, and how concerned she was for Ryan now that he had been injured so many times. I reassured her, as best as I could, that I was taking care of him.

Although I couldn't make any promises that he would be sent back home from his injuries, I did promise that I would pull Ryan from the rifle platoon, off the front lines, and assign him to the company head-quarters platoon. There, at least he would be spared the daily fray.

I told her, "I know this isn't much of a comfort to you, ma'am, but he'll be a lot safer there than out on patrol. It's the best I can do for now. But don't worry about Ryan, he's a real fighter and has done more than his share over here."

Kimberly exhaled heavily and said, "Thank you."

She continued to talk—telling me about all of the deployments her boys and husband had completed, of the fighting and injuries they had endured, and how hard it had been for her.

She said, "Scott, you know something? You are the only one that has ever called me over all of the years my Marines deployed in combat. So, thank you. It means a lot to me."

I was a little choked up by her gratitude for my simple gesture of making a phone call, and somewhat astounded that no one had ever before taken the time to call her. I reassured her again and then hung up the phone.

Ryan was a little bent out of shape when he found out I called his mom. No badass Marine wants his CO to call his mommy. Deep down, though, I think he appreciated it.

He took the news about his reassignment to headquarters platoon a lot harder. He pleaded with me to stay with his platoon and keep fight-ing. I didn't budge and had made my decision. Just as I expected, Ryan proved himself as capable and dedicated in his new billet as he had been in his old one.

■   ■   ■

Kimberly's struggle didn't end as the war in Iraq came to a close.

Post-traumatic stress (PTS) had taken hold of her boys. Justen and Ryan would burst into fits of rage at the slightest annoyance. They were like walking time bombs ready to explode, and she was always scared and on edge around them.

Kimberly initially waited, hoping the psychological effects now etched into her boys' memories would fade. After three years, Kimberly could not see any signs that Ryan was coming back. The survivor's guilt lingered from the war. He couldn't hold down a job. He wanted to leave his pregnant girlfriend. He'd lock himself up in his apartment where he'd drink excessively and play video games.

As a nurse, she knew he was slipping into a deep depression, perhaps irretrievably—and was at high risk for suicide like so many other returning warriors. She knew the statistics.

She went to Ryan's apartment and confronted him.

"Ryan," she said sternly. "You need to get your act together and go to the VA Hospital for help because if you don't, I'm going to sign you up myself for the lockdown ward. Is that understood?"

Words only a mother can say to a U.S. Marine without repercussion. Ryan heeded her advice.

Kimberly humbly professes that she is only a mom, and just happy to have all of her Marines back home. Ryan, Justen, and Jeff will always be her heroes, and she is proud that they protected her.

They are equally fortunate that she was their protector as well.

CHAPTER 11

Fallbrook

Operation Sackets Harbor was our last big push while working with Task Force 1-9 Infantry. We'd be operating in the Sufia District, a section of the city on its northeast side, south of the Euphrates. We called it Area of Operation (AO) Fallbrook, after the small town in Southern California just east of Camp Pendleton. Echo Company took the northern half, and Fox Company had the southern one. The dividing line between us was a dangerous road called Route Apple.

We planned to sweep from west to east through the area, clearing buildings and looking for weapons, contraband, and high-value individuals (HVIs). My executive officer, First Lieutenant Bobby Lee, traveled in a convoy that included our mobile command post which we called "The Jump." The convoy carried combat engineers who would blast open the gates and doors of any sealed compounds we needed to search. We would work during the day and go firm when night fell.

The first day of the operation was my birthday. Not the best way to celebrate, but it wasn't the first time I had missed out on special events while in the Marines—like the birth of my daughter while deployed to Baghdad in 2004.

Lee was twenty-five years old. Born and raised in Corpus Christi, Texas, his dad worked construction, and his mother was a nurse at the local high school. By pooling their money with what Lee earned from odd jobs, the family sent him to study at Hastings College in Nebraska where he played football until he blew out his knee his final year. At six-two, 225 pounds, and heavily muscled with broad shoulders, Lee was physically imposing. But the effect was softened by the friendly, mischievous grin he usually had on his face.

Although only a thousand meters from the heart of Ramadi, the Sufia District seemed a world away. Palm groves stood along the banks of the Euphrates River, providing shade and lush scenery amongst the homes that were more spread out. Families walked the streets and traffic moved regularly.

The operation painted us a different picture of insurgent tactics in stark contrast to events of the previous weeks. Snipers, or those who thought they were, would take arbitrary shots and attack Marines from hiding spots. They never hit with much accuracy. When the firing was over, the Marines would push hard into the homes looking for the shooters.

We always outnumbered them. When smaller groups attacked us, they didn't last long. They'd scatter like cockroaches when we came at them in force. They figured out that the best course of action was to go to ground and wait us out.

I began to think that the Sufia District was where many of the hard-core fighters who fought in the Industrial District lived. They'd commute to their jobs in the Industrial District, clock in, fight, and then clock out and head home—a kind of insurgent 'nine to five.' When they returned home, they didn't want to make trouble in the neighborhoods in which they lived, and so they kept off the streets.

Air strikes were out of the question. Too many civilians lived in the area. We relied heavily on the aerial observation from the U.S. Army—lethal Boeing AH-64 Apache Gunships provided most of the coverage while we moved during the day. They flew low and aggressively, different from the U.S. Marine pilots. They were powerful, armored flying machines—cannons and rockets jutting off any available space on the airframe, and the pilots loved to support the Marines on the ground.

The people were as different as the landscape. Many volunteered to discreetly provide us with information about the insurgents who hid in their neighborhoods. They did so because they wanted peace and stability and were willing to do whatever it took to get it. They offered us orange slices and scalding hot chai in tiny cups with as much sugar as there was tea. It was sickeningly sweet, but we never refused it when locals poured us a cup.

Some of the locals were scared but would ask the Marines to come back after dark, and we did.

Our new network of informants paid off by the third day of the operation. We'd gotten a tip about a compound, about an acre in size, in which there was a stockpile of weapons. The information the locals provided was detailed. We had the address and targeted the building by the number on our map. We zeroed in on it. I set plans to raid it that very night at midnight.

Even though my Marines were exhausted, the knowledge that we had hard information on a specific target seemed to revive them. I could sense their anticipation building. They were hungry.

■   ■   ■

Lee and his team pushed north with an Army armored personnel carrier (APC) in their convoy for support.

They crept up warily to a position close to the raid site. The roads were all dirt, unimproved, and were not designed or constructed for the size of our Humvees or APCs.

His driver gunned the gas pedal of the vehicle. The terrain was steep. They backed up and tried to gain some momentum to climb the steep embankment. Collectively they prayed to muster every ounce of horsepower out of the truck as it began to bog down again. Tires slipped and sprayed dirt from the road. They made it.

Lee called back to the others to let them know it was a treacherous climb and to be careful. The APC followed.

Lee sat on the other side of a steep dike by the Euphrates. He envisioned the APC flying over the road embankment like an episode of *The Dukes of Hazzard*, the massive armored vehicle sailing through the air, soldiers yelling in excitement. For Lee and his convoy, it was much like stunt driving on those roads—except the explosions were real.

■   ■   ■

Around midnight, we were in position. However, Lee and his convoy—along with the APC—had not arrived. He had not sent word as to why he wasn't there. Nothing. No communication.

Friction.

I couldn't wait for the Jump any longer. It was midnight. I gave the order. We raided the compound.

I heard the loud cracks of semi-automatic shotguns as Marines blasted the locks on the gates. As men rushed into the complex, others hopped over the large broken cinder-block wall that surrounded the compound.

We quickly made entry into the house and secured all the occupants. It didn't take long until they began to talk. Our tip paid off.

The Marines outside began unearthing large blue plastic thirty-gallon water drums. Each drum contained its share of AK-47s, ammunition, IED-making materials, and body armor. Insurgents often put their contraband inside the drums to keep it watertight and dirt free. They sat buried a few inches below ground covered with a light layer of dirt on the lids. Essentially, each drum was a ready-to-go weapons locker. They were clever. But we'd nailed them again, denying them from the much-needed supplies that fueled the insurgency.

I was pleased by the raid's results.

Still, I was concerned that I had no communication with Lee and his men.

■   ■   ■

Lee's convoy had missed a turn and tried to find another way to link up with us. As they moved down a dark road, Lee's Humvee hit the edge of a giant sinkhole that forced their vehicle into a slow rollover.

In a Humvee, the seatbelts didn't fit around the Marines and all of their bulky gear. The turret gunner sat precariously on a sling-type seat made of nylon, similar to that of a kid's swing found on a playground. They sat and swung in it behind the machine gun.

The five-thousand-pound vehicle had begun to roll. Lee turned around to try and grab ahold of the gunner's leg, but it slipped out of his hand. It was over in an instant. The vehicle was upside down.

Lee turned around instinctively to help his gunner from the sling. He wasn't within Lee's reach. He began to panic. Lee's first thought was that he'd been tossed out and the vehicle had rolled over and crushed him to death.

Through sheer instinct, the gunner had curled up into the fetal position, tucked neatly as the vehicle flipped, and popped through the turret back inside the vehicle as if he were a human donut hole being dropped gently back into the truck. He was thrown right behind Lee.

The Humvee lay there upside down like a turtle stuck in the mud—the tires like stubby little legs and the unarmored undercarriage of the truck exposed like the smooth belly. None of the Marines were hurt. The barrel of the heavy .50 caliber machine gun sat thrust deep into the ground like a giant lawn dart.

Despite failing to link up and all of the friction, thirty hours later, Lee managed to get the vehicle pulled out. It started right up. His vehicle that served as his protector had proved worthy that night.

■　　■　　■

At the end of Operation Sackets Harbor, we were exhausted. We were also elated. Our tactic of applying relentless pressure on the enemy and forcing them to react to us provided measurable results.

We had detained dozens more suspected insurgents and confiscated more weapons and contraband than we could count. Matched with the combined results from Fox Company, the task force commander was more than pleased with how his Marines performed.

CHAPTER 11.1

Rollup

Echo Company had made a definite impression on the insurgents after only a short time in Ramadi. We had been in direct contact with the enemy two to three times a day ever since we arrived. We could almost set our watches by when we'd get attacked—after morning and evening prayers. The mosques' call to prayer broadcast from loudspeakers on the minarets and served as our alert system to stand ready to fight.

Throughout the action, the Marines had expended over fifty thousand rounds of 5.56mm, 7.62mm, and .50 caliber ammunition combined. We'd devastated the enemy with countless 120mm main tank rounds and shoulder-fired rockets and lobbed dozens of M-67 high-explosive hand grenades into enemy positions in addition to the multiple GMLRS rocket strikes we'd called in on enemy positions.

The task force had already credited the Marines of Echo Company with over fifty enemy AIF killed and dozens more enemy wounded. The numbers were impressive. We detained countless more that were on the task force's most wanted list of HVIs.

Echo Company had lost one Marine, and we were fortunate that we'd suffered just over a handful wounded in action. As satisfied as we were with our performance, we knew that more hard fighting was ahead of us, and the Marines were ready.

CHAPTER 12

Captive

It was not a matter of *if* a unit would get investigated, but *when* a unit would get investigated for alleged detainee abuse in Iraq. After the massive scandal in Baghdad with the Abu Ghraib Prison in 2003, handling detainees during combat operations became a sensitive subject.

In Ramadi in 2006, we raided so many houses during clearance operations that we inescapably had to detain suspicious persons.

On the occasions when we did, the minute that we put the flexicuffs on them, they became our responsibility, and the clock started ticking to get them processed.

Inevitably, transportation got delayed, and we were forced to move them back to our firm bases. We never kept detainees at our firm bases because there was no way we wanted them getting an inside look at how our company operated or listening to our radio communications and because of the sheer fact that we didn't have the physical space to accommodate the process.

We always pushed them to the IA compound across the street that we shared with their soldiers to safeguard them. Doing this, however, left us vulnerable to allegations. First, the detainees would make up any story to discredit U.S. forces to get their case thrown out. If they were "card-carrying" members of the insurgency, they had been trained on exactly what to say. Second, if we were short on the manpower to guard them, it was a task left up to junior Marines with no training on how to handle them—a dangerous position to put any young Marine in.

The bad guys we caught with stacks of contraband in their possession made it easy to justify detaining them. Our Terps would inform them of suspicion of being an insurgent due to possession of illegal materials and wanted for further questioning. They'd always try to plead their case and make excuses, giving some far-fetched story, like, "I'm just a radio repairman and the wire is for my business."

Detainees would plead with us, "This stuff is not mine. The insurgents told me I had to keep it or they'd kill my family and me." Sometimes they were on the brink of tears.

Normally, the ones who cried only did so in fear that we'd hand them over to the Iraqi Police. If that happened, they knew that it would only get worse. The Iraqi Police had no Rules of Engagement—they were brutal and dictated their own terms of justice.

Regardless of the excuses, we had to detain them. We'd gather up all the materials, photograph them, and then put the suspects in plastic flexicuffs, with their hands behind their backs. Then we waited for transportation to get them back to the THT unit at Camp Corregidor or Camp Ramadi.

The problem we faced was the fact that we never had sufficient training on how to carry out the process. The lack of training was evident at every level of command. It was no different when we started working for TF 1-9 Infantry. Even though the war had been going on for years, the U.S. military did not have enough trained personnel to deal with this issue. Marine infantrymen are trained to locate, close with, and destroy the enemy. But that only scratches the surface of the tasks they had to do on a daily basis.

It was not uncommon for an infantry Marine to go from engaging enemy targets to acting as a policeman, handing out claims cards for damaged property like a "would-be Geico insurance adjuster," to corralling youngsters off the street who threw rocks at our patrols or giving candy and school supplies to the well-behaved ones. They had to be trash collectors as well—cleaning up the debris, dead bodies, and wreckage that cluttered our battlespace often used as concealment for IEDs by the insurgents. The job list was endless.

Although detainee facilities were located at Camp Corregidor and Camp Ramadi with trained soldiers from Tactical Human Intelligence Teams (THT) to handle them when they arrived, it was an area of expertise that was so in demand the manpower structure couldn't keep up with the need.

What we needed were trained correctional officers to get the job done properly. It would have been ideal if this type of support was around at the onset of operations in Iraq, but it seemed to be an afterthought from the operational level planners.

Like much of what Marines and soldiers do in combat to survive and succeed, they had to learn new skills as they went along. It wasn't like learning how to use a new rifle or radio. It wasn't like being able to simply change a flat tire on a Humvee for the first time. These were people's lives we were dealing with, and it was incredibly complicated.

In addition to the lack of trained personnel to handle the detainees, we faced numerous other hurdles. Echo Company was, for the most part, a foot-mobile infantry company with limited ground transportation assets. We had eight Humvees that sat five Marines in each—every seat filled on every mission. We didn't have the organic lift capability to move detainees from the battlespace to the rear areas for interrogation at the drop of a hat.

When we did request ground transportation for detainees during clearance operations, we faced the problem of clearing the roads of IEDs and allowing the safe passage of the trucks. The massive amount of undetected IEDs added to the complexity. I had to decide on the scene whether the suspected insurgents were worth detaining and, if they were, I still had to figure out a way to get them moved under a strict timeline to the holding facility.

Moving detainees back to the rear meant a couple of things. One, it slowed the momentum of the clearance ops as we patrolled for weapons and high-value individuals. And two, I had to balance the value of the detainee with the risk of putting my Marines on roads scattered with IEDs. It was a constant dilemma of risk versus reward as a commander.

When they were available, armored 7-ton trucks would be dispatched to our locations as we picked up detainees. It took hours and sometimes days for them to get to us.

Friction.

It left us with another problem—either sit on the detainees and cough up the extra manpower from Echo Company to guard them, or release them and potentially let some shady assholes back into the fight that we'd have to face at a future time. Not to mention the fact they'd also know who we were, how we operated, and what direction we were traveling and pass the word to set us up for future attacks and possible ambushes from other teams of insurgents operating in the area.

As disjointed and unresponsive as it was, there was a process in place. I just don't think anyone really knew what the hell it was. It wasn't as if we had time to stop fighting and patrolling to have an academic discussion or formal class on the procedures. It just never happened, and everything was constantly reactionary instead of proactive when dealing with detainees.

In addition to the ROEs that we followed, we also had vague guidance on what the criteria were for detaining individuals within our area of operation. It ranged from weapons possession to the amounts of contraband on their person—that included spools of wire for command-detonated IEDs, Maytag washing machine timers, key FOBs for cars, dozens of Nokia cell phones in one location, homemade explosives (HME), unexploded ordnance, and tripwire. Or it could have included having anti-coalition propaganda or breaking curfew at night. The list was exhaustive, and it was ultimately up to the on-scene commander to make the call.

If it sounds subjective, it's because it all was.

We also had to rely heavily on the experience and instincts of our interpreters and Iraqi Army counterparts to gauge whether or not the people in question were legitimate bad guys. It was not a science by any means, but something of an art form based on experience and the evidence found on the scene.

We were fortunate at times to have trained Human Exploitation Team (HET) Marines and THT soldiers with us on patrols to conduct tactical questioning (on-the-spot interrogations) of suspected insurgents. They had training on how to look for signs of suspicious behavior from those they questioned and make more educated assumptions regarding the importance of the individuals. They'd have a good idea if we decided to detain them whether they'd be of some future intelligence value.

In the absence of HET or THT, we were left to our own devices to determine whether or not we'd detain persons from the houses we raided. It frustrated me at times. I hated having to process detainees in such a haphazard fashion when we didn't have the support structure in place.

I found myself making decisions sometimes based on arbitrary facts—if we found a pile of weapons or IED-making material, that sealed the deal for me, and we'd process them. Other times we'd find small amounts of contraband, but the demeanor and attitude of the suspect were enough to piss us off sufficiently, and we'd detain them—again, it wasn't a science.

Sometimes we'd raid houses, and the occupants would try to run out of the house or hide or feign sleeping. They'd get a rude awakening if they tried any of that shit.

■　　■　　■

In late December 2006, during a clearance operation in the Sufia District, we raided a suspected insurgent's house. As we cleared it, I found myself on the verge of snapping.

Our team made entry into the house, and the noise startled the occupants. The Marines began to clear the first floor, pulling AK-47s out from behind the furniture, complete with fully loaded thirty-round magazines—a strong indicator that bad guys lived there.

With a team of Marines, I made my way upstairs and began to search the rooms.

With my SureFire flashlight on, connected to my M4 carbine, I turned the corner of the room—a suspicious occupant hid in the back of the first bedroom, and he dashed from a pile of blankets on the floor toward the doorway, like a frightened rabbit.

He bounced right into the muzzle of my rifle. He's lucky I didn't shoot him, but he didn't have a weapon in his hands. Stupidly, he tried to run for the back of the room. I grabbed the pistol grip of my M4 with my right hand and quickly reached up, caught him around his throat with the other, and pinned him up against the wall.

The fire team flooded into the room and covered me. Jake followed after them and began questioning him on the spot.

I told Jake, "Ask this idiot why he was hiding, why he tried to run, and why the fuck he's got so many AKs in his house."

Jake translated, and as the dialogue between them went on—my hand still clenched around his neck and my index finger running alongside his carotid artery—I felt his pulse race.

When one of the Marines shined his flashlight directly on him, and I could see his face clearly, his blood pulsed faster. He was fully clothed in an Adidas athletic tracksuit with a gray winter coat over the top. I could tell he hadn't bathed in a while. The foul, pungent body odor hit my nose when he moved even slightly.

Jake told me that the man said he wasn't going to cooperate and that the weapons weren't his, according to his story. He had an arrogant look of disdain on his face, coupled with the fear that was evident from the sweat now collecting on his brow and sideburns. I was on the brink of losing control. I wanted to smash his head into the wall for thinking he had any sort of upper hand on us.

My temper cooled as quickly as it rose. I released my grip from his thin, weakly muscled neck and told the Marines to cuff him. They spun him around, pulled his arms behind his back, strapped the thick black plastic zip-ties around his wrists, and hauled him out of the room.

He made the decision easy for me that time. His obstreperous, smug attitude and the stack of automatic weapons and ammo sealed his fucking case that night.

■   ■   ■

My dilemma of risk versus gain was tested that same night when Mac and the QRF were radioed to come and pick up the detainee. I couldn't afford to wait to have 7-ton trucks pushed to our location. The clearance op was scheduled to end the next day, and we had orders to pull out of the area of operation. I had to risk sending a convoy to Camp Ramadi on the west side of town.

Mac was part of the team of Echo Company Marines who picked up all of our QRF vehicles from Camp Ramadi when we arrived in the city. Our vehicles and equipment remained plagued with problems from the onset. The Humvees lacked the proper FRAG 5 armor kits on the turrets. They didn't have the right radios or any of the mission essential gear.

Our drivers lacked training and only had a handful of hours behind the wheel in most cases. When they did pick up detainees, they had to do so at night, and I realized none of the Marines had driven the vehicles with their NVGs. It was astounding to think how effective we were on the roads in these Humvees despite the lack of training they had in them.

Our success, most likely, was attributed to the fact that the Marines understood the seriousness of their responsibility whenever they got behind the wheel of the trucks. The Marines have this strange, innate ability to adapt quickly—in the absence of any formal training they would always figure a way to succeed at everything they did.

Friction.

■   ■   ■

Mac arrived at the house where the detainee was held, and I greeted him in the courtyard. It was late, around 0200 hours, and the transit to take the detainee across town was a ten-mile drive, but it would take them hours to do it because they had to drive so slowly to scan for IEDs.

Mac and his team loaded up the detainee in their four-vehicle convoy. He was in the lead truck as the convoy commander. The Marines sat the detainee in a back seat in the second truck of the convoy. They left the house and navigated their way a few kilometers south to Route Trans Am so they could push west over to Camp Ramadi.

Route Trans Am was a main avenue for MNF units in Ramadi. The road was south of the Ma'laab District and the Ramadi soccer stadium, an unmistakable terrain feature. The route itself was habitually known for being laden with IEDs. Mac and his team were well aware.

The road itself was nothing to speak of—an unimproved road on a raised berm of compacted dirt. But its composition made it easy for our enemies to slip in and burrow into the side of the road and bury 155mm shells packed with explosives—most of the IEDs were command or pressure detonated.

There was a false sense of security on Route Trans Am, however, because it was continually patrolled and used by coalition forces. M1-A1 tanks sat in overwatch at a tactical control point (TCP) and used their thermal imaging devices to look for any movement at night to ensure insurgents weren't placing IEDs along the sides of the road. One tank sat at Entry Control Point 3 at the junction of the Euphrates River and was a strong show of force. It was not an easy post for those soldiers since the tank was a massive target for constant RPG and machine gun fire.

The tank, a hulking mass of machinery, was a domineering sight, shielded with seemingly impenetrable armor and machine guns and a massive cannon. It even sounds menacing idling—as its engines hiss. Its presence alone should have scared off even the most determined enemy.

On occasion, however, it was reported that the tank's crew were fast asleep during the most crucial times of day, usually at night, when convoys would pass by their position. The carelessness allowed the insurgents the opportunity to slip through the farmlands to the south and plant their destructive IEDs successfully under cover of darkness—waiting for the mounted patrols that drove by.

Mac's convoy crept west about five miles per hour, as they approached the east side of the Euphrates River at 0300 hours. The vehicle and its occupants hit a searing wall of pain as a sub-surface IED exploded with force.

Mac instantaneously felt like he was nonexistent.

The Marines inside the truck couldn't see as dust whooshed through the tight cabin. They couldn't hear. They couldn't breathe.

Mac was alive.

He began to hear yelling and screaming as the Marines called each other's names in a panic. Mac instinctively reached in between his legs to a small tan backpack that was on the floor. He rummaged through it and fished out a couple of chemlights. In the blackness, Mac couldn't see what colors they were.

He reached for his M4 carbine that he had clipped into the rifle rack on the doorframe. It snapped in two. He grabbed the top half, turned on the Surefire flashlight and tossed a couple of green chemlights outside through the gun turret. Green chemlights meant everyone was good to go. Red meant casualties.

Time had slowed down—what felt like hours were only minutes as Mac scrambled to assess the damage. He reached forward to get the radio. It wasn't there.

The entire dash and center console of the vehicle were blown backward—the radios were destroyed.

Mac checked on his driver, Lance Corporal Kenneth Clark, a twenty-year-old SAW gunner from Orange County, California. He was six-two and 200 pounds, with dirty blonde hair and blue eyes. Clark was a natural fighter. Fierce in every action he took.

Clark was groaning in pain. His left arm had been lacerated and crushed by the steering wheel and console as they had been blown back. Lance Corporal Cortez, the turret gunner, was cussing. He'd taken bits of hot shrapnel to the face.

Lance Corporal Ivan Montez, a twenty-year-old rifleman from Dumas, Texas, and HM3 David "Doc" Andresen, a red-headed nineteen-year-old from Davenport, Iowa, were both in the back of the Humvee during the blast. They were shaken up, but uninjured.

Mac and Clark tried to exit the vehicle but found they were trapped inside. The doors of the heavily armored Humvee had jammed shut from the blast of the IED, making it inescapable. They piled over the debris that lay in the center of the truck and crawled to the back to exit by the rear doors. Montez and Doc moved to the second vehicle for security.

Doc stood outside the Humvee, seemingly unfazed, and relieved himself on the front tire despite the madness that had unfolded around him.

Mac regrouped the Marines and began to set up a perimeter of security. He was bracing for impact and scared to death of a secondary IED explosion. A common tactic for insurgents was to blow the lead truck with one bomb, and as the Marines scrambled in the chaos, detonate a second device to kill more troops—which was a psychological mind-fuck if executed properly.

A second device never went off.

Mac moved to the other vehicle, opened the front passenger door, reached inside, and grabbed the radio handset. He called in the attack to the TOC at Camp Corregidor—relaying the casualty report. He could hear small arms fire in the distance. It was uncertain if the convoy was under attack again. The enemy fire was poor, and the rounds were ineffective, missing the Marines that were the intended targets.

The Marines in the other trucks held their fire. They looked in the direction of the muzzle flashes ready to suppress the insurgent attack. Mac stood there dazed. He heard the distinctive high-pitched whining of the M1-A1 Abrams as it pushed close to their position.

The tank stopped close to them. The hatch on the top of the M1-A1 popped open, and the tank commander (TC) stuck his head out. He said, "Marines. You guys need some help?"

Mac replied, "Yeah, we're good, but definitely need some help."

The TC gave Mac his radio frequency and told him they had him covered until more help arrived. The tank scanned the area with its thermal optics, looking for the insurgents who had set the trap. They were gone.

The sun began to rise, and Mac sent the Marines back over to the damaged Humvee to start the strip procedures—ripping out all the radios, sensitive equipment, weapons, and anything salvageable from the truck.

The survivors of the IED blast looked at the truck. A couple of them smoked cigarettes trying to calm their rattled nerves.

They surveyed the damage. The entire front end of the Humvee was completely gone. Both tires and the front axle were missing. The engine had been pushed back into the cabin of the truck, and the turret was peppered black from the blast with shrapnel. The bulletproof windows were all cracked but had remained intact. The Humvee's sturdiness had undoubtedly saved their lives that morning.

Mac and his team sat on Route Trans Am for six hours until a wrecker recovered the vehicle. Mac made his way back to the TOC at Camp Corregidor. He rolled into the Echo Company workspace still not able to believe they had survived the attack.

One of the Marines in the COC was sitting there in his chair and rolled around to Mac as he stood there. "Hey Mac, did you hear that one of our vehicles got blown up by an IED this morning?"

Mac glared back. He didn't dignify the comment with a response after all he'd just survived.

CHAPTER 13

Tigers

Echo Company was ordered to the west side of Ramadi to support another U.S. Army unit: Task Force 1-77 Armor Regiment (TF 1-77 AR), call sign "Steel Tigers." They deployed to Iraq out of Schweinfurt, Germany, comprised of M1-A1 Abrams tanks. Their area of operation made up the southwest corner of Ramadi.

The unit we were supporting had changed, but the mission remained the same—kill or capture Anti-Iraqi Forces.

We turned our posts in the Industrial District back over to Task Force 1-9 Infantry.

Most were apprehensive about leaving. The Marines had made tremendous gains. We knew the area and had a solid battle rhythm. But orders were orders.

■　　■　　■

I reported to the command post, which seemed like a ghost town that day. Most of the soldiers and the battalion commander were out in the city.

The workspace that we were assigned was not typical, by any stretch of the imagination. The compound which TF 1-77 AR worked from reminded me of an old Wild West fort. It was a single-level, U-shaped building that stood inside Camp Ramadi.

U.S. Army personnel had rightfully occupied all of the good work areas. The Echo Company staff was relegated to work out of a dilapidated 7-ton box truck converted into a planning space. It made us feel as if we were scab labor, but honestly, we didn't mind—Marines were used to improvising, and we were eager to get back out into the city.

The truck was, to be frank, a piece of shit. Its camouflage paint was chipped off, and a big, rusty tow chain wrapped around the front bumper. The grated, aluminum ladder used to climb in and out of it routinely fell off, and anyone climbing the ladder ran the risk of being knocked off it if those inside weren't careful when opening the large metal door.

Appropriately, the handle on that door was like that of an industrial meat locker because the interior of the truck was a small, square, and sparse box. Any Marine who stood more than six feet tall bumped his head frequently on the ceiling. The room held tables, chairs, maps, and other gear—utterly jam-packed inside. We called it "the *A-Team* van," a reference to the 1983 television action series with Mr. T, though not always affectionately, and, like Marines always do, we made the best of it.

We immediately got to work on the capabilities brief for the commander—a fancy PowerPoint presentation highlighting the firepower that Echo Company was bringing to the game, and how our numbers had grown.

I recruited more attachments at Camp Ramadi before the push—former Green Beret Special Forces contractors, a half-dozen interpreters, MWD teams, and a team of civil affairs specialists. I added a combat camera crew, and two teams of THT soldiers that conducted biometric scanning of the population in Ramadi. All told, we rolled in with over two hundred fifty-eight Marines including the additional gunfighters.

I was unabashed at employing anyone from the rear area that was willing to fight—if they had a rifle and wanted to get in the mix, they were welcome to join the team. My strategy ultimately proved successful.

I met the task force commander, Lieutenant Colonel Michiotto "Bear" Johnson, in his office before the command brief. We chatted formally for a while, but I could tell he wasn't much for standard protocol. He put me at ease right away.

He was a thick man, about five-nine. He was forty-two and had a thinly trimmed mustache that ran neatly to the corners of his mouth. He had a big, bright, toothy smile underneath it all. Clad in the traditional Army-gray digital BDUs, he wore a tan, leather pistol holster strapped to his back—his Beretta 9mm service pistol dangled under his left armpit, and two ammo mags under the right.

At first glance, he reminded me of the famous actor and comedian Cedric Kyles, better known as Cedric the Entertainer. But there was nothing comical about him. He was aggressive and proved to be one of the most skilled commanders I ever supported.

The Steel Tigers were the largest armored task force in the brigade—and in recent U.S. Army history. They had a vast resource of tanks, armored vehicles, and Humvees at their disposal. Bear proudly led over eight hundred thirty-five soldiers in addition to the massive armored arsenal under his command—but now he also had an additional two hundred fifty Marines ready to unleash in the city.

While I sat and spoke to Bear, he quickly understood what Echo Company was bringing to the fight—a team of highly-trained warriors with substantial combat experience.

He referred to us as his "Blunt Instrument" of war. He then asked, "How many vehicles do you want to start the clearance ops, Scott?"

"None," I replied.

Probably a bit stunned by my response, he asked, "Well how the hell are you boys planning on moving around the city then?"

"We'll walk."

A look of admiring disbelief crossed his face as he let out a one-syllable laugh through his nose, exhaling sharply.

I continued, "I want to break this area of operation into three sectors and have Marines crawling around every corner, building, alley, and street located in the Ta'meem District and scare the living shit out of any insurgents that think they have a safe haven here. If they stick their head around a corner, they're going to get it shot the fuck off."

Bear smiled. He seemed excited to have us in the fight.

The Steel Tigers had arrived in Ramadi four months before Echo Company and had developed a good battle rhythm in their area—but they still needed more help. M1-A1 tanks were great machines, but they were even better with hundreds of Marines integrated around them.

Bear's predecessors had made significant gains in western Ramadi, but he and his men still had work to do. When Echo Company arrived, he let me in on his plan.

Bear knew that to gain a foothold in Ramadi, he had to achieve two objectives. First, he had to get out into the heart of the city and set up functional forward operating bases (FOBs). Simply pushing out tanks and patrolling the streets wouldn't achieve the results he wanted.

The second was that he knew he had to plan and execute a major offensive that would allow the task force the opportunity to seize the initiative for his men to occupy the city seamlessly. He was successful.

By the time Echo Company joined the Steel Tiger Task Force, there were already multiple FOBs and outposts in key positions that we used to our advantage to have ammunition and supplies pushed to our maneuver elements. Bear needed Echo Company to go into the Ta'meem District and systematically and aggressively clear and hold the area.

The Ta'meem District was an austere section of Ramadi. It had suffered the same devastation from the war that most of the cities in Al Anbar Province had endured. The Ta'meem was another perfect image that reflected the crumbling cityscapes of Iraq—semblances of what used to be a community.

Bear was a little hesitant about our approach when Echo Company began the clearance of the Ta'meem District. He thought we were too violent and our actions might diminish any advances the Steel Tigers had made concerning local support garnered before our arrival. Our relationship over the course of a few weeks inevitably changed the tide of the war, but the methods in which we did it seemed too radical for some.

I abated his concerns as we planned and executed a disciplined and methodical approach while conducting our patrols. We knew what we were doing—controlled chaos.

The Marines moved through the city with fierce determination every step of the way. They helped those who needed it. They crushed others that stood in our way with violence of action.

We were in contact with the enemy every night as we pushed from the southeast corner of the Ta'meem District in a westerly direction. We cleared every single structure that we encountered in our zone. The platoon commanders met with me every morning, and we went over our maps and compared notes.

I took a yellow highlighter pen and marked every building we cleared. We left nothing untouched. As we did, we fought and killed the insurgents. We raided their safe havens, disrupted their supply routes, and collected every single weapon we found hidden or buried in the ground. We took some casualties but managed to make it through without a single fatality.

We knocked the enemy off balance. They never saw us coming. When they did see us, they knew it would be a bad day if they tried to engage the Marines of Echo Company. We simply never gave them a chance to breathe. There was never an hour in the day during our time in the Ta'meem that there wasn't a Marine or soldier on patrol fighting and taking it to the enemy.

Echo Company never left the zone. We lived out in the city. We never rested or returned to Camp Ramadi. We cared only about mission success.

It was hard for the boys. Living in that environment for such an extended period was extremely tough and unforgiving. The Marines and soldiers made it through it all, though—because they had each other. The focus was always on the unit, not the individual. They executed every day singly focused on their mission of destroying the enemy.

There was never any rivalry between the Army and Marines in Ramadi. It was always one team—one fight. I think everyone believed that, and they respected each other for it. Ultimately, our success and lives depended on it.

Echo Company continued to dominate the insurgents in the Ta'meem District. Our tactics were different than the Army's, and our violence and audacity shocked the enemy.

We moved fast and deliberately to confuse and disorient the enemy—we constantly kept them guessing.

As we continued to apply pressure on the insurgents in the Ta'meem, it allowed Bear and his men to set up a more permanent presence in the city. It enabled them to focus on creating IA compounds and Iraqi police stations the city desperately needed. I was determined to eradicate the enemy from the Ta'meem District without compunction to allow Bear to expand his control.

Bear's blunt instrument proved to be just the tool he needed.

CHAPTER 14

Jump

If I pushed my platoon commanders hard, I pushed my second in command, Bobby Lee, even harder.

I had to. Our implicit and expressed relationship as CO and XO was vital to the success of the company. More importantly, if anything happened to me, he had to be ready to take command. I knew that every chance I had needed to be used to develop him into a company commander.

Lee's gregarious nature made him very likable to those around him—his peers, the Marines, and especially me. He never missed an opportunity to find the levity in a tough situation and had a knack for brightening everyone's spirit in tough times.

It was hard for me to stifle his charm. I didn't want to, but I also had to make sure that he knew there was a time and a place for letting his hair down. I'm quite sure I saw a lot of myself in him, and that made it more difficult for me at times. I counted on him to be "The Heavy." The enforcer. I think it went against his natural style, but I was training him the way Marty had trained me. Relentlessly.

I am certain he felt frustrated and overwhelmed at times. He was a relatively new lieutenant with only a shade over two years of experience under his belt in the Marine Corps, and I often had an abrupt way of tasking Lee in the midst of the chaos.

Despite any look of exasperation on his face, I was famous for telling him, "XO, just get it done."

I failed to factor in his lack of experience when I saw the frustration. I simply saw a bear of a man standing in front of me, and I expected results. Lee never let me down in that regard, and he thrived—notwithstanding my limited guidance at times.

Ramadi was Lee's first combat deployment. After a short time in the city, his nervousness disappeared—he became desensitized by the combination of emotions and constant stress.

Lee had assembled a team of Marines that functioned as the company Jump, a mobile command post of sorts. It consisted of a couple of armored Humvees, but it was highly effective and provided critical support to the entire company. Lee and his team drove fearlessly around the war-torn city in their trucks and Echo Company could always count on them.

He identified and chose one of the new Humvees for his headquarters team, and over the course of the deployment, that vehicle became his house, office, bedroom, and protector.

I thrust a lot of responsibility on Lee, and he handled it well. His team of characters in the Jump were constantly on the move as our dismounted platoons patrolled throughout the city. I relied heavily on them to be the forward eyes and ears of the company. They scouted out safe zones. They served as a resupply for ammunition and chow, and pushed detainees back to the rear for questioning after we'd capture them on raids.

They were left alone and unafraid at times. Vulnerable and without the support of the rest of the company, they moved on the battlefield encountering all, if not more, of the same perils everyone else did. Their biggest threat was their constant exposure to IEDs on the roads. It was a feeling of impending doom every time they drove anywhere in Iraq. It had been that way since the initial invasion.

Lee and his team pressed on through the turmoil of tight living conditions inside the truck. They were always on call and would go for days without sleep. It wasn't uncommon for them to take a handful of Excedrin PM to force sleep when needed then awaken on a moment's notice to push to a platoon's location for support. They'd instantly wash down another handful of tiny white ephedrine pills with two or three highly-caffeinated, fizzy Rip It energy drinks to get back in the game.

We went firm in the Ta'meem District. Lee and his crew navigated the unknown streets of western Ramadi and pushed support as we cleared in zone, going from house to house. They'd frequently stop at houses we'd just raided. They dropped off chow and boxes of tiny CR125 SureFire flashlight batteries that we burned through daily. They'd pick up stacks of confiscated enemy weapons, or a detainee we'd been holding and race back to Camp Ramadi, make a drop-off, grab some more supplies and repeat the cycle.

■   ■   ■

Lee and his men had been up for over thirty hours when they headed back to Camp Ramadi to turn over a detainee to THT. Lee's driver slowed the truck to a stop.

"Sir, take a look up there. It's an IED off the side of the road," he said, pointing to what looked like two small aluminum baking sheets pressed together.

They studied the device. There were wires visibly protruding from the side of it. They ran for twenty meters toward a house on the east side of a street named Route Cindy—just sitting out in the open.

Lee called over the radio, advising a squad out on patrol in the area of the device. They were blocks away. The squad pressed closer to the suspected IED and cordoned off the area, keeping a safe distance from the unknown object.

The squad leader found the wires that led from the device to the side of the house. They were bare. There was no battery or detonator attached to the ends. Unwisely, he grabbed the wires and gave them a solid yank.

The wires spooled back loosely in his hand, like a string from a kite that had broken loose in the sky. The device lay in place in the middle of the road. Nothing happened.

"Has to be a decoy," Lee thought.

Not being EOD experts, they didn't want to take any chances. They tried to test the IED just to be on the safe side.

The turret gunner skillfully threw cans of Mountain Dew at the square aluminum target with great aim. After hitting it directly with several cans of soda and expending a few precious Rip It drinks, they deduced that it had to be a decoy.

With the wires now out of the device, Lee and his team approached the plate and determined that it was harmless, but thought they'd best take it back to the EOD experts at Camp Ramadi so they could show them that the insurgents were placing this type of decoy out on the roads. It looked different from any they'd seen before.

They picked up the two-by-two-foot piece of aluminum plating and strapped it securely to a pile of camouflage netting that was always on the back hatch of the Humvee.

After they turned over the detainee to THT at the camp, Lee and his men drove over to the EOD compound.

Outside the compound, the EOD team had set up an impressive and educational display of dozens of IEDs they had picked up and defused throughout the city so soldiers and Marines could learn what the enemy was using.

A master sergeant stood outside of the EOD compound as Lee got out of his truck. He gave the master sergeant a quick recital of how he'd found the decoy and walked him to the back of the Humvee. He unstrapped the plate and sat it on the ground by the truck. The master sergeant began to take a closer look.

He said, "Hey, sir. Where'd you find this?"

Lee pulled out his map and showed him. "It was placed as a decoy on the road right where the rest of our company is clearing."

"Well, I got news for you, sir. This ain't no decoy," he said, with certainty garnered from twenty years of experience handling explosives under every condition. "See that white, flakey stuff right there? That's what we call homemade PETN (Pentaerythritol Tetranitrate, one of the most powerful explosive compounds, commonly known as plastic explosives), and if you look real close, jammed in there you can see the blasting cap shoved in."

Lee, suddenly flushed, shook his head. He instinctively knew that he'd made a grave error in tampering with the device in the first place. He left the IED in the capable hands of the master sergeant.

When Lee told me about the event, I was shocked. Then I was enraged. I'm quite sure I ripped into Lee for his lapse in judgment that afternoon but was also keenly aware that sleep deprivation and fatigue always played a hand in everything. In retrospect, I was grateful that no one was hurt, and I had to acknowledge that Lee and his team's actions, although slightly misguided, probably saved lives despite risking their own.

Chance plays a significant role in war, but so does experience. We were all learning as we went along. There were no standard operating procedures for dealing with the unknown and the massive amounts of chaos and uncertainty placed in front of young men.

The Marines always did a superb job under those circumstances. They made a lot of the tactics up as they went along—something not that uncommon in combat in a continually changing environment.

Ramadi proved to be an unforgiving battleground that taught them while they fought, and they did it extremely well.

CHAPTER 15

Mopeds

The Marines had patrolled as hard as I have ever seen since we'd been in-country—going house to house, rooting out weapons and engaging the enemy every day. Although capable of killing the enemy at distances of up to five hundred meters, most of the fighting was close-up in the city—fifty to one hundred meters.

In addition to racking up enemy kills—Echo had an informal rivalry with Fox Company as to who could find the most insurgent contraband—we found rockets, RPGs, rifles, ammo, body armor, intelligence, you name it. Whether it was buried in a hole in the ground, stashed under a house, shoved into the trunk of a car, put underneath a bongo truck, or stuffed up the ass of a camel, my boys would find it. It got to be such a competition they wanted to patrol all night and sleep all day; that—and killing insurgents—was pretty much the order of business for months on end.

One night, we raided a known insurgent house in the Ta'meem District. Insurgents had been cooking their evening meal as we moved in on the site—a small plate of uncooked goat meat sat next to a tiny stove.

We must have scared the living piss out of them right before we made entry and they fled—we'd missed them by seconds.

The house itself was no more than twelve hundred square feet, small by American standards, made of big red bricks—globs of mortar oozed from the cracks from the primitive construction—and was surrounded by a ratty, wrought iron fence.

As most of the team scoured the interior for weapons, other Marines searched outside. In the house, Bam-Bam found some small, strange-looking items lying next to the goat meat. They looked like tiny triangle paper footballs—the kind kids make in grade school and kick with their fingers through imaginary goalposts or use to pass notes in class. They were wrapped tightly in plastic Saran Wrap. When we unraveled them, we discovered they were indeed secret notes—crude messages that insurgents used to share information. They safeguarded them in the caches.

We were applying the most advanced military technologies in the world, and the insurgents were using the most basic. It's called "asymmetric warfare," a fancy way of understanding that the enemy often didn't afford us the courtesy of engaging in a stand-up fight, allowing us to bring our superior firepower, technology, and manpower to bear.

As advanced as our technology evolved to be on the battlefield, the insurgents always found a way around it. They believed in the basics of how to get things done at any expense, no matter how rudimentary it was, or if it took more time to do so. Time was always on their side.

A clamor out in the front yard pulled our attention away from the notes.

Sergeant Ken Liesche came inside. "Hey sir, you got to come and check this shit out."

Liesche was a twenty-year-old rifleman and the only sergeant in his platoon. He was from Kansas City, Missouri—a self-assured, bold physical specimen at six-two, 200 pounds, with brown hair and blue eyes.

When I strode onto the front porch, I saw Liesche standing there with a huge 120mm mortar round in his hand.

I said, "Where the fuck did you find that?"

Liesche replied, "In the garden."

"Garden? What garden?"

He responded excitedly, "In the front yard. The whole front yard is a fuckin' garden full of unexploded ordnance, sir."

I made my way out to the "garden."

Six Marines had already broken out their entrenching tools—the small, collapsible shovels that Marines and soldiers have been carrying since World War I trench warfare—and were digging vigorously. Every single scoop of dirt they turned up revealed mortar rounds, RPGs, rocket booster motors, cans of ammo, and, amazingly, even the wings of a downed U.S. drone. They dug and dug and kept finding more stuff popping out of the garden.

It was a weird harvest.

By 0300 hours, the boys had finished the three-hour excavation. They climbed out of the chest-deep hole and stood in the front yard, with hundreds of pieces of ordnance stacked around them. Dirt was piled high around the eight-foot-long cache and thrown onto the sidewalks and over the front wall. They looked like a pack of hound dogs that had dug up a pile of bones.

The Marines were filthy—dirt is a close companion to most Grunts, and it's also a vocational aspect of the nature of our work. Their cammies were soaked through with sweat. The digital camouflage pattern of their uniforms was almost indistinguishable by now—their grime-soaked cammies looked like solid, dark khaki trousers from continually wiping their hands down the front of their pants.

By this point, all I could think was, "Man, how the hell are we going to get rid of all of this shit?"

■   ■   ■

We called on the radio for a team of explosive ordnance disposal (EOD) technicians for several hours as we sat staring at the mountain of unexploded ordnance (UXO).

In 2006, EOD teams were probably the most in-demand experts in the entire country. The country was awash in weapons and ordnance of all sorts, and, when we found it, we had to destroy it. EOD teams worked more, slept less, and blew up more unexploded ordnance than any other soldiers. Military working dog handlers and Terps came in at a close second because of their extremely unique and specialized skill sets.

I was always impressed by those in their right mind who sign up for a job in which their entire mission is based on stumbling across bombs and massive piles of explosives and get paid to detonate that stuff—EOD techs are those guys.

By a sheer stroke of luck, an EOD unit came up on the net and requested permission to cross through our area of operation.

Standard courtesy when going through another unit's boundary is to do a face-to-face link-up with the unit's commander to identify yourself and, by doing so, reduce the chances of "blue on blue"—that is, fratricide between friendly forces. It's critical to know where all of the pieces on the battlefield are at all times.

When the EOD team arrived, they hopped out of their trucks. We introduced ourselves and played the "name game" for a bit. As we spoke, I discovered that this particular unit happened to be a U.S. Marine EOD team based out of Camp Pendleton, California—a sheer coincidence for us that night.

I didn't take the time to tell them how we'd come across this massive weapons cache. All that mattered was that we had no way of hauling it back to a firm base and we obviously couldn't leave it in the middle of the street. It had to be dealt with.

Daylight was around the corner. I asked the EOD team if they had any C4 (military-grade plastic explosives) in their Humvees so they could manage to set a charge and destroy the cache in-place.

Dawn crept closer as the Echo Company QRF, led by Lee, rolled up, bolstering the security we had from the Marines manning rooftops in overwatch positions.

Most of the locals were aware of what we were up to—we had made enough noise. All of the commotion we made in the early hours brought snooping eyes to see what was happening. Some flicked on their front porch lights and others were peeking through their windows.

I knew they were curious—and probably pretty annoyed that we'd awakened an entire neighborhood. I was also keenly aware that now the locals had been alerted, some might give away our position to nearby insurgents to try and ambush us as we worked to detonate the massive stack of ordnance.

Even if the insurgents didn't mount a full-scale attack, snipers could work themselves into position. As the daylight came close, they'd be able to see who was huddled up with their radio operators who carried backpacks from which projected long whip antennas—the equivalent to a big neon sign that read, "Shoot me first! I'm important."

We felt exposed and extremely vulnerable. The longer we stayed in one position, the higher the risk was for us to start taking fire. We were racing against the clock.

Round by round, rifle-by-rifle, RPG-by-RPG, the EOD team and the Marines laid the ordnance out in neat rows. Then they put every block of C4 they had on top of it. They placed detonation cord and primers in the bricks of C4 and daisy-chained them together. One more step needed to be taken before they could unleash what would certainly be a massive and spectacular explosion.

The staff sergeant in charge of the EOD team wandered over to me casually and said, "Sir, we're cool on C4, but we got one problem: we don't have any way to tamp this det."

They needed a huge counter-weight on top of the ordnance that would ensure that the C4's blast would be directed down onto the UXO. Otherwise, everything would get tossed into the air, and a lot would not be destroyed.

I told him to hold on. I had the solution.

While clearing out the front yard of weapons, we had come across a minivan the insurgents were modifying to use as a VBIED. The leaf springs were welded flat, the shocks removed, and the back seats were taken out, and the trunk was completely bare. Not a normal piece-of-shit ride, even for Iraqi standards.

Insurgents knew tricks like this to make sure that the cars they packed full of explosives didn't sit low in the back as they were driving them to the intended targets. Despite their efforts, we had figured this out long ago after hundreds of VBIED attacks. We had developed a keen eye for which vehicles looked out of place.

I directed the Marines from HQ Platoon to tow the minivan over to the pile of UXO using one of the Humvees. Once they had it situated next to the UXO, a squad of Marines pushed it over on its side onto the heaping mass of ordnance.

I turned and said to the staff sergeant, "I went to Illinois State, so it's safe to say I don't have a degree in physics. Is this going to be enough weight to tamp this down?"

"I don't know, sir," he replied. "You don't need a degree to know that this is going to make one hell of a crater in the ground once it blows. It'd be better if we had some more weight on it."

Two moped scooters sat parked on the side of the house where we'd dug up the cache—probably the insurgents' intended get-away vehicles. Quickly, a couple of Marines retrieved the scooters and hefted them on top of the ordnance in addition to the minivan.

The staff sergeant came back over to me. "You guys might want to get some video of this. It's going to be one hellacious fireworks show."

I ordered my men to move back several hundred meters and to take cover wherever they could. The Marines in the vehicles were pushed back to the top of an elevated road, a safe distance away but still with a good line of sight to the blast.

I told Lee to get on the radio and call the task force HQ and tell them there was going to be a controlled det in our zone in twenty minutes. Before detonating a charge, we always passed it over the radio network so that all friendly units in the area knew it was friendly fire and not some random IED going off.

We expected the worst every time we heard a loud boom in the city. If it wasn't a controlled det, it would always give pause for the inevitable bad news of a friendly casualty.

The det was approved.

I got back on the company net and passed the word, "Controlled det in five minutes. Everyone stay covered. Over."

The EOD Marines pulled the time fuses and walked back calmly and confidently to their vehicles as if they'd done this a thousand times before—which, of course, they had.

The countdown began, and almost to the second, we felt the overpressure. A smooth wave of heat and force rolled over us. There was a deafening noise, and a massive fireball, fifty feet high, shot into the sky. Bright sparks scattered into the breaking morning light, and yellow-orange shrapnel, all that was left of the UXO, whistled down range.

Cheers erupted from Marines, many of whom had obviously not heeded my command to stay undercover but peeked out from wherever they could to watch the show. They screamed and hooted—like a crowd at a high school football game.

From the rooftop of a building to my right, there was a team of Marines in overwatch. One yelled to his teammate, "Holy shit, did you see the fuckin' size of that blast? Fucking unbelievable!"

They giggled like adolescent pranksters—the Marine Corps unintentionally bred a high school mentality in most cases.

The Ta'meem District proved to be as busy for us as we were in central Ramadi. There was never any relief for the Marines. They stayed busy, but that's how they liked it.

It may be hard to understand for those who have never been in the military how men thrive on the continual need for risk and danger. The best example I ever provide is to imagine a professional football team that practices all week, and there is never a game on Sunday. For the Marines that's how they viewed it.

Echo Company trained for months on end, and it was their game day—every single day—and they were winning.

CHAPTER 16

Rafts

Camp Ramadi had turned into a massive sludge bucket of dirt roads in late December. It had been raining for several days on end. Every vehicle inside the one-square-kilometer compound was covered with mud. Marines and soldiers walked around with huge dirt clogs caked to the bottom of their boots. It splattered up the backside of their uniforms as they walked and left tiny, wet dirt speckles—the kind similar to those you get when riding your bicycle through a puddle.

25 December 2006

Christmas day in Ramadi was as good as could be expected, seeing as we weren't home and weren't with our families and friends. We had each other, though. That seemed to help ease the separation. We were missing one member of our Echo Company family now, but we still were incredibly grateful to be together.

As we had on Thanksgiving Day, all of the Marines gathered together in the DFAC. The men made their way around the tables to wish each other a Merry Christmas. We gorged on turkey and Baskin-Robbins ice cream and tacos and anything else we could devour. I broke from my normally strict diet without an ounce of guilt, figuring that this might be the last chance I would get to eat foods that I now considered indulgences. I was thirty-seven years old, and my days of stuffing my face with massive quantities of pizza and guzzling soda without guilt were long gone.

It also was the first Christmas dinner at which I had to fill sandbags before I could eat.

But this was a hard and fast rule for the "Ready First" Brigade Combat Team at Camp Ramadi. Every Marine or soldier had to grab a shovel, fill ten sandbags, and stack them on metal pallets outside of the DFAC before getting served.

A four-by-six plywood sign at the entrance of the DFAC read, "Do it for THEM."

"Them" referred to the real "door kickers," the soldiers and Marines who usually were out on the streets, patrolling and fighting, and who rarely had the opportunity to have a sit-down meal like the soldiers and Marines who worked at the forward operating bases (FOBs). A good share of these "warriors" permanently parked their asses on the FOBs and never went beyond the wire—never leaving the relative safety of their positions. Infantry types referred to them derogatorily as "*Fobbits*," a spin-off of the little home-loving people from J. R. R. Tolkien's *Lord of the Rings* novels.

For the infantry Marines and soldiers who were the ones out in the city doing the fighting, it galled the grunts—the ones who were in danger every day—to have to fill sandbags.

I made it all the way through the chow line with my tray full of food, ready to sit, when I reached down to adjust my M4 carbine, to make sure it didn't clank on the bench as I sat down.

It wasn't there.

I dropped my tray on the table in a panic and backtracked my route through the DFAC the way I had entered, all the way to the entrance where a couple of soldiers were checking ID cards.

I blazed past the soldiers with the dread that I had lost my rifle. I started scanning the area around the pile of loose sand where I had filled my quota of sandbags. A knot hit my stomach as I feverishly looked around for my weapon. It wasn't there. I knew where I had rested my rifle precisely when I filled my bags, but it was gone. I sprinted a couple of meters back to the podium where the soldiers were standing.

I asked, "Excuse me. Has anyone turned in a…" Before I could get the rest of the sentence out of my mouth, one of the soldiers turned away from the podium and reached into a stack of maybe seven or eight rifles.

"Sir, can you tell me your serial number on your rifle?" he asked politely.

I quickly recited my rifle serial number, and the sergeant handed me my M4. I thanked him profusely for safeguarding my weapon.

The soldier who returned my weapon said, "Sir, don't worry about it. It happens all the time."

It was apparent he was right as I glanced again at the stack of abandoned rifles behind the podium from which mine had been pulled. In my sleep-deprived state, walking around in a daze, I had left my M4 abandoned sitting only feet away from the soldiers at the podium.

I was mortified. In combat, your rifle is your life and something you never take for granted. Thankfully, there was an unwritten rule—nobody fucks with anyone else's weapon in combat, deserted or not.

■   ■   ■

New Year's Day 2007

Echo Company had been pressing hard for several days, conducting clearance ops in the Ta'meem District. Lee had orders to take elements from the mobile QRF and set up a firm base on the south side of the Euphrates River.

By now, I had learned the best way to operate in Ramadi. I spread my platoons throughout our battlespace, allowing each platoon commander the ability to gain particular familiarity with his unit's area of operation and also de-conflict our fires by terrain (meaning we wouldn't have friendly forces shooting at one another because buildings would serve as protective barriers between them).

It wasn't a complicated process. I studied a map of the area we worked in and plotted all of the friendly units, main roads, and checkpoints with a black Sharpie marker. Then, I divided by three.

Platoons were never more than several hundred meters apart at any time. That way, although they were protected from fratricide, they could mutually support each other in the event of a coordinated attack from insurgents—which, we knew by now, they were fully capable of conducting.

As my dismounted platoons swept through the Ta'meen District methodically, I sent Lee and his team ahead to a key piece of terrain near a place we called End Road Bridge.

Over the course of our time in Ramadi, we had received intelligence updates that insurgent forces used a technique to shuttle weapons, ammunition, and bomb-making materials across the Euphrates River from one zone to another. They did so in order to avoid the numerous vehicle checkpoints that the Army and Marines had established.

Lee and his team provided overwatch east of End Road Bridge from the compound they occupied, a half-completed bridge abutment that sat on the sandy bank of the Euphrates—not usable by any vehicle traffic. Built of concrete and with large support pillars, it had been under construction when the war began. Had it been completed, it would have served as a main artery for transportation from northern Ramadi to the south.

Lee had a great vantage point. It was an ideal spot to observe enemy movements across the river.

They often spotted weapons and ordnance floating across. Insurgents would create makeshift rafts by filling large truck inner tubes with air, and line the bottom with netting or rope. They'd build the rafts in the city, pack them full of weapons, and then sneak them into the tall reeds near the river. When they deemed the time right to cross the two-hundred-meter-wide expanse, they'd launch them, hoping they'd sail safely across and be picked up by their fellow insurgents across the river.

Lee and his men would park their Humvees near the river, sitting like hunters waiting for deer to come out of the edge of a tree line into a razed cornfield. Mounted on Lee's vehicle was an MK-19—an impressive weapon. It is a belt-fed, blowback operated, 40mm grenade launcher capable of shooting sixty rounds per minute out to fifteen hundred meters.

He made easy target practice of the insurgent's futile labors. Using the MK-19, his gunners unloaded multiple strings of fire of high explosive, 40mm rounds at the rafts, sinking them to the bottom of the Euphrates.

■   ■   ■

From the onset of the fighting, we'd stumble across the most bizarre occurrences.

We targeted a house for a nighttime raid while conducting clearance ops in Sector Bravo 13 in the Ta'meem. I was patrolling with 3rd Squad, 4th Platoon, when we isolated the building.

It was pitch black.

The house was a one-story affair surrounded by a high concrete wall pierced by a high metal gate. A Marine moved toward the gate wielding his Mossberg 12-gauge. He racked the pump action on it and, standing at a 45-degree angle to the target, blasted the gate's lock. The squad flooded the compound through the now-open gate. Fire teams dispersed, looking for entrances to the house.

My team was out back.

With me was Corporal Brian Lee Dickinson, the platoon's radio operator. He stayed by my side so that I would have the radio at my disposal. A twenty-year-old rifleman, he was a big kid, weighing in at 220 pounds, probably 265 with all of his kit.

Dickinson grew up in Locust Grove, Oklahoma—population: 1,571—fifty miles east of Tulsa. In high school, Dickinson was a troublemaker who wasted most of his time partying and evading run-ins with the local sheriff rather than focusing on a plan for his future. He was quickly lured into the Marines when the recruiters came by his high school his senior year delivering their best sales pitch. His graduating class was less than one hundred. Four joined the Marines, including Dickinson.

There was a heavy, white, steel screen door that appeared to lead into the kitchen. We could hear the other Marines up front banging on the door. No one answered. Dickinson turned his back to the door and cocked his leg forward and thrust it back into the handle, mule-kicking the door.

Nothing. It didn't budge.

Dickinson turned to me with a look of defeat on his face. "Sir. Fucker won't budge! Wanna' blow it?"

I knew the Marines were close to entry up front. My patience was thin, but my team didn't have a shotgun and were short on sledgehammers—but not on great ideas.

I walked over to Dickinson. I slid my hands up inside the back of his sweaty body armor, high, behind his armpits, squeezing tightly, digging my fingertips into the nylon material.

"Dickinson, on three we're going to bust this fucker in. You got it?"

Dickinson responded with the typical, "Roger that, sir."

We hugged our bodies close together.

I was guiltless using Dickinson as a human battering ram.

We took three steps back. "One...two...three." We yelled out loud as we hurled ourselves at the door.

The latch gave way, and the door flung violently open from the combined force of 500 pounds of Marine. The door's glass shattered from the impact and shards sprayed us as we landed on top of one another on the kitchen floor.

We were in.

The Marines behind us flooded into the house, stepping over us with little regard as I lay there on top of Dickinson, now flattened to the ground.

I pressed myself off of him like I was doing a push-up. He grunted as I shoved off him. I reached down to grab his hand as he looked up at me.

"Well, sir, it worked," he said.

We heard the call "Clear! Clear," throughout the house as the men checked room by room. Dickinson and I made our way to the rest of the squad, as two Marines stood watch over a family kneeling on the ground. The terrified occupants sat hidden as we made entry but were quickly discovered by the search team. The Marines shined their flashlights in their faces as they knelt on the ground.

We combed through the house, searching for weapons and other contraband. We searched every room, pulling AKs out of closets and from behind sofas.

A Marine called out, "Sir, you gotta get down here."

I went through a door that led into a cellar-like room in the basement. Basements were not common in Iraq.

I stopped in my tracks. I looked down in bewilderment to see a man in his mid-thirties with Down Syndrome. That wasn't all: he was bound to the pole of the staircase with a large, stainless steel chain and a medieval shackle around his ankle. Like some animal in a circus.

Another "Holy fuck" moment washed over me.

Chaining people with disabilities in basements may have been more commonplace than I knew—albeit eerily disturbing. But because there were no functional special needs facilities in Iraq, I think folks just didn't know any better and seriously thought that this was the solution for caring for them. We were shocked at the sight, but our only recourse was to report it once we got back to the firm base.

We had seen a lot so far: rafts, cleverly disguised IEDs, suicide bombers, full-on firefights. There were times we thought we had seen it all. But there always was a new madness waiting for us the next day—most of us simply thought, "You just can't make this shit up."

Often, it became more insane than we ever could have imagined.

CHAPTER 17

Millions

The days of letting families stay in their homes had come and gone as we gained experience in the city. It became evident that letting them stay didn't make sense. We had to sequester them in the house all day and guard them at all times—they just became a massive burden and even bigger risk. Additionally, it took Marines off the streets or pulled them from security duty. If the insurgents attacked the house, the locals would be exposed to greater danger as well.

We were blunt. "Hope you have some family or friends nearby because you can't stay here, but we'll make sure that you get back home safely the next day. It's not safe for you if you stay here with us now."

We always added that if the insurgents thought they were helping us they might be targeted for later retribution. That usually served as an added incentive for them to vacate. They also could tell the insurgents in all honesty that we kicked them out. The next day, we generally gave them a few hundred dollars for their troubles from our Commander's Emergency Reparation Funds (CERF) that we always carried with us. I had a few thousand U.S. dollars in my stash.

We pushed through the Ta'meem to Route Cindy; we found a great position to go firm. It had good observation and plenty of room for the whole platoon. It always helped if the houses contained oil heaters and a pile of faux mink blankets to help keep us warm as we tried to get some sleep. Allowing ourselves some creature comforts when we had time to rest—instead of toughing it out—was another lesson we took a while to learn.

The house did have one problem, however: a grove of reeds across the street. It was a huge ditch—five football fields long and another one hundred yards wide—dense with reeds, grass, and brush. The plants stood twenty feet high in spots, obstructing our view across the ditch to the buildings on the other side of the town, limiting our observation of any enemy movement, and severely restricting our ability to identify insurgents and return fire.

We knew we had to stay there for more than a day to allow the other platoons to catch up to us. Early that same morning, we started taking sporadic small arms fire from across the ditch. The rumor mill had spread news of our presence pretty fast. It was kind of hard keeping a platoon of Marines a secret as they occupied any house. We'd also observed military-aged males (MAMs) running in and out of the ditch, presumably grabbing weapons they had hidden in the cache.

I got on the radio to the Steel Tigers and relayed my concerns. I requested that the task force send a refuel tanker to our position and soak the reed-filled area with gas so we could burn out the vegetation.

Most of my guys thought this was crazy, including my XO, Lee, but the Steel Tigers approved my request, and dispatched the tanker truck from Camp Ramadi.

A couple of hours later, around 1500 hours, the truck crew raised "Longhorn" on the net and requested permission to enter friendly lines. Most soldiers or Marines didn't feel completely safe driving through Ramadi in an M1-A1 tank. But the tanker crew did it in a vehicle protected only with light-skinned armor on the doors and a bulletproof windshield. Not to mention they were towing a tanker trailer filled with two thousand gallons of gasoline. In broad daylight.

One of the crew, a private first class, maybe nineteen years old, reported to the command post and asked what he needed to do.

I said, "Thanks, warrior. You have some steel balls rolling around town in that rig. I need you to run your lines as close and as safe as you can to that ditch and hose it down with fuel so we can torch it. Can you handle it?"

He didn't even hesitate. "No problem, sir. That's why I'm here. Just give me plenty of security, and I'll be ready to push two thousand gallons into it for you."

I was utterly astounded by how calm he was.

With Echo Company Marines in overwatch from multiple buildings and protected by two teams of infantry, the soldiers flooded that field just as I asked. It took less than a half hour. They were gone before I could thank them again.

Now we had another dilemma to sort out: how the hell were we going to light this particular candle? After kicking around some less than stellar ideas, I decided to launch a couple of 40mm high-explosive grenades into the ditch and hope they would trigger the fire. I went to the rooftop and grabbed Corporal Jonathan Yenglin, one of the fire team leaders.

"Alright, let's see how good you are with that thing." I gestured to the Colt M-203 40mm grenade launcher that was attached to the bottom of his M16-A4 rifle. "I want you to park one round at each end of the ditch and light this bitch up right where that soldier hosed it down. Got it?"

"No sweat, sir." Yenglin flipped up the leaf sight on the M-203, shouldered his weapon, and took aim.

He smoothly cupped his hand around the ribbed tube and slid open the breach, inserted the high explosive grenade, and locked it shut. Without hesitation, he took his trigger finger and flipped the safety switch forward. He took one cool, collected breath, exhaled slowly and squeezed. There was a low, muffled pop and the round left the tube. It sailed three hundred yards, hitting dead center of the reed field, and let loose a massive explosion.

The entire field instantly became engulfed in flames. As the fire roared and smoke boiled up, we felt the heat wave and overpressure, even from a distance away. I'm sure the locals were thinking the Arabic equivalent of "What the fuck?"

I wasn't too concerned. I'd achieved my objective.

As the field continued to burn, Marines crept out of their hibernation dens to see the blaze. We heard the cracking of ammunition cooking off and the booms of secondary RPG detonations from the midst of the inferno. My suspicions were correct. The insurgents had stockpiled weapons and ammunition in there for months.

It was a perfect spot—sitting only a few hundred meters southwest of the Euphrates River and End Road Bridge where they ferried weapons and ammunition across.

It was one hellacious fire, and it burned for hours, well into the night, throwing a surreal light over the area.

The next morning the field was burned to the ground. Only a smoldering gully of ash remained. We could now clearly see from our position in Building 15 to Millions Street and the rows of houses from which we had taken sniper fire. We also could see some MAMs running around.

One of the biggest challenges when fighting an insurgency was figuring out who the bad guys were. It took us a few weeks in Ramadi to crack this one.

Obviously, the ones who shot at us were bad—they definitely needed killing. But the longer we fought in Ramadi, the better we became at picking those little clues that identified a man as an insurgent as clearly as if he were wearing a military uniform.

That afternoon, I was called up to the roof.

Muscle was hunkered down behind the shoddy wall, sitting on a dilapidated bucket seat that had been torn out of some car and now was propped up on a couple of concrete cinder blocks. It looked uncomfortable, but Muscle didn't seem to mind. He handed me a set of powerful Steiner binoculars.

"Sir, check this out. Look for guys running in between building 243 and 245 off Millions. You see them?"

I stood at the edge of the concrete cinder-block wall, rested the binos on the ledge, and scanned the area. It took a few minutes, but I finally saw some runners.

Muscle said, "You see the guys running wearing tracksuits and running shoes under their man-dresses? None of the other *hajjis* wear running shoes. They're all wearing sandals."

It made sense now.

Let's face it, if you were going to get into a fight with a bunch of Marines, you didn't want to be doing it wearing flip-flops. It made sense to wear running shoes. It also was a dead giveaway. They were smart, but we were the smartest on the battlefield. Being able to identify the "uniform" they chose to fight in had just made our job that much easier to target the guys who needed killing.

I spent a short time observing the insurgents' movement. Then a Marine yelled up the stairs, "Sir, you need to get down here now!" I handed the binos back to Muscle and headed downstairs.

■   ■   ■

The night we'd moved into Building 15 we told the owners of the house to give us the keys to their vehicles. We also let them know we would leave them the keys in the driver's seats for them the next day. This was another tactic we had developed through trial and error.

We needed a way to block the access roads on the streets of the houses we occupied in order to prevent the insurgents from running a VBIED into our position and detonating it. Our solution: we'd take the cars from the houses' owners and park the vehicles several hundred meters apart, creating a hasty roadblock at either end of our position. The family's white Chevy Suburban and red Opel fit the bill that night.

When I got down to the first floor where the radio operator had set up, he told me, "Sir, there's a taxicab headed east, moving slow down the street toward the red Opel that's parked out there."

I immediately grabbed my interpreter, Jake, and a fire team for security. The Marines on the roof were now on alert and had posted 360-degree security from every angle of the rooftop.

Jake yelled in Arabic at the driver and told him to get out of the car with his hands up.

The driver's eyes were wide, and a look of fear crossed his face. He had good reason: a half dozen Marines had their rifles trained on him.

According to Jake, the taxi driver said that he had a passenger who was going to her family's house, but they were lost. Things got more interesting when the passenger, an elderly woman, probably in her seventies, got out of the back of the cab and began shouting frantically and waving her arms. She stood confused in the middle of the road in broad daylight attracting attention.

Then we began taking fire from across the field. I heard the cracking of rifles and then the sharp snaps as the bullets hit the dirt—I could see several rounds splinter as they hit the ground right next to me. Quickly we took cover.

I opened the door on the red Opel sedan for cover and grabbed Jake by his gear and jammed him to the ground behind me. The old woman was terrified. Still wailing frantically, she crossed her arms across her chest in terror, trying to curl herself into a small silhouette, unable to move. One of the Marines quickly grabbed her and moved her behind the Opel.

The enemy fire increased. Automatic fire came from the vicinity of the buildings off of Millions Street. The Marines on the rooftop of Building 15 began returning fire—suppressing the enemy attack.

I looked around and ordered the Marines to bound back to the house and get inside. In a smooth, well-trained motion, they did so, taking the shaken woman and the cab driver with them.

A few minutes passed before I realized I was now *alone* behind the door of the Opel with Jake hunkered behind me—I could feel him cringing as he used my frame as a human shield. As a company commander, I normally directed the fires of the Marines I led. It took a moment or two before my training overtook my delayed reaction as I thought to myself, "Hey, dumbass. You have a rifle. Now would be a good time to start shooting it!"

Through the window of the Opel, I could see muzzle flashes from multiple floors of the buildings on Millions Street. I flipped my M4 off "safe" and rose up to return fire and sighted in. I aimed in on two targets and squeezed the trigger twice, and tiny shards of glass shattered all around me.

"Fuck me!" I thought. They were zeroing in on me. However, in my adept aiming technique at the time, I didn't compensate for the muzzle on my rifle and had inadvertently shot out the side view mirror on the car. That's what shattered.

Friction.

"Rookie move," I thought.

The cover fire picked up, and Jake said, "Sir, what the fuck do I do?"

"When I'm shooting, you move. Got it?"

This time, I scooted to the back of the sedan behind the trunk to fire. As I suppressed, Jake and I made our way quickly back inside the walls of the house. Within minutes, all firing ceased.

We told the taxi driver and elderly woman to stay inside the house with us since it wasn't safe to drive out on the streets. They'd be safer leaving after dark—so would we.

It was never smart to stay in one house too long. It gave the insurgents the advantage of time to formulate a plan to attack us. It's what I would have done. I told the boys to start prepping our gear to move out of the house.

■   ■   ■

Before we left, I took a moment to promote Staff Sergeant Mackenzie to Gunnery Sergeant in the living room. We had scribbled out a makeshift promotion warrant on an MRE box with a black felt-tip pen. We got the wording as close as we could and gathered a handful of Marines to witness the ceremony.

Lee read the warrant. "*To all who shall see these Presents. Greeting: Know Ye that reposing special trust and confidence in the fidelity and abilities of James W. MacKenzie, I do hereby appoint him a Gunnery Sergeant in the United States Marine Corps...*"

We pinned his new rank insignia chevrons on the collar of his uniform. It was official—well, as official as it could be under the circumstances. Mac smiled and thanked me as he shook my hand. He knew I could have easily waited until we were back in the rear area to promote him. I could have—I had a lot of important things to worry about right then besides promotions—but I didn't want another day to go by without having my new Gunny in the company.

■   ■   ■

The Marines on the roof started calling for me again.

When I got there, Muscle told me that there was a lot of activity going on in the area. I moved from various sides of the roof keeping a low profile behind the four-foot wall that protected us. Across the way on Millions Street, several men with weapons in their hands were moving from house to house.

A couple of rounds popped off in the distance, but they weren't shooting at us. Yet. But between the massive blaze in the morning and the firefight behind the Opel, the enemy knew where we were and were gearing up for a fight. We could feel it.

Rounds then began to sting the sides of the building. I slid to the south wall and peered over the side. I had a clear line of sight behind the house into an alleyway. Men darted out of the houses directly behind our position.

Two houses down, a blue steel door swung open. A man popped his head out from behind it and looked directly at our location. He repeated the motion twice.

I looked through the Trijicon ACOG scope of my M4 to get a clearer view. The third time he popped out I saw he had an AK-47 in his hands.

He crouched down as if he were about to sprint across the alley; the muzzle of the AK peeked past the edge of the door. I clicked my weapon off safe and fired two rounds through the blue door. It swung open a few inches.

I readied my aim for another shot. I saw another enemy fighter through my scope approach the edge of the door. He bent down and pulled the downed insurgent inside. I saw his limp feet protruding from the edge of the door. Running shoes. The man was dragged slowly back inside. The door closed and I heard a loud clank as the latch dropped.

We had worn out our welcome on Millions Street. It was time to move.

CHAPTER 18

Damage

Uncontrollable variables occur in war and, sometimes, innocent people die. It is unfortunate, but true. These people and their deaths aren't just statistics to Marines who fight—or those that wind up as some sensationalized news story on cable news. They are terrible realities that we have to live with for the rest of our lives.

Military doctrine defines collateral damage as the injury inflicted on something other than an intended target—specifically, civilian casualties of an operation. In a perfect world, that definition seems pretty clear, but for those of us who have fought for years in combat, it is never cut and dry.

Like many units that fought during the surge, Echo Company was not immune to the grim reality and damage caused on the battlefield by both sides. The collateral damage didn't result just from the actions of the Multi-National Force (MNF).

The insurgents committed their share, along with the deliberate violence they often inflicted on the locals. I'm confident when I say that when we did the shooting, collateral damage was avoided as much as humanly possible. We adhered to the rules of engagement. Knew our targets, determined positive identification (PID) before firing a shot, analyzed patterns of life (POL), and made collateral damage estimates (CDE) before we squeezed the trigger, dropped our bombs, or launched our rockets to destroy the enemy. We had years of training, self-discipline, and a moral code that guided our actions as we fought.

For the insurgents, killing their own people was business as usual. They did it with wanton disregard for the people they harmed and for nothing more than getting their hateful point across. To them, civilians were obstacles on the way to their objectives—or pawns to use to gain an advantage on the battlefield. Time and again, we encountered the effects of their callousness and blatant disregard for human life.

■　　■　　■

The winter skies over the desert were gray and overcast as the enemy sprayed fire at us from buildings northeast of our position. Mid-day, Echo Company came under heavy attack as we staged near ECP 8 to conduct a targeted raid on an insurgent stronghold to the west.

McLaughlin's platoon maneuvered to a set of buildings close enough to gain sight on the enemy, and returned fire with more than two thousand rounds of machine gun fire and about a dozen 40mm grenades, to suppress a concentration of insurgents who tried to close the distance on our position.

I called up Somerville and the Quick Reaction Force. When the four Humvees and four M113s arrived, they opened up with their .50 caliber machine guns with devastating effects to support McLaughlin and 1st Platoon as they fought back the attack.

A squad of insurgents who survived our fire ran south down Route Apple and took up positions in some of the abandoned buildings and re-engaged us, apparently determined to keep up the fight. The Army M113s' crews saw a few teams not able to run fast enough to take cover and cut them down. No one is fast enough to outrun the .50 cal—epitomizing the adage, "You can run, but you'll only die tired."

A barrage of small arms fire came from the insurgent stronghold from the buildings to our west. The accuracy of their fires surprised us and slowed our advance as we tried to close in on their positions.

We figured that in Ramadi we'd be up against a well-trained enemy. After several weeks in the city, we knew we were. I often found myself thinking, "Man, these fucking guys know what they're doing."

They weren't a bunch of pussies either. No one willing to go toe-to-toe with the Marines and the Army could be. We knew they'd lose in the end, but we never underestimated their will to fight.

As our QRF sat in overwatch, its vehicles began to take hits, suffering some minor, cosmetic damage. We were holding the enemy tight and suppressing them, but we had to find a way to close in on them.

The mission of the Marine rifle squad is to locate, close with, and destroy the enemy by fire and maneuver, or repel the enemy assault by fire and close combat. Marines never have difficulty locating or repelling. Destroying is second nature to them. But closing with—that was the most inherently dangerous part of the mission, the time when Marines were most exposed to enemy fire.

The secret to closing successfully with an enemy was suppression of the bad guys—keeping them pinned down with indirect fire or machine guns to the point where they were too scared to pop their heads up. Then they had only two choices: try to run and get torn to shreds by the rockets, artillery, mortars, and machine guns, or be drilled with rifle fire from the Marines who were closing with them.

Standing atop ECP 8, I had a superior vantage point and solid radio communication with McLaughlin as he and his men continued to repel the enemy's assault toward our position. He had his Marines tucked back on the east side of Route Apple.

I raised McLaughlin on the radio. "Do you think you're far enough back for me to call in a GMLRS rocket strike?"

We'd become familiar with the accuracy and destructive power of the GMLRS rockets during our fight on 6 December and relied on them again to get the job done.

He replied, "It looks like the buildings they're in are a good 150 meters or more from our location, sir. I think we're good to go."

I checked the map and plotted all of the friendly locations. We had some intervening terrain, mostly concrete buildings that would mitigate the blasts from a rocket strike.

McLaughlin made it clear there was at least an enemy squad or two moving from between two buildings and taking well-aimed shots at us. I requested two GMLRS rocket strikes, one rocket for each building. The task force approved both missions.

I got the "read-back" of the fire mission from ANGLICO at Camp Corregidor. As our vehicles continued to suppress the enemy with machine gun fire, we informed all of our units that a GMLRS strike was inbound.

Within minutes we heard the distinctive low, bellowed sound of the strike. The rockets echoed as they hit their targets dead-on. They drilled through the tops of the buildings, exploded, and sucked the life out of everything inside.

There was a deafening silence after the strike. The enemy ceased fire, and so did we.

I walked out of ECP 8 with a fire team of security and my interpreter and linked up with McLaughlin and the other Marines from 1st Platoon, and we began to close on the buildings in order to clear them out.

The first site we went into had been rubbled to the point where it was nearly impossible to make entry. As we entered through the carport, a silver four-door sedan sat parked underneath. The roof and hood of the car had been crushed by the concrete and brick debris that had fallen on it from the blast. A cinder-block wall was smashed down on the other side of it. Despite the damage, the car's hazard lights were flashing. For whatever reason, the blinking lights irritated me, and I ordered one of the Marines, "Turn that shit off!"

Once inside the first floor, we could tell that if anything was living in the building before the rocket hit, it wasn't now. The effect of the rocket had painted the walls with a pink mist from the blood of the insurgents holed up inside. Blood mixed with the dust from the rubble pooled in parts of the house along with burnt and twisted AK-47 rifles, household effects, clothing, and furniture. Everything was demolished.

The roof, or what remained of it, had a gaping hole in it, made by the rocket when it punched through. Steel reinforcement bars were broken and bent and poked out of the remaining concrete like a strange, mangled spiderweb.

We pressed to the houses not yet engaged. I walked through the entranceway of the first one. There was a large smear of blood—three or four feet long—streaked alongside one of the concrete walls on my left-hand side. It looked like someone had taken a rough brush used for white-washing a fence and tried to make some sort of abstract painting.

I moved to the living room and found an Iraqi family, gathered around someone on the floor and wailing uncontrollably. I moved closer and saw they surrounded a man in his mid-forties lying on the floor—it appeared that he had a single gunshot wound to the head. His face and head were dark purple and grotesquely swollen. But he was still alive.

The platoon's corpsman rushed to his aid and began to triage the victim. A woman stood next to me, holding a child half dressed in a loose-fitting shirt that came down past its waist. The baby had long, thick black hair. I couldn't tell if it was a boy or a girl. The child's legs were covered in someone else's blood, but it wasn't crying—in shock, I suppose. But the child's silence lent a surreal air to the situation.

My Terp, Bruce, began to question the dying man's wife.

Bruce was a five-six, 135-pound warrior who had supported hundreds, if not thousands, of patrols with other units before being assigned to Echo Company. He fashioned himself a little bit after the martial arts fighter Bruce Lee. He was fiercely loyal, and, if given a chance, I'm sure he would have enlisted in the Marines at the drop of a hat. He begged me for a weapon on every patrol so he could kill insurgents. I never gave him one.

The woman told him that the insurgents we'd been hunting had burst into their house, and demanded the keys to the family's car so they could use it to escape. When the man of the house refused to surrender the keys, an insurgent shot him at point-blank range in the head with a pistol.

Blood pooled around the man's head through the pressure-dressing that Doc had applied. His face had become completely discolored. We managed to get him into one of the M113s and drive him back to the Combat Outpost for treatment, but he never made it—he was dead on arrival.

The wife asked Bruce a question after watching her husband die in front of her eyes.

He turned to me. "Sir, she wants to know if it is safe for her to remain here in their house."

I was a bit stunned at the ridiculousness of the question given the circumstances.

"Look. If she hasn't figured it out by now," I responded, "I have been parking rockets closer and closer to her house, and it's not safe. If she knows where any of the other insurgents are holding up, she'd better tell us now. Otherwise, I'd suggest she go find some family to stay with elsewhere."

The woman stood there silently with a blank look on her face, sobbing softly. I don't think she understood the gravity of the situation.

After we finished searching the houses we hit with the rockets, we headed back to ECP 8 walking south on Route Apple. As we left, I walked past one of the rocket-smashed buildings. It was a rectangular, single-story building, probably no more than a thousand square feet. The flat concrete roof was completely caved in and sagging in the middle. It looked like a half-pipe ramp at a skateboard park. The remaining walls on the ends of the building were still standing.

At the far end of one wall sat a mangy, yellow dog. It watched every Marine as we passed, turning its head each time each one of us walked by, like it was checking us off. To me, it was another random event so common in Ramadi.

■   ■   ■

Bam-Bam was on watch in charge of the company operations center and received information from the TOC at Camp Corregidor that a blue four-door sedan needed to drive through our area in order to transport a woman who had miscarried her baby to Ramadi General Hospital, a thousand meters west of ECP 8.

Bam-Bam's primary responsibility was to be our FAC, directing the actions of fixed- and rotary-wing aircraft in our support. He had also picked up a lot of the administrative tasks. He relayed requests for ammunition, food, water, CASEVACs, and any other support to Echo Company's other platoons.

When the TOC advised us of the request to allow movement of the family to the hospital, it represented an important opportunity—to help a local family and give some credibility to our messaging campaign to win "Hearts and Minds" and give it an additional meaning beyond killing insurgents. It also would stand in stark contrast to the insurgents' preferred method of gaining support and cooperation: fear and intimidation.

Some believed that the best way to win an insurgency is not to fight the insurgents—but to fight the insurgency. At the end of the day, I never subscribed to that theory.

That meant making the majority of the locals hate the murderous, callous insurgents who didn't give a shit about the locals' well-being and who had zero respect for human life in general. As I saw it, our mission was to kill or capture the enemy, and that's what we perfected on every patrol—if we gained some support from the locals along the way, even better.

Bam-Bam contacted the radio operators at all of our positions and relayed the specifics of this important request to ensure the family's safe passage to the hospital. The call went out to all stations on the radio net: *A blue four-door sedan would be passing through our area directly past OP South House and then ECP 8 on Sufia Road with four passengers, bringing a woman to the hospital for emergency medical attention.*

Everyone was explicitly advised that the car would be marked with glowing green chemlights taped to the roof and behind the windshield. Bam-Bam also expressly instructed each radio operator to pass the word to their respective platoon commanders, platoon sergeants, and the Marines on watch and to report back when they completed the task.

After double-checking with each platoon to reconfirm 100 percent notification, understanding, and acknowledgment, Bam-Bam felt certain that he'd done all he could to ensure that the Marines would not mistake the vehicle for one possibly packed full of explosives with a suicide driver behind the wheel—and allow it to pass safely.

Bam-Bam went back to his normal routine and listened to the radio transmissions intently. A few minutes later, he was startled by the distant sound of machine gun fire.

A sinking feeling hit the pit of his stomach.

Bam-Bam called each platoon for an update. They all confirmed they had not opened fire.

OP South House and ECP 8 verified that the sedan had passed by their positions safely. But when he checked with a U.S. Army radio operator that was adjacent to our position, his worst fears were confirmed.

The sedan had driven clear past our positions as slowly as it could into the boundaries of another Marine unit to our northwest. It crept up the unimproved road and directly in the line of fire of some Marines on post. The ones who had manned the post earlier were aware of the sedan's passage, but, when they conducted a turnover of the post, they didn't pass the word about it to those who relieved them. Fearing for the safety of their fellow Marines, when the sedan came into view, they opened fire on it.

Multiple three- to six-round bursts of 7.62mm machine gun fire blazed from the muzzle of the weapon and ripped through the car, bringing it to a halt. The driver, who was the husband of the woman who'd miscarried her child, survived. She and her sister did not.

I later talked about the incident with Bam-Bam.

He knew he had done everything within his power to ensure that the Marines of Echo Company let the sedan through safely, and they had done so.

He said, "If I could go back and do it all over again, Scott, I would have checked with the battalion headquarters next door to verify that the adjacent units were notified between higher headquarters. I did everything I could."

I told him, "You did."

Hindsight is always twenty-twenty in combat, and it's often the only way to learn some hard lessons to pass on to other warfighters.

Later, the husband received payment for the deaths of his family from Civil Affairs personnel. It wasn't a disgrace to accept the money by Arab standards. The Diya (*Dee-Yah*)—essentially a non-negotiable payment of blood money—is customary, if not downright expected, in cases of accidental deaths.

The grief-stricken man left with the handful of cash, a menial amount considering what had happened. I only imagined the level of disgust and contempt he must have felt for us.

I could have been wrong, however.

Iraqis had a very fatalistic view of life. You often heard them say in response to an event or when proposing a plan, "*Insha'Alla,*" basically "If God wills it," or as we might say, "God willing." This man believed that if God willed that his family would die, that's exactly how it had to be—and it was forbidden to question the will of Allah.

Although we'd done everything humanly possible to mitigate the shooting I still felt terrible about the incident.

Afterward, the family's vehicle was towed over to our firm base at ECP 8 and parked in the middle of the cul-de-sac comprised of dozens of concrete barriers.

Burnt-out plastic chemlights sat still intact underneath the windshield wipers. A white cloth flag—symbolic of truce or surrender—had been used as a signaling device, and lay crumpled up in the back seat of the car. Bullet holes had punctured the grill, hood, and windshield. The blue velour fabric interior of the sedan was stained with blood, the seat backs mottled with dark red blotches. Fragments of shattered safety glass from the windows were scattered about the interior and on the dashboard.

The car sat outside of our position for days on end as a constant, bloody reminder of how things can go so fucking wrong in war. As hard as we had tried to do good that night, things turned out badly. The car served as a physical, daily reminder of the damage that a moment of inattention or the smallest of mistakes could cause—and of our inability to fix it.

We carry those grave events with us forever.

After a little while, I couldn't stand looking at the car anymore and made a point to have the task force drag it away.

The car was gone the next day.

CHAPTER 19

Ta'meem

We had been patrolling hard throughout the night and had gone firm in one of the houses we cleared at around 0300 hours. One of my men went outside to relieve himself in a building that looked to be some sort of an outhouse. He turned on his flashlight before he took care of business and looked down a four-inch hole in the concrete slab he was about to piss in.

Something caught his eye. He knelt down and shined his flashlight into the hole. It was hollowed out, and there was a strange looking object at the bottom. He called to the other members of his team, and they came out to inspect. They spotted what looked like a pile of weapons, unexploded ordnance, and ammunition that lay at the bottom of the latrine.

They exited the tiny building and made their way outside. The structure's concrete slab foundation sat on an elevated wall of concrete cinder blocks. The Marines called for sledgehammers and specially designed Halligan tools—and began pounding and smashing the cinder blocks until one of the walls collapsed, revealing a hole in which was packed a huge weapons cache: dozens of RPGs, AK-47s, rocket motors, ammunition, body armor, flares, grenades, and a variety of other makeshift explosives. It was a big win for the team that night. The Marines always reveled in denying weapons to the insurgents, and they liked proving that they were better at the hide-and-seek game than the enemy.

As some of the Marines dug out the weapons, the security teams posted on the perimeter began to shout. I made my way over and saw they had detained a local Iraqi on the ground. He was on his knees in black plastic flexicuffs. He was in his late twenties, with a beard and mustache, and wore a brown traditional men's dishdasha robe (or "man-dress" as the Marines called it), a blue lightweight winter jacket, and, despite the freezing temperature, he wore blue plastic flip-flops.

They brought him inside the house and Jake began to question him. I wanted to know what the fuck he was doing on the street at three in the morning and why he was skulking around the house where we had found the cache.

He provided us with little information other than his name. He told us he was out for a walk—or, going to his brother's house for a visit.

Bullshit.

We asked him what his brother's name was and where he lived. He couldn't come up with a good answer.

More bullshit.

I had a suspicion he was either the occupant of the house or a spotter for the insurgents who had stockpiled the cache. I wanted to know where the insurgents were.

The sun was nearly up. I knew that if we let him go, he would most likely alert the enemy to our presence which would almost certainly lead to an ambush later that morning. Not the way we liked to start our day. We kept questioning him while we called 3rd Platoon to come to our position and transport the detainee back to COP Steel.

I told Jake to tell him, "Look. We've already detained you for being out after curfew. If you don't tell us which buildings the insurgents are in now, I'm going to call the Iraqi Police to come get you, and you can tell them."

He became physically flustered at this threat and began to whimper. The Iraqi Police were ruthless, and the way they handled detainees reflected it. This guy knew that if I turned him over to the Iraqi Police, his fate might very well be sealed.

This time, I was bullshitting. We didn't even have a direct link to the Iraqi Police in Ramadi when we were out on patrol. It wasn't as if we could simply call 911 and they'd appear. But those facts never stopped us from using the police's reputation as leverage to get people to provide us information on the spot. The detainee still said nothing and was carted off by our QRF for processing back at COP Steel—now, with tears visibly running down his face.

■   ■   ■

One of the toughest challenges we faced was stomaching the bureaucratic party line referred to as, "Putting an Iraqi Face on it." That meant when we conducted an operation we had to make an effort to have Iraqi soldiers or policemen with us. It was designed to give some sort of legitimacy to their army and police, and give the population more confidence in the Iraqi government, and turn them against the insurgents. I never got it. Too often, putting an Iraqi face on it was equivalent to putting an incompetent face on it.

Despite the years of training that the Marine and Army Mobile Transition Teams (MTTs) and Police Transitions Teams (PTTs) had given them, the Iraqis had never taken ownership of their duty to be professional soldiers. They were steadfastly proud to wear a uniform and be Iraqi, but never really got what it meant to serve their country for its greater good. They simply wanted the status, legitimacy, and authority that a uniform afforded. They didn't grasp the responsibility that came with it.

The uniform was a bobble—like a brightly festooned costume to them. The Iraqi soldiers and police were not Patriots akin to our American Revolutionary War fighters in any way, shape, or form.

The Iraqi Army's soldiers were underpaid and ill-equipped, its logistics efforts were inefficient, and its officers were incompetent, corrupt, and demeaning to their subordinates—and prone to bickering among themselves. It led to a constant breakdown in authority, and their command and control was a joke. Soldiers and police would often abandon their posts and units without notice. Some would even take off in the middle of a patrol. Sometimes, they'd just flat out refuse to work. It was so dysfunctional the Marines would use them at the beginning of an operation and then let them lay back while we got on with the task at hand—and relegated them, like cannon fodder, at the onset of an operation since Echo Company always did the lion's share of the work anyway.

■　　■　　■

As Echo Company patrolled in the Ta'meem, First Sergeant Foster, my senior enlisted Marine, was in charge of the HQ Platoon. I posted him at a forward operating base in the middle of the city at COP Steel which served as a main re-supply point.

Foster was one of a handful of Marines who lived at COP Steel—the majority of Echo Company lived out in the city. The soldiers living there agitated him easily because they didn't have the same standards he did. He was always needling them to pick up after themselves. The mess drove him crazy.

Throughout our time in Ramadi, we had been subjected to very few enemy mortar attacks. It was a luxury we enjoyed after the local tribal leaders stamped them out for us in return for our unyielding assistance to stabilize their tribes. Foster's luck ran out late one afternoon as he made his way to one of the resupply trucks to get gear to start improving the company position.

He walked between the vehicles and the outer wall of the building toward an Oshkosh 7-ton truck. In an instant, he was slammed violently against the side of the vehicle. Dirt sprayed him. Dust filled the air. His Kevlar helmet flew off his head and rolled unevenly underneath the vehicle. Foster lay on his side from the brunt of the explosion. A peaceful feeling washed over him as he lay there, stunned. His ears were ringing. A high-pitched hum wouldn't go away. He had no idea what had happened, but he knew he was alive.

Foster pushed himself to his feet within seconds and crawled toward the front tires of the truck—instinctively knowing that he was in the worst possible spot during a mortar attack.

The ringing in his ears dissipated and he could now hear yelling. He got to his feet and made his way to the top floor of COP Steel where three 120mm mortar rounds had struck. Ironically, the U.S. Army had mounted a brand-new radar system and counter-ballistic computers designed to detect incoming mortar rounds on the building's roof—it lay in pieces, destroyed.

Foster jumped over a pile of cinder blocks and rubble and began to dig through the debris with his bare hands looking for injured soldiers. He looked down and saw blood on his hands. His first thought was that he'd found a wounded soldier. He found no one. He paused. A stream of warm blood trickled from his nose. He was thankful it was his blood and not someone else's.

Foster looked around to assess the damage. A portion of a wall had collapsed on top of where his Marines normally slept. Fortunately, they had all been awake during the attack and not in the area.

■   ■   ■

January 2007

We continued to push out of COP Steel and were tasked to patrol and provide security for an assessment at a proposed site for a new Iraqi police station in the Ta'meem District. A team of U.S. Army engineers were going to determine the suitability of a building that they thought might do the job. The site was close to a massive apartment-housing complex called the White Apartments. It was different from other such places in Ramadi in that criminal activity was equal to, if not greater than, the insurgent activity in it—and one often overlapped the other in this urban ghetto.

The police station grand opening was designed to be a showcase event to let the citizens of southern Ramadi know that the Iraqi Police

(IP) was back in town and had taken control. It was another "Iraqi Face" operation that reeked of disaster and disappointment from the start.

By the time we arrived, the insurgents had gotten word of the planned event and had blown up both ends of the building, leaving only the center of the structure, rubble-filled, but tenuously standing.

McLaughlin, Bam-Bam, Jake, and I surveyed the building. It was in shambles. Chunks of cinder blocks and loose concrete covered every inch of the floor. The ceiling looked as if it would cave in at any second and had pieces of metal re-bar jutting out, still clinging onto blocks of concrete at the tips. There was no power, and cut wires hung randomly from the overhead. My team of Marines looked around and shook their heads in disbelief that the IP and the U.S. Army still entertained the idea that this could be made to work.

Bear and some of his soldiers arrived on the scene shortly after we surveyed the area. I met him on the street and gave him the run-down on where Echo Company was. We'd linked up ahead of time with the Army and Navy SEALs who were providing overwatch for the event and coordinated to avoid any "blue-on-blue."

A loud boom echoed closely.

It sounded like a mortar impact, but when Bear and I turned around, we saw smoke billowing from the top floor of a building across the street.

Bear asked if I had enough Marines to run over and sweep the site. A squad of Marines from McLaughlin's platoon was close by, and I led them cautiously over to the house.

Two teams set up an outer cordon on the building as we pressed inside. We were leery. We'd heard too many stories of insurgents who booby-trapped buildings, waiting for unsuspecting Marines and soldiers to walk into them and then detonate devices inside. We checked every inch of the building, looking for trip wires and suspicious devices. Some of the Marines took out small cans and sprayed Silly String into the doorways to uncover thin trip wires. Silly String wasn't issued gear, but would always show up in care packages in the mail from family members at the Marines' request.

Desert Storm care packages of Corn Nuts and grade-school letters had been upgraded to meet more mission-essential needs of Operation Iraqi Freedom: Silly String to check for trip wires. Fresh socks to keep our feet clean and dry. Flashlight batteries, eye protection, custom Oregon Aero helmet pads, and even embarrassing Tampax feminine hygiene products to carry on patrol to fill bullet wounds and stop bleeding.

Our families and friends realized the severity of the environment we were fighting in and supported us with things needed to help ensure everyone made it home alive.

When we made it to the second floor of the building where we'd seen the smoke, we quickly figured out the cause. The room was a mess. It had a damp, charred odor to it. There was little furniture in the house itself. It almost looked abandoned. There was fresh blood spattered on the walls as if a water balloon had popped, but there wasn't a body in sight. A metal kitchen table stood in the room. The floor was cluttered with pieces of junk, like someone had dumped a box of spare radio repair parts all over the place—spools of unraveled wire scattered around.

It was clear to us that an IED maker was in the process of building a device in the room, and it had accidentally gone off.

The locals had already made off with the body in less than the twenty minutes it took us to get on site. They were quite effective at policing up their dead. In the end, it was one less IED we'd have to face and one less insurgent we'd have to worry about, judging by the amount of blood on the floor and walls.

By the time we walked back to the police station, the celebration had already begun in the ghetto. Iraqi Police and Iraqi Army were driving around the large center square of the White Apartments, flying IP and Iraqi national flags from, respectively, the beds of white Chevrolet pickup trucks with blue doors, and atop the Humvees, both given to them by the MNF. Most of the men had their faces covered with red-and-white-checkered shemaghs. They were screaming and shouting fanatically and doing victory laps.

It was a spectacle, but it was farcical.

I never knew if the Iraqi Police ever occupied that police station. It wasn't my problem, either way. That was Echo Company's final mission with the Steel Tigers.

We had orders to head west.

CHAPTER 20

West

January 2007

Echo Company departed Task Force 1-77 Armor and Camp Ramadi and headed to Camp Korean Village (CKV), forty miles west of our ultimate destination: Rutbah, Iraq. We'd move in ground convoy and, once there, begin supporting the 15th Marine Expeditionary Unit (MEU) Command Element (CE).

Bam-Bam planned for Army AH-64 Apache attack helicopters to escort the first half of our movement. They'd hand off midway to UH-1Y Hueys and AH-1W Cobra gunships—that we called "Skids"—of the 15th MEU's Air Combat Element (ACE) that were operating out of a Forward Arming and Refueling Point (FARP) at CKV.

The Hueys and Cobras never showed up. We had to travel the rest of the way to CKV without air cover.

Bam-Bam was enraged and felt a little betrayed—until he contacted the 15th MEU's Air Officer, who told him that the pilots were just finishing their flight brief for the convoy escort mission.

Bam-Bam realized that he had made a rookie mistake: when he made the air request, he used local time (the actual time zone we were in) instead of Zulu, or Greenwich Mean Time, which is the standard time zone used for the military because units are so widely dispersed over several times zones.

Although Echo Company had been exposed during the movement, I was less upset about it than Bam-Bam. I knew he had been running on fumes for weeks in Ramadi. As a pilot, however, he trained to be meticulous, and he was embarrassed by this lapse in attention to detail.

To add insult to injury, during the drive west, Bam-Bam's Humvee died—the hood of his truck spewed into flames with the engine completely blown out. His vehicle had to be towed into CKV by another Humvee.

Friction.

CKV was the main base of operations for the 15th MEU Command Element and where our rotary-wing CAS was sourced from while we were in Rutbah. CKV sat in one of the farthest western parts of Al Anbar Province, roughly forty miles west of the city of Rutbah. It reportedly got its name because it was where Korean laborers who helped build the Amman-Baghdad Road (which we knew as MSR Michigan) during Saddam Hussein's regime were housed.

In addition to the tactical support, CKV also provided a place where Marines could relax every few weeks, shower, get supplies from the PX, make phone calls, and use the Internet.

People often wonder how the Marines had comforts like this in a combat zone when the majority of their time was spent fighting. But we did. We had iPods, Sony PlayStations, and Internet service at times. Marines had to have some sort of release in their downtime—they needed to decompress. To me, it was equivalent to what Marines and soldiers in previous wars did when they went back to the rear area.

In World War II, when the Marines rotated off the front lines, they probably did similar things to take their minds off the madness. They played cards or checkers. We used PlayStation. They'd write letters. We typed emails. In Vietnam, they'd take snapshots with Kodak film. We used our phones and digital cameras. It's simply relative to the generation and technology available at the time. Either way, in any era, it's essential to include some normalcy to keep the chaos in check.

Despite the amenities, CKV was still an austere place, and the buildings were dilapidated concrete structures, while the exterior walls were white with a three-foot swath of trim painted around the top in a horrible shade of turquoise green.

■   ■   ■

Rutbah itself was a city in the middle of nowhere in the desert of Iraq. With twenty thousand residents, almost all of them Sunni Muslims, it was the closest population center in western Iraq to both Jordan and Syria, roughly seventy miles from each border.

I jokingly referred to Rutbah as the "Truck Stop of Iraq" since it was one of the only towns that had a functional gas station right on MSR Michigan. When it was open for business, maybe one or two days out of the week, it was always jam-packed with customers. They'd line up for more than a mile.

Many Americans would throw a fit if they had to wait in line at a gas station for more than five minutes. In Iraq at the time, however, it was not uncommon for locals to wait in line for a half day for fuel. The Iraqis would fill up not only their vehicles, but also fuel jugs they carried in their cars' trunks to make sure they could get through the weeks or months between the chances to gas up—ironic in a country where gas only costs less than fifty cents per gallon.

There were inevitably many contentious moments on the days that the gas station was open. It was not uncommon for fistfights between the locals to erupt while they waited in line. My Marines thought the entire spectacle was utterly hilarious.

Besides having a working gas station, Rutbah also had some large mansions and many well-preserved smaller homes. It was a welcome contrast to Ramadi, in which every structure bore some mark of the war that waged there.

One thing Rutbah did not have was a functioning infrastructure. It had once, but the fighting had taken its toll. Power was intermittent at best. To run lighting in any of the homes, we were like the locals, dependent on gas-powered floor generators. Garbage was everywhere, and raw human sewage flowed through the streets.

In an attempt to correct these horrible conditions, we were ordered to orchestrate "Team Garbage Cleanup." The idea was to get the locals engaged in taking care of the city and give them a sense of pride. For me, it meant reducing the garbage piles and removing the broken-down vehicles on the shoulders of the roads that could easily hide IEDs and weapons.

My Marines were more than incensed at the thought of having to pick up the Iraqis' trash and debris. I wasn't too crazy about it either.

I continually put in requests to have U.S. Marine TRAMs with buckets and forklifts come into the city. I needed them to scrape the shoulders of the roads to remove the piles of garbage and to haul away the abandoned, shot-up vehicles to a consolidated dumping location.

My requests were constantly denied because the vehicles didn't have sufficient armor to operate in the city. I pleaded my case that if my Marines were willing to patrol every day in the town in nothing but their body armor, a TRAM driver could wear his and be equally safe if we provided security during the cleanup and debris removal. I made my point, and the requests were finally approved.

When we weren't picking up trash, Echo Company spent its first week at CKV planning and preparing for Operation Gateway: a citywide clearance operation scheduled to kick off on 19 January 2007.

Although several 15th MEU and other Marine units had patrolled in and around the city, they had been engaged only sporadically by insurgents who operated from the bowels of the city. This activity kept the Marines on the outskirts of town controlling the main Traffic Control Points (TCPs) in and out of the city from the east, west, and south. To root out the insurgents who remained embedded in the town, they needed more manpower.

Clearance operations had been our bread and butter in Ramadi. Piece of cake, I thought.

Go in. Hit hard. Get the job done. I soon found out though that the landscape would not be the only thing in Rutbah that was different than Ramadi.

■   ■   ■

During our stay in Ramadi, it was an infantryman's game.

If someone was digging a hole in the road, they were assumed to be planting an IED in the ground—shoot them.

If there was a car driving down the street toward your position, they were assumed to be driving a car bomb into your operating base—shoot them.

If someone was out walking around at night past curfew, they were considered an insurgent on patrol—shoot them.

If someone was using a cell phone during the daytime it was presumed they were about to detonate the trigger on a roadside bomb—shoot them.

If they had a weapon of any kind, they were the enemy—shoot them.

This interpretation of the ROE in Ramadi was not cavalier, but the standard routine since all of these events were commonplace in Ramadi and what we witnessed firsthand.

■   ■   ■

Our mission in Rutbah was focused more on support and stability operations (SASO) rather than the daily raids and constant firefights in Ramadi.

In Rutbah, we would fight what the Marine Corps called a "Three-Block War." The idea was that, in the space of three city blocks, you would go from full-scale, conventional war to police and peacekeeping operations to providing humanitarian aid. It was a fluid concept. Any Marine could find himself in any part of that spectrum at any time. My men had become used to doing all sorts of tasks that weren't in the job description of Marine Corps infantry.

The ROE, however, went from extremely permissive in Ramadi to painstakingly restrictive in Rutbah.

Not only the mission and the ROE, but also the atmosphere was vastly different in Rutbah. It was a shock to our senses. Traffic drove freely and local shops were open for business—which we used to our advantage. When we patrolled the streets in any city in Iraq, the children also stood out to me. Children roamed the street freely during the day in Rutbah since none of the schools were functioning.

As in Ramadi, some would taunt us and others would beg for candy. The incorrigible ones would throw rocks at our vehicles and Marines. They could be an annoyance, but they sometimes provided a welcome distraction. Besides, the children made us smile.

Iraq was a war-torn country with a host of problems, and the people lived a rough life, but children are children anywhere in the world. They had ways of finding mischief and time to play. Despite the language barrier, kids were kids. They grew on us in the areas we patrolled, and we were always delighted to see their familiar faces.

■　　■　　■

A few weeks into our stay in Rutbah, Corporal Brian McKibben was on a two-hour patrol. He was out front conducting double-point coverage to protect the alleyways with overlapping fires as he led the patrol.

The mission had been quiet, almost uneventful, until McKibben halted his squad no more than a few hundred meters from our firm base. They were almost back.

McKibben conducted a head count and realized that Lance Corporal Brackamonte wasn't with the patrol. McKibben was frantic. He had no idea where Brackamonte had gone or what had happened to him.

Brackamonte was a nineteen-year-old from Las Vegas, Nevada. He was five-ten and weighed 150 pounds. He came from a long line of veterans in his family, but none were Marines. He lied to his parents about being in the infantry. He told them he was going to be a military firefighter, thinking it would be easier for them to understand. His mom cried when she found out the truth. She pleaded with his recruiter to change his orders, but it was a done deal.

McKibben halted the patrol. His squad posted security, and he took a team of Marines to backtrack their route. He pressed no more than three hundred meters from where they had come and peered around a corner.

McKibben spotted Brackamonte squatting down on the side of the street. He was talking to some little kid and giggling with him. He seemed oblivious as McKibben advanced toward him. Brackamonte was in his own little world with this kid. He'd just stopped, connected, and forgot about everything else that was going on.

McKibben laid into Brackamonte when they got back to the firm base and threatened never to let him go out on patrol again and take away his SAW and ammo for the stunt. He was furious with him for not staying with the squad. The warning brought Brackamonte to the threshold of tears.

When McKibben told me about the incident, I wasn't shocked. I empathized, in fact, with what Brackamonte must have felt: the need to be human if just for a short amount of time—albeit at the most inappropriate moment on patrol—but human nonetheless. For some Marines, it was quite easy to lose that side of themselves after everything they'd been through.

CHAPTER 21

Gateway

17 January 2007

The 15th MEU's assistant intelligence officer, Captain John Kelly, arranged for me to conduct my first leader's reconnaissance from the air. The flight proved invaluable as did Kelly's briefing. He gave me a detailed lay of the land where Echo Company would be working in Rutbah. In the future, I would come to depend on his solid, unvarnished intelligence updates and the phenomenal pictures he took with a digital camera.

The following day I was scheduled to conduct my second leader's reconnaissance. This time I'd see things from the ground.

I was happy to be greeted outside my command post by a friendly and familiar face, that of Captain Giles Walger, the commander of Charlie Company, 2d Light Armored Reconnaissance (LAR) Battalion. Call sign, "Chippewa Six." Giles made his way toward me with his wide-mouthed smile, clean-shaven head, and tall, athletic frame.

Giles and I had known each other for years. We had cut our teeth together in Virginia at Officer Candidate School, The Basic School, and the Infantry Officer Course in 1997 and 1998. We followed each other to the operating forces stationed in Twentynine Palms, California, and then again in 2004 as young captains at the Expeditionary Warfare School.

We spent the entire day combing the outskirts of Rutbah in his eight-wheeled, armored machines assessing the city. Giles pointed out the areas of most concern in the city. The patterns. The traffic. The people. I still felt like somewhat of an outsider looking in. It was strange not to hear a single gunshot fired as we patrolled along. It gave me an odd feeling, and I wondered what lay buried inside Rutbah.

The 15th MEU operations officer, Major Paul Nugent, had tasked Echo Company to conduct a daytime clearance operation from east to west to clear the city. That did not go over well with me—or anyone in Echo Company. We were all justifiably paranoid at the time, having moved out of Ramadi.

When we patrolled in Ramadi during the day, it wasn't a matter of whether we would get shot at, it was a matter of when and by how many insurgents. So, we patrolled during the dark. Everything we had done up to that point had been at night. With our advanced night vision devices, we owned the night. We used it to our advantage.

I was apprehensive as well about taking Echo Company into a zone not fully cleared. The Maritime Special Purpose Force (MSPF) with the 15th MEU that operated out of CKV had tried to assault the insurgents in Rutbah and had come under sporadic enemy fire. They tried to root out and kill the enemy during coordinated attacks with limited results.

The MSPF was comprised of a small group of specially trained Marines, about fifty, from the USMC reconnaissance community and other intelligence specialists, but lacked the firepower and large numbers of a traditional Marine infantry company.

While planning Operation Gateway, I'd been briefed by a good friend of mine, Captain A. J. Goldberg. He told me his platoon with MSPF attempted to push into the city from east to west. They were engaged by a team-sized element of the enemy, four to six fighters, with a single RPG attack and small arms fire—effectively halting their advance on the far side of a dried-up wadi, a sandy area washed out by rain. They had to re-group to formulate another route of advance since the terrain was not in their favor.

Paul Nugent was thirty-nine years old. Bulky, with brown hair and sharp green eyes, he was from Philadelphia and had received his degree from Pennsylvania State University. He was another familiar face. He had been a mentor and friend of mine, as well as my advisor when I was a student at the Expeditionary Warfare School. He was a Marine that I could confide in and trust completely. He was one of the best officers I ever met.

After we had gathered for the operations order for Gateway, I voiced my concerns about operating during the day and recommended we modify the plan to execute it at night. Major Nugent was gracious enough to give me the autonomy to come up with a different concept of operations and allowed me to construct it in a way that would best suit the mindset and combat capabilities of my Marines.

My company staff and I sat around a map of Rutbah on a four-foot-high planning table made out of plywood and two-by-fours in our company headquarters at CKV and came up with a new scheme of maneuver. It better supported how we would clear the city. It took some thought, and once I felt comfortable with the plan, I took it back to Major Nugent for approval.

It was a simple plan. We would move in at night by truck, dismount in the southern part of the city, and push north. Our platoons would disperse and move in a manner that would allow us to swiftly and efficiently comb through the city. On our western flank, we'd have the support of Captain Stan Hawk and his Bravo Company, 3rd Reconnaissance Battalion. Stan was a solid leader, and his men were well-trained and highly experienced. I trusted them unreservedly to get the job done as we conducted the operation.

I gave Major Nugent a guarantee after I pitched the plan: within forty-eight hours we'd have the city stamped "Clear," and we'd be able to start regular patrolling operations.

19 January 2007

Echo Company's strength was more than two hundred Marines that night. We rolled in heavy with a ton of combat power—two AH-1W Cobra attack helicopters, a platoon of LAV-25s armed with 25mm Bushmaster chain guns, eight up-armored Humvees with .50 caliber machine guns and 40mm MK-19 grenade launchers, and six massive Oshkosh 7-ton trucks, fully armored and strapped with turret-mounted machine guns.

The Marines in Echo Company were loaded down with ammo to feed our ten M240B medium machine guns, thirty 5.56 Squad Automatic Weapons, and five Shoulder Fired Multiple Launch Weapons (SMAW) rocket systems, as well as the ammo that they carried for their M16-A4 rifles and Colt M4 carbines.

We staged at CKV and loaded up the 7-ton trucks that would drive us forty miles east and then into the southern part of the city for insertion.

It was an incredibly cold night as we hopped off of the vehicles and assembled into our staging area. We shook from the cold as we fought off the effects of the sharp wind that cut through our bodies.

We began to conduct our communication checks across the board, to include those with the Skids—already hovering at two thousand feet.

No joy.

Despite our best efforts, we couldn't get solid communications with our adjacent units or the helos that hung in the overhead.

After several fruitless attempts, I made the command decision to abort the mission and head back to CKV to sort out the communication issues. It was demoralizing and frustrating, to say the least. All of the Marines in Echo were ready to take the fight to the enemy that night. But without reliable communication, the risks would have been significant, and I was unwilling to accept them.

Friction.

After sorting out all the communication problems when we returned to CKV, we planned to execute the mission two days later.

We knew it was going to be a long, painstaking process to clear the city. The Marines were confident that we would encounter less resistance in Rutbah than in Ramadi. Nothing could be worse than Ramadi, we told ourselves—turned out we were wrong.

■   ■   ■

21 January 2007

The bone-chilling air cut through us as we stepped out of the trucks into the obscurity of Rutbah just past midnight. Once again, I divided the company into three platoons of dismounted infantry, and Somerville's 3rd platoon served as our QRF at TCP 2 on the eastern end of the city.

We formed up and stepped off, sweeping north, knowing there was plenty of work ahead of us that first night.

Six hours later, I dropped down on the cold marble floor of the building in which we had just gone firm: Building 504, Sector C2, at the southern part of the city. I was exhausted. We had worked our asses off. I stared up at the plastered ceiling, dizzy, yet feeling relieved and excited that we had pushed so far in one night.

I was still in my gear and lay there stretched out trying to get my second wind. I was pretty sure I could have fallen fast asleep if I wanted to.

Then, I heard a call across the net that we had a casualty. An adrenaline rush instantly flooded my body, and a gut-dropping feeling—a combination of anxiety and rage—hit me hard.

The Marines came in and gave me the news—Lance Corporal Sanchez was down, shot by a sniper. For some reason, bad news always seemed to happen in the morning, typically after you woke up—a perfectly shitty way to start a day in a shitty place.

I jumped up and asked for the details and the location. I ordered the platoon I was with to move to the scene, ready to exact revenge on whoever had the balls to shoot one of my boys.

■   ■   ■

In the early morning hours at Building 500—in which two of the platoons had gone firm, after a draining night of clearance operations—they had been taking sporadic enemy small arms fire.

Corporal Brian McKibben led 1st Platoon's 3rd Squad. A twenty-five-year-old infantryman from Lakewood, Colorado, his age and experience made him one of the most dependable leaders in the company. He was tall, with a serious look about him. A deep, single frown line cut in between his eyes until someone around him cracked a joke. Then his odd upside-down smile crossed his face, the kind where the corners of his mouth would point down until his teeth crept through his lips.

McKibben's maturity and relaxed nature and the unquestioned respect he commanded among the other Marines in the company allowed our senior leaders to trust him completely with any mission.

I talked with McKibben more than I did with other Marines because he seemed to be in the action where I was. He'd give me that cool nod of approval when he'd see me jocked-up, ready to go out and patrol with the boys. He'd also normally add some unprovoked, sarcastic comment, "Oh, great, the CO is going out with us again boys. Hope you're all ready to get some—and get shot at."

For whatever reason, I seemed to attract fire when I was out on patrol. I think the Marines actually liked it because it gave them a permissible opportunity to bust my balls.

McKibben was comfortable telling me what he and the other Marines were thinking, whether we were on patrol or while I sat in Building 500, playing a blue Johnson acoustic guitar that I had "acquired" from the 15th MEU's chaplain. McKibben and I had always seemed to be on the same page.

In addition to being one of the best small-unit leaders in the company, McKibben was without question also the sweatiest Marine I have ever met. I don't care how cold the day, how late the hour, how short the duration of a patrol, McKibben would be drenched in sweat. He could sweat through body armor like no one's business. His filthy cammies became crusted with white salt rings around his shoulders and hips from the sweat always soaking through and then drying repeatedly.

On this day, McKibben was off post at Building 500 on the first floor of the three-story house when he started hearing shots fired outside around 0700. McKibben immediately pressed to the roof—not knowing one of his Marines lay wounded.

Concerned there might be a sniper about, he did a turkey-peek around the corner of the doorway that led out onto the roof. He saw Marines racing around yelling, "Corpsman! Doc! Doc! Get the fuck over here, Doc!"

The top of Building 500 was a large, flat concrete slab with a massive gray cinder-block ledge around it that stood nearly six feet high. It provided excellent protection and concealment, for the most part, for the Marines on post. He raced over to the back wall where four or five Marines and Docs Lee and Lleva were already performing first aid on Lance Corporal Sanchez.

McKibben stepped in and helped take off Sanchez's gear. As he did, he spoke to Sanchez.

"Sanchez, hang on, man. We're here. We've got you. Just blink or squeeze my hand if you understand!"

Nothing from Sanchez.

McKibben heard the other Marines on the roof shouting. "What the fuck! Where is the shooter?" No one had located the sniper.

It was not the first time McKibben had been in a firefight or seen his brothers get shot, but he still felt scared and helpless at the moment—the sight of it all took his breath away. The Marines moved Sanchez off the roof to a convoy that would carry him to TCP 3 where he'd be transferred to a helicopter that would fly him to a medical station. As he watched the vehicles leave, he felt a sense of responsibility, and his heart felt broken. Not knowing if Sanchez was alive or dead weighed heavily on him that morning.

■   ■   ■

Foster rode in the convoy with Sanchez as they rushed to TCP 3. The Marines gently moved him from the Humvee to the landing zone as the radio operator made contact with the inbound CH-53 helicopter that was providing the CASEVAC.

TCP 3 was a barren piece of property the 15th MEU had staked out at the southern part of the city. It was fortified with a wall of huge, sand-filled HESCO barriers—and defended by the artillery Marines from Sierra Battery, 3d Battalion, 11th Marines.

Foster sat beside Sanchez and could see clearly the hole from the bullet that pierced the right front side of his Kevlar helmet. Sanchez was silent, but Foster could see the agony on his face. As Foster listened to the radio transmissions, he knew it was only minutes until the CASEVAC would arrive. The Corpsmen and other Marines from the MSPF platoon tried to stabilize Sanchez—his breathing was labored. As they inserted an intubation tube to free his airway, Foster held his hand.

Sanchez gripped Foster's hand and rubbed it feverishly as he fought through the pain of his wound. His hand was warm and dry. Foster rubbed it gently, trying to smooth off the caked dirt, but as he looked down, Sanchez's hand lay soft in his own, covered in dried blood.

The smacking of the helicopter's rotors was loud as it approached the LZ. The CASEVAC team moved Sanchez so they wouldn't get pelted with loose gravel kicked up by the helicopter's downwash. Foster instinctively knew Sanchez would not let go of his hand when they moved him to the helicopter. Foster held on and moved with him.

The hulking CH-53 Super Stallion was on final approach to the LZ. Thirty seconds out. Sanchez stopped rubbing Foster's hand. Foster felt it go still. It slipped out of his grasp as the aircraft landed.

■　　■　　■

As we geared-up for another fight, a second, gut-wrenching call came across the net. Another Marine was shot and was being CASEVAC'd to TCP 3 to the south.

Again, my heart sank. I could not believe that in less than twenty-four hours in zone, we'd suffered two casualties.

■   ■   ■

After McKibben had watched Sanchez carried out of Building 500, he went to his squad on the first floor. "Hey, I need someone to volunteer to get up on the roof now and take over Sanchez's post."

Without delay, Lance Corporal Andrew Matus chimed up. "I got it, Corporal."

Who does that? What kind of person unhesitatingly jumps to the task and challenge of assuming a post where another Marine has been shot? What kind of character do young men have that drives them to go in harm's way without a second thought?

Matus rustled around in the pile of blankets and sleeping bags strewn out on the floor in the modest room that was packed tight with twelve other Marines. He threw on his boots and grabbed his gear and followed McKibben back up the stairway to the top of Building 500.

Lance Corporal Andrew Matus knew at age thirteen that he wanted to be a U.S. Marine. He was muscular, 190 pounds and five-eight. He came from Chetek, Wisconsin. His family had a strong military background. His great-grandfather served in the Army in World War II. His father, grandfather, grandmother, uncle, aunt, great-uncle, and cousin also had served their nation. Military service was in his blood.

When it was his time to serve, Matus read books about the Corps. He worked out in preparation for boot camp because he was determined to be in the best shape of his life when he arrived. When he was seventeen years old, his parents signed a waiver so he could enlist before his eighteenth birthday.

Tough and solid, Matus excelled as an infantryman. He also had an aptitude for mechanical and engineering tasks that made him an invaluable asset to Echo Company.

While on the *Boxer*, he was assigned to the Combat Cargo Detachment. Matus, along with a select group of other Marines, helped the sailors maintain all of the equipment and gear that we had stowed inside the massive amphibious assault ship.

When we headed into Iraq, Matus returned to 1st Platoon to join the fight. His parents thought he was still on the *Boxer*. Matus wasn't much of a letter writer, and he never called to tell his folks he was even in Iraq.

■   ■   ■

McKibben walked with Matus over to the wall on the back side of Building 500, almost exactly where Sanchez had been shot. Matus was armed with his M16-A4 with M203 40mm grenade launcher fixed to the bottom. The wall was too high for Matus to see over. He found an ammo can and slid it close to the wall to use for a step so he could view his sector of fire that McKibben laid out for him. He placed a hand on the edge of the cinder-block wall and pulled himself up for a peek.

McKibben said to Matus, "Keep your eyes open. There's a lot of windows and doors out there, brother."

McKibben took five or six steps away when he heard a strange noise, like the sound of a hammer cracking the bottom of a frying pan. McKibben turned back toward Matus, and, as he did, he saw Matus standing facing the wall, almost floating. He fell backward, slowly, as if someone was behind him waiting to catch him in a game of Trust.

"Doc! Doc! Get over here!" McKibben shouted in panic.

Matus lay on the roof motionless. His eyes were bloodshot, and he wasn't breathing. His face began to swell, and he was limp as the other Marines quickly moved him onto a blanket to get him off the roof as fast as they could.

The Marines on the first floor had already jumped into action and were dumping dozens of confiscated weapons and gear out of a high-back Humvee. Corporal Thao, a veteran of Ramadi in 2004, met McKibben when he came downstairs. Always a quiet, steady presence, Thao reassured McKibben that Matus was being taken care of and was on his way to TCP 3.

The rest of that day McKibben was stunned. He constantly stopped to catch his breath. McKibben again felt lost and helpless. Survivor's guilt had already begun to feed his thoughts.

■   ■   ■

Along with Nicholson and 4th Platoon, I pushed north to Building 500 to link up with McLaughlin and 1st Platoon. I wasn't happy to find out the tenants of the house were still there when I showed up, but I quickly kicked them out—the building was going to be my new command post for an indefinite period. They were pissed off, but I honestly didn't give a shit about their problems at the time.

Echo Company was under sniper fire daily in Ramadi, but we did not expect the same relentless attacks when we moved into Rutbah. It was evident to us now that the local insurgents knew we were in town. It was equally evident that they were testing us, challenging our resolve, and gauging our reactions to the demoralizing effects of sniper fire.

Tensions were high throughout the company. We had stirred the enemy—a faceless enemy we could not locate.

I went to the roof of Building 500 with McLaughlin. I immediately saw the dark, stained concrete that had soaked up the pools of blood from my fallen Marines.

I went around to all of the posts and talked to the boys. They were fractious and kept a low profile. They knew a sniper was taking precise aim on their positions. I tried to reassure everyone and keep calm. I sensed the anxiety in everyone.

Corporal Simon Litke was on the back side of Building 500. He had taken a helmet from one of the boys off post and balanced it on a short pole. He slowly raised it above the roofline, hoping to bait the sniper into taking another shot. It reminded me of something out of World War I trench warfare. Another Marine sat next to him with his back to the cinder-block wall. He held a mirror in one hand and positioned it out of a mouse hole—a makeshift shooting position made from punching a hole in the wall—to view the direction of fire where Sanchez and Matus had been shot.

Litke was six-one and 165 pounds of lean muscle and a squad leader in 1st Platoon. He was a handsome kid with brown hair and striking blue eyes. Litke had a malicious squint most of the time—not for acuity of vision, but as part of his demeanor, the kind of way he let everyone know that he was the real deal. And he was. He was a legitimate badass who never took shit from anyone.

McLaughlin and I made our way over to the position and quickly shot a heading on a lensatic compass to try to refine the direction of the shots that had just killed two of our Marines.

Everyone wanted to exact swift vengeance on the shooter that had taken two of our brothers from us that day, including me. It's a natural reaction under those circumstances.

I made my way back down to the second floor and gathered McLaughlin and his team around the map. We had a good idea of the buildings from where the shots had originated. I generated a plan to mount a hasty raid on them. I never liked using the word "hasty" to do anything, although that was the accepted vernacular in the Marines. For me, the word meant "half-assed" and improperly planned, and I hated anything like that.

I walked out of the room where we'd been planning the raid and stood at the banister on the second floor for a moment. I looked down trying to gather my thoughts. A couple of squads stood on the large red Persian rug in the living room. They were ready to go. I knew they were waiting for me to cut them off the leash.

I went back to the command post and got on the radio to the 15th MEU operations officer and briefed him on the situation. I decided that the timing wasn't right. My men were just too keyed up, and that could lead to unnecessary bloodshed. It wasn't as if we were going out to fight a "like-force." Who we were looking for was more elusive, and they had now blended in with the local Iraqis, most of whom were innocent bystanders.

I decided on a more deliberate course of action to take advantage of the limited amount of time we had to catch the shooter. I task-organized the patrol to move out to the targeted raid sites and form an outer cordon to observe any possible "squirters"—enemy fighters fleeing on foot.

Within minutes, we sealed the area, cleared the target sites, and began raids on all of the suspected houses. The shooter was nowhere to be found, and the locals gave us shit as far as information was concerned.

I had reneged on my guarantee to Major Nugent. It took us seventy-two hours to clear Rutbah, because of our casualties. But Rutbah was clear.

CHAPTER 21.1

Pueblo

In late January of 2007, Lance Corporal Emilian Sanchez returned home. A fellow Marine from his tribe, the Keres people of the Tamayame, or Santa Ana Pueblo, New Mexico, as it is more commonly known, escorted him from Dover, Delaware, to his family. Local police shut down a five-mile section of Interstate 25—a courtesy normally reserved for the president of the United States. Thousands of locals lined the streets. Huge U.S. flags draped the overpasses as his procession moved down the highway.

To say that I knew Emilian, or "Sancho," as the Marines of Echo Company called him would be a bit of a stretch. I was his commanding officer and spoke with him only on occasion. Sanchez acted reserved around me. But his peers considered him a jokester—constantly smiling and clowning around with them. It wasn't until I made my journey to his home that I would come to know who he was, how he had lived, and how much he meant to his family.

■　　■　　■

It had been almost nine years since I'd last seen the Sanchez family. I'd always promised to visit, and they always invited me each time I'd call, but I never went. But it was time. Something I felt compelled to do.

I arrived early in the morning to witness the festival to pay tribute to Saint Anne, the patron saint of the Keres tribe and partake in the feast they had invited me to. I stopped along the way on a bridge as the sun came up above the Rio Grande. It was a perfect time to take a photo as the sun crested the river, so I did.

The Keres tribe, like many in the area, are Catholic, and their formal religious beliefs are tied to their long spiritual heritage. They believed in two worlds: a physical one in which they balanced between their historical, cultural beliefs and those of Western society, and a spiritual one, the world of one true God that encompassed their Catholic and cultural beliefs and practices.

When I arrived, the residents of the Pueblo were milling around—others moved from house to house with a definite purpose preparing for the annual festival. Some carried vibrantly patterned umbrellas to defend against the intense New Mexico sun. As they walked, their steps kicked up the fine powdery sand, forming little dust clouds around their feet. The unnamed dirt streets were lined with small tents from which local merchants were selling everything from food to traditional handmade jewelry, especially turquoise and sterling silver ornaments.

Large families were the norm. The Sanchez family had six children, but others had more than that. The sizes of the extended families were filled with ranks that blurred beyond my comprehension. Aunts, uncles, brothers, sisters, and grandparents—the children knew them all by name and addressed them all with the proper honorifics.

The children had been taught the language and customs of their unique culture at early ages, and they all practiced it. The tribal elders made sure of it. Everyone had a role within the tribe of more than eight hundred members. Some might think that it is a little too insular. To me, it seemed to be a community of equality and mutual respect.

The Keresans have lived in the Pueblo for more than five hundred years. The Pueblo sat at the basin of desert mountains in a vast expanse of scenery. It sat on eighty acres surrounded by high mesas. Streaks of reddish sand streamed down the northerly face of the hills as if they had been weeping for centuries. The ground was freckled with creosote bushes. Rains, when they came, cut distinct lines from top to bottom. In the sky, bright blue that day, thick white and gray clouds loomed in the distance and crossed the sky slowly. Lightning zigzagged brightly and struck on occasion.

When I entered the modest family home in the Pueblo, I was introduced immediately to all who gathered inside. Mrs. Jennie Sanchez, Emilian's mother, announced, "This is Emilian's Major. They were in the Marines together." The fact that I was a captain in Iraq didn't matter. She always referred to me as "Emilian's Major."

The air inside the house was rich with the smell of breakfast cooking and coffee brewing. With no power lines running into the Pueblo, anything electrical ran off of a generator. There was no running water. Water was brought in by the bucketload from a spigot outside and dumped into a large, gray plastic bin.

Everyone trekked to the family outhouse to take care of bathroom business. A key fastened to a blue piece of wood belonged to a small lock that secured the outhouse. It hung in the kitchen like one found at an old service station. I was gently scolded later that morning when I walked back in the kitchen after using the outhouse—I had drunk more than my share of coffee.

Mrs. Sanchez saw the keychain jutting out of my pocket. "Oh, you have it. It goes back right there." She pointed to a small wooden key rack no bigger than the size of a six-inch ruler with five tiny cup hooks screwed into it.

Joey Sanchez, Emilian's elder brother by eighteen years, sat down at the long wooden table with me. The table could accommodate eight comfortably with two long wooden benches on both sides and an armchair at each end. There was never an empty chair as they fed more than one hundred family and friends who circulated the house through-out the entire day and well into the night.

Joey invited me to sit and talk. He was the third child of David and Jennie Sanchez. Aubrey was the eldest brother, Bernadine or "Berna" the only sister, then Joey and Adrian. Emilian had been the baby, but the pride of them all.

When Joey spoke, his voice swelled with emotion. He had been more than a brother to Emilian because of the age difference, more like a father. In fact, he was often mistaken for Emilian's father when the boy was young. Emilian would take exception to the mistake saying, "Nah, man, he's not my dad. That's my brother." Joey didn't mind as much.

When Joey continued to speak of his brother, he told me that Emilian was the only Keresan to die in combat while in the U.S. military. He also whispered to me, "The spirits called Emil to the other world for a more important reason."

I loved hearing that. It made me feel as if Sanchez was still with us, just on a new mission.

Those words gave me comfort as I got up from the table and walked to the adjacent room where there was a shrine to Emilian. His certificates and pictures hung on the wall. His medals and an encased American flag sat as the centerpiece. Two small bowls were on the table, one filled with a bit of fine, yellow cornmeal, the other an empty bowl. The traditional way to pay tribute to the fallen was to take a pinch of the cornmeal and sprinkle it into the other bowl. The rest of the living room was decorated with traditional colorful blankets that hung from the walls. A bison and two large deer heads with massive racks also hung prominently on display, trophies from family hunting expeditions.

Time passed leisurely, and I occupied myself mostly by sitting on a small wooden bench on the front of the concrete porch to take shade from the sun. I imagined Emilian sitting there as a young boy.

When I knew him, Emilian was five-ten with the average build of a U.S. Marine—160 pounds. Lean. His hair was cropped short and black. He had clever brown eyes that were squinted most of the time in an inquisitive fashion.

His family had filled in some of the blanks for me. When he was young, all he ever wanted was to claim the title of U.S. Marine. He, like many, had a long family history of Marines who had served their country. His grandfather was a Marine in World War II who fought on the iconic island of Iwo Jima in the South Pacific. An uncle was in Vietnam, and his cousin served in Desert Storm. So eager was Emilian to join the Marines that he tried to drop out of high school and enlist. The recruiters from Rio Rancho, New Mexico, told him to get his diploma first and then come back.

■   ■   ■

The Keres prayed for rain that day. The tribal members danced in two groups—the colors pumpkin and turquoise—each consisting of more than a hundred dancers. All wore traditional attire for the elaborate and well-performed ritual. Shirtless men danced, covered in light blue body paint on their torsos with armbands, animal pelts tucked into the back of their waistbands, and a small evergreen branch wedged into the belt that wrapped their waists. The women wore black dresses and had two red circles painted neatly high on their cheekbones. They carried an evergreen branch in one hand.

The music from the drums and the synchronized chanting in their native tongue of Keresan lulled me. The bells that the men wore fastened above their calves rattled as they walked and danced. They had tan gourds filled with dried beans and tiny handles bound to them and shook them in rhythm with the deep booming of the animal-skinned drums.

They danced for hours on end in the hot sand of the Pueblo square. They marked time. Moving slowly, they performed for the residents and visitors that were welcomed to observe. No photos were allowed. No sketches. No videos either. It was a part of their culture that was to be respected. Some thought it just a suggestion and had their phones and cameras confiscated on site by the Tribal Police who were out in force.

■   ■   ■

I was peaceful taking it all in.

A hot breeze blew periodically throughout the day giving mild respite from the blazing temperature. I was happy to sit. I thought about the new experience, and it made me content. My enjoyment was bolstered by the laughter of the children around me eating colorful shaved ice served in paper cones—oblivious to the heat of the noon sky as they devoured the ice-cold treats.

Periodically, my eagerness took over and I would roam about, trying to chat with some of the tribe, asking questions. They never had much to say. My natural inquisitive nature was something they didn't share. Things were the way they were, and that's just how it was. They were taught not to ask why—if I were ever a member of the tribe they would have shunned me. I never possessed the ability not to ask questions. I'm sure I was labeled a chatterbox.

I left the Pueblo late in the evening. I thanked my hosts, hugged Mrs. Sanchez and kissed her gently on her salt and pepper hair.

Joey walked me to his dad's truck and reminded me of the road to follow out of the reservation. I thanked him again. He extended his arms, and we shook hands while patting each other on the back. He called me brother. I instantly felt the heat rush to my eyes as they teared up slightly. I was humbled and honored that he said that, and grateful to the darkness of the night that masked my emotions clearly visible in my eyes.

I drove off the Pueblo. The pickup truck that Emilian's dad graciously let me borrow carried me back to my hotel. I thought about Emilian. We were brothers as fellow Marines, but I knew the bonds he shared with his family reached far beyond to a different dimension that I was now fortunate to be a part of.

CHAPTER 22

Anthem

After the shocking loss of Sanchez and Matus to sniper fire on 21 January 2007, my boys weren't too keen on the new Rules of Engagement. It frustrated them when I had to tell them to use more restraint.

As an infantry commander, it is not a significant challenge to train a nineteen-year-old how to fire a machine gun, give him a box of ammo and a target, and get him to go from zero to sixty, employing his weapon and killing the enemy, in about three seconds. It's a whole different story after weeks and months of intense daily fighting to get him to go from sixty to zero in an instant and think before he shoots.

Building 500 was different than any other house we had occupied in Iraq. It was an elaborate structure decorated gaudily with mismatched furniture in every room. Tacky gold plastic chandeliers hung in most of the rooms but didn't work. Massive Persian rugs decorated the floors, and the windows had big thick draperies. But we didn't choose it for its interior décor. We did so because it was tall—three stories high—and so offered panoramic views of the entire city and provided interlocking fields of fire with Marines from two other Echo Company platoons who used what we called "The Bank" as their firm base.

Throughout our stay at Building 500, we occasionally allowed the original homeowner, Ali, to pay quick visits during which he'd gather up some of his personal belongings and other minutiae. At first, I felt a bit guilty about what we had done to his house. The two platoons of Marines were jam-packed into that place. To accommodate the tight living conditions, they had stuffed all of the owner's clothes and personal effects into one of the smaller rooms. Whenever the owner showed up, I thought, "Man, that sucks for him, having all of his family's shit tossed into a tiny storage room." I never let it bother me for long. Again, we had bigger problems at hand.

Days after we'd raided the houses from the sniper that had shot Sanchez and Matus, we'd received intelligence reports that the shooter and some of his accomplices might have been holed up somewhere on the south side of town, west of Building 500. The 15th MEU command element readily supported my desire to seek out these High-Value Individuals (HVIs), and I coordinated a daytime raid to exploit the information.

The target was a small row of houses that sat on the west side of MSR Mercury, the main street on which Building 500 was located.

We launched the raid in the early morning hours supported by armed Humvees and a few additional fire teams in overwatch from Bravo Company, 3rd Recon Battalion, the unit responsible for that part of the battlespace.

We split up into squads, and as dawn broke, we moved quickly to the target site and cordoned off the house. As soon as the Marines from the other squads were in a position to cover us, we kicked the door in. Two teams entered the front door and another through the back. Whenever we made entry, one team immediately began to clear up the staircase to secure the second floor.

"Clear! All Clear!" We could hear yelling from the second level.

We cleared each room quickly hoping to find our target. Nothing. Either we'd hit the wrong house, or the insurgents had abandoned their safe haven. It was times like these when our faith in the intelligence section wavered.

I stayed inside the vacant house and sent a fire team of Marines a couple more houses down to advance the movement and keep up the momentum of the raid. We wanted to press through quickly to keep the element of surprise on our side.

Litke, along with one of his fire team leaders, Corporal Matt Scott, moved out along the narrow walkway in order to secure a house a few doors down.

Scott was twenty-one and on his second deployment to Iraq. He was thin and lanky, from Darrington, Washington. He had a boyish look about him and was unmistakably recognizable from behind on any given patrol as his protruding ears tended to jut out from the sides of his Kevlar helmet. It wasn't uncommon to find him and Litke as ringleaders engaging in random acts of horseplay in order to lighten the spirits of their men.

I stayed with Lance Corporal Dereck Carpenter, or "Carp," as most called him, with one of the fire teams in the house we had initially cleared. I got on the radio and tried to contact the 15th MEU command element to update our position and status.

Carp was a dynamo, at five-eight and 140 pounds with brown hair and large, round brown eyes. He was unassuming and normally had a closed-mouth smile that ran across his face with deep lines that cut into his cheeks.

He was from a two-horse town in Libby, Montana, population 2,648, which was tucked into the northwest corner of the state due east of Idaho and south of the Canadian border. Carp was a jock in high school, like many Marines. But like many in high school, myself included, he'd strayed and begun hanging out with the wrong crowd. He knew he was going off course and needed direction.

His family had all served in the military, but Carp was attracted to the Marines. Just before graduating, he drove almost a hundred miles to the nearest U.S. Marine recruiter's office in Kalispell.

The recruiter looked at Carp with seriousness. "Nowhere else will you be challenged as much as you will be in the Marines—and you will get paid to run around in the woods and shoot guns."

Sold.

He volunteered for the infantry, too. Wise choice. He turned out to be a shit-hot rifleman, a term of affection and notability not thrown around lightly in our community.

I grabbed my Thales Multi-Band Inter-Team Radio (MBITR), and all I heard was a constant beeping. No comm again. We moved around the house trying to troubleshoot the radio problem, but it was no good. The radio was dead.

"Fucking typical!"

I had been cursed with comm problems my entire life it seemed. There were times when I would tell my radio operator to get someone on the hook for me, and they'd call him up, have great comms, and, the minute they passed me the handset, it would go to shit.

Friction.

I didn't want to waste any time. Litke and Scott had a radio a few houses down.

I told Carp, "Stay here. Don't move. I'm going to run next door and try to link up with Litke and Scott to get comms."

"Roger that, sir. We're not gonna move."

I made my way to the front door and cracked it open. We'd heard a few shots fired at that point but thought the area was contained.

I identified the house in which Litke and Scott sought cover. I checked my left and right and bolted out the door onto the narrow sidewalk and ran down the path. Almost immediately, I began to get shot at. A couple of solid streams of small arms fire smacked into the sides of the houses as I ran. I tripped along the way. My knee went down, and I almost face-planted but quickly recovered in one not-so-smooth motion.

They were shooting at me from the far end of the street from behind a parked car. After I got back to my feet, I raised my M4 and shot back at the car to suppress the enemy as I continued to run.

Most of the children and locals dashed into their homes to avoid the crossfire. Others just stood there taking in the show.

I never understood how oblivious Iraqis could be to what was going on around them. It took being literally caught in a crossfire for them to get the picture and get the fuck out of the way. Sometimes they didn't even do that. They'd just stand around like a bunch of spectators, like it was some sort of sporting event. Maybe they had become totally desensitized. After all, they'd been living in the midst of a war zone for years.

I tried to push through the door of the house that Litke and Scott were in and couldn't get the handle open.

"Fuck."

I finally busted in. Muzzles glared at me in the face. Litke and Scott both had their rifles trained on me. They dropped their weapons from their shoulders and pointed them downward.

"Goddamn, sir! We almost shot you!" Litke exclaimed.

"Yeah, thanks. That would have sucked. You guys up on comms?" I was still sucking air into my lungs after my brush with death in the street.

Litke replied, "Yeah, sir. We're solid."

I got on the MBITR and radioed back to the 15th MEU command element Humvee that was sitting in overwatch a few hundred meters away. I told them we were taking fire from the north and to press up in their vehicles, identify the shooters, and cover us while we continued the raid.

Carp was still holding fast in the first house. I was in the courtyard with Litke and Scott and could hear yelling. It was Carp shouting at the 15th MEU Humvee gun truck to open fire on the targets to the north. The Humvee wouldn't return fire.

Aggravated and cut off from the rest of the squad, Carp and his team decided to push up to Litke's position and run into the house. Four Marines entered, all of them winded from making the short dash to safety and security with the other team.

Carp entered first and blurted, "Fuck sir, we thought for sure you got shot. Once you took off, we saw you hit the ground, and we ducked back inside. We couldn't shoot back, so we decided to push up to make sure you were OK."

I passed the radio handset back to Litke and glared back at them. I wished they had stayed put as ordered, but I was heartened to know that they were willing to take care of their CO in the midst of the chaos.

The skirmish ended, and we continued to clear the row of houses. Not a single shot was fired after that. Aside from gathering up a few dozen weapons that had been stashed throughout the homes, we never found the HVIs we were hunting. But that is how it went most of the time, especially during daytime raids. We always seemed to have more luck nabbing bad guys while they slept.

Despite their reputations of being labeled "fighters" on the most wanted list, the insurgents were inherently lazy. They lacked discipline, and when they were caught, normally fast asleep, they would always default to trying to lie their way out of being detained like any criminal would.

Our stay in Building 500 remained plagued with friction for several weeks. After we'd cleared the city, we essentially began routine patrolling to maintain a presence and continued to collect information on the locals. The lack of active engagements—or the absence of chaos—still rattled us as we readjusted our patterns of action to best help the citizens of Rutbah.

■   ■   ■

Marines have a sense of humor. An awfully quirky sense of humor that often manifests itself at the oddest times and in the weirdest ways.

We had received a Long Range Acoustical Device (LRAD) from the 15th MEU supply section after we occupied Building 500. It was just a big speaker—a large tan dome about three feet wide in the shape of a hexagon that stood on a pedestal. We were never given any instructions on what to do with it—although we understood it was intended to be a "tactical broadcast system."

Almost immediately, my boys figured out they could hook up their MP3 music players to it—true to their ingenious nature of problem-solving.

The next day, and several after that, at the crack of dawn, they played *Start Me Up* by the Rolling Stones. That song and the others they played could be heard several blocks away. Word of our music selection got back to the command eventually, and I was sternly admonished for misusing the equipment for other than its intended purpose. I was told to play the Iraqi National Anthem instead.

Initially, the Marines were riled and contemptuous about the order.

Weeks later, as the anthem played, we would see Iraqi children coming outside of their homes and marching around in the street to the music, feet stomping and arms pumping back and forth like little soldiers. It made my Marines smile.

Between Building 500 and The Bank, Echo Company was sending out six to eight dismounted combat patrols a day. Sometimes we would patrol with the support of a single Humvee with a .50 caliber machine gun for overwatch and backup. I liked it. It gave us the protection of a big gun, CASEVAC if needed, and allowed the Marines to stay foot-mobile and connected to the locals.

Jets and attack helicopters would fly overwatch missions as the Marines patrolled. They conducted intelligence, surveillance, and reconnaissance (ISR), sending live video from their high-powered electro-optical lens straight to Bam-Bam's Panasonic Toughbook, as he sat on the roof of Building 500 keeping an eye on us.

Our company headquarters at Building 500 was in one of the larger bedrooms. All of the windows had been sandbagged. A large table made of plywood stood in the center of the room. We used it to spread out our maps and set up our computers for administrative work.

Electricity to run the computers came from power cords that were duct taped to the walls which ran out of the cracks in the windows down to the first floor where gasoline generators ran our power. They'd constantly go out, normally right when I was in the middle of something.

Immediately after a power outage, I would inevitably let out a loud, exasperated call: "Yaaaansky!"

Lance Corporal Chris Yansky was five-seven and 155 pounds and from Fort Wayne, Indiana. He'd been wounded only weeks into his first deployment with Echo Company in 2004 and received a Purple Heart Medal. He was a rifleman by trade, but was blessed—he might think cursed—with knowledge of small engine repair and became my go-to guy to fix the unreliable generators that we had purchased in Rutbah.

All of the officers, Foster, and a couple of others slept in the COC. Lee, Bam-Bam, and I took turns sleeping in a tiny five-by-eight-foot closet in the back of the room that was partitioned off with a curtain. The Marines only came in there to wake us up in case of an emergency. It was musty and smelled of sweat and dirty socks. The foul, pungent aroma was a byproduct created from patrolling through the human waste that flowed freely through the streets of Rutbah.

Every street we patrolled down stood littered with trash and a river of gray liquid waste that clung to our suede boots. The backup was so bad in front of Building 500 that we had a small pond of sewage that accumulated daily in front of the entrance where all of the Marines and vehicles entered and exited the compound. It got to the point that we had to send work details out front with shovels to dig muck out of the gutters so the sewage would drain off. Everyone took turns digging through that disgusting mess, myself included.

A large John Deere military tractor with a bucket, called a TRAM, had dug a huge pit in the backyard of Building 500—we'd been using it to dump waste in for months. Imagine construction contractors coming to your house to dig an Olympic-sized swimming pool in your backyard and never finishing it. That's how big the hole was.

It was jammed full of trash, food, dead animals, and tiny green WAG (Waste Alleviation and Gelling) bags full of human feces. Since there was no running water and the sewage system was worthless, we had to go to the bathroom on a campstool, lined with tiny little green bags filled with a cup or so of the equivalent of kitty litter. The real trick was, you couldn't piss in the bag while doing your business. Otherwise, it wouldn't burn.

During my time as a young lance corporal during Operation Desert Storm, I took my turn burning shit in fifty-five-gallon drums doused in diesel fuel. In Rutbah, we set pallets or trash on fire and then tossed the daily human waste onto the flames. It was all done outside in the open for obvious reasons, but at the end of the day, no one wanted the task for fear of getting shot.

Nobody wants to die burning shit.

Lance Corporals Calvin Spencer and Nick Velez eloquently recited a story to me one day about an experience, which I remember them calling, "The WAG Bag Cycle of Life."

Marine shits into Bag. He then has to do the "WAG Bag Walk of Shame" past his fellow Marines and toss it into the fire. Fire burns the shit bags. Bag burns. Ashes rise. Wind blows ash. Ash sprinkles into his unzipped MREs. Marine eats. Marine gags. Marine shits into bag.

Spencer, much like Sir Isaac Newton who had an apple fall on his head, came up with this theory when he came back from a patrol and was sitting out back of Building 500 eating an MRE. Exhausted and starved, he cut the top of the bag open and began to eat when he noticed tiny, gray sprinkles falling into his meal.

It was then Spencer backtracked his theory to discover that he was essentially eating shit powder on his MRE.

Despite the austere living conditions in Building 500, Gunny Mac had a way to make things more livable. He set up a makeshift cantina and stocked it with chips, soda, and candy that he'd procure from CKV on his logistics runs. The boys loved it, and anyone who visited the position was impressed by it. My Marines were very territorial about the cantina and scowled at any outsiders who thought they were entitled to help themselves to snacks—especially those who lived at CKV, which served hot chow twenty-four hours a day.

After a logistics run, Mac procured a huge chunk of beef from CKV. He roasted it and sliced it up for the boys as a special treat. The thinly shaved meat sandwiches were served on tiny buns. He'd also concocted some special mustard au jus sauce to dip them in as he called out to all of the Marines in the house. They gathered around, and each helped himself to one of the gourmet sandwiches, dipping them in a bowl Mac had placed in the center of a large, silver serving tray. I heard the boys' excitement from below as I sat upstairs in the COC.

I stepped out of the COC and peered over the railing. I was happy. Nothing made me smile more than seeing Marines taking care of each other.

Mac came into the COC later. He called to me as I sat reviewing a patrol report.

"Sir, you have to try this," Mac beamed. He had saved me one of the sandwiches, complete with sauce. It tasted better than anything.

■　　■　　■

The next morning, a chorus of screaming and commotion interrupted the normal jocularity among the Marines on the first floor. I didn't pay much attention to it, figuring it was a couple of the boys getting into it.

I was wrong.

I leaned over the railing and could now see smoke coming from inside of the building. A couple of Marines raced to the back of the cantina bar that sat in front of the kitchen.

We used the kitchen to store all of our ammunition, pyro, and grenades. It didn't get much other use outside of Mac's sandwich extravaganza, which we later affectionately referred to as "Operation Arby's."

The Marines were conducting a turnover of posts from the roof as they made their way down the staircase. Two of the Marines exchanged gear. One handed the other a tiny, black aluminum pen flare as part of his relief procedures. Used as a signaling device, a pen flare is no bigger than an ordinary ink pen. It had a small spring-loaded cocking lever on it and a red flare screwed into the end of it.

The cocking lever got caught on the Marine's gear, releasing it and the flare shot out in a hiss. It sailed right by Bam-Bam's face as he stood on the staircase, headed downward, hit the floor, and ricocheted into the kitchen.

The flare by itself wouldn't have been much cause for concern. Flares don't explode. However, the cooking oil that was also in the room with all of the ammo was the real problem. The four-gallon cans of oil stacked in the room had been leaking, and when the flare hit the ground in the room, it ignited the oil. The ammo could have cooked off had some of the men not extinguished the blaze immediately.

Friction.

Foster laced into the Marines for their part in the near catastrophe, to say the least. I'm quite sure he had plenty of "volunteers" to burn shit after that episode.

CHAPTER 23

Mosques

We were well aware that the insurgents were using the mosques as hiding spots and safe havens. Under the coalition forces' rules of engagement, we weren't allowed to fire on a mosque unless someone was shooting at us from it, and even then, we had to request permission from higher command for authority to engage.

The ROE also placed five-hundred-meter no-fire areas (NFAs) on top of every mosque in Iraq. An NFA is a graphic symbol on a map, a red circle with little hash marks in it. It's a restrictive measure—nothing in an NFA may be targeted by artillery or air support. To get an NFA lifted from any building, mosque or otherwise, required a decision from the highest command and that took at least forty-eight hours—by then it was more than likely a moot point.

The insurgents exploited these restrictions to the fullest. Most mosques stood in compounds that were surrounded by ten-foot-high concrete walls and steel gates, making them ideal safe havens. They stashed weapons, ammunition, and explosives in mosques—often getting imams' "permission" by means of intimidation. They also terrorized these clerics into broadcasting hateful propaganda from the loudspeakers inside the minarets that towered over every mosque.

Our Terps always listened keenly to the messages recited during morning and evening calls to prayer. If they heard any anti-coalition messages, they told their commanders. Most of the messages were so vague that we couldn't act on them from a tactical perspective. In time, they just became part of the background noise of Iraq.

One of the largest mosques in our area in Ramadi was the Al Haq Mosque. We commonly spotted insurgents running to and from, most likely in order to re-supply their forces with ammunition from their stockpile in it.

It was no different in Rutbah. The restrictions on targeting mosques remained the same, and the insurgents made full use of them. For us, the restriction was a continuing source of frustration. We hated that the insurgents could—and routinely did—take refuge in these holy shrines. For Marines, using a place of worship as a shield went against a fundamental moral code.

■   ■   ■

Echo Company established two firm bases from which to conduct patrols after Operation Gateway in Rutbah was complete. We patrolled up to ten times per day and developed a good handle on the atmospherics of the city—what the locals were up to, reports of any insurgent activity, and the general sense of security the locals thought about our presence.

After a night of patrolling, one of my squad leaders came into the COC in Building 500 with some information. Our Terps, Big Sam and Ford, accompanied him.

Big Sam was holding a piece of white paper in one hand. It was a little crumpled up and had Arabic writing on one side of it. Big Sam looked concerned and a little proud at the same time.

I asked, "OK. So, what's up? What do you got?"

Sam began to explain that during a raid on a house, they confiscated a bunch of AK-47s and some other contraband, but, more importantly, found the note he was carrying.

He translated, *"Bring all of the weapons to the mosques. We need all weapons brought to the mosques so the Americans can't get them and we can strike back at them when we choose."*

I asked Big Sam if he thought the letter was legitimate and if he was certain that he'd translated it correctly.

He said, "Yes, sir. That's what the letter says. I think that the insurgents are staging their weapons at the mosques so they can launch an attack."

Despite having little more than an unverified note to go on, I immediately passed this information to the 15th MEU operations officer, Major Nugent. After I told him about the letter, I requested that he pass on to the 15th MEU Commander, Colonel Brian Beaudreault, a request to raid the mosque that was directly next door to the house where we'd found the letter.

Permission came back in less than an hour. I told McLaughlin to get a reinforced squad ready to move out as soon as possible. We were going to raid the mosque.

There was excitement in his eyes when I gave McLaughlin the news. He and the other Marines were about to enter forbidden territory, and they were keen to see what lay on the other side.

I was eager to mount the raid, too, because I was sure it would yield great results for Echo Company. I got on the radio and began advising the other units in the area that we were going to conduct a raid on the mosque based off of actionable intelligence.

After the platoons responded, I requested that all units in our zone of operation give a position report (POSREP) to see where everyone was that night. We normally had two to three patrols out at any given time. As they called in, I saw that two other squads were within a block of two other mosques that lay within our zone's boundaries.

After careful consideration, I decided to have all three squads raid all three of the mosques at the same time in a coordinated effort to exploit the information at hand. I didn't make this known to the 15th MEU COC that was forty miles away at CKV. I was going with my gut feeling. We had to strike while the iron was hot.

On my orders, the squads raided the three mosques simultaneously.

Unit leaders reported they'd found massive caches of weapons, body armor, bomb-making materials, communications equipment, and other supplies the enemy planned to use against us. Big Sam's discovery had turned out to be a gold mine in terms of intelligence.

Reports continued to filter in from the squads—the raids were a success.

As good as the mission was going it took a turn for the worse when a message came across the net. There was a casualty in one of the mosques to the northeast—a female civilian.

She'd been shot in the elbow by Lance Corporal Joseph Raney.

"Holy fuck," I thought.

■   ■   ■

Earlier, Raney had been in his room when his platoon sergeant came in and said, "Get your shit ready. We're raiding a mosque." Raney scrambled to get all of his gear together and passed the word to the rest of the squad.

So quickly had I ordered the raid that Lance Corporal Robert Thompson, a SAW gunner in Raney's squad, had his weapon completely disassembled for cleaning. His platoon sergeant said, "We don't have time to wait. Thompson, you'll have to stay back."

When the time came for Raney's squad to exit the firm base at The Bank, he felt a certain unease leaving Thompson behind, not only because his squad would be one Marine short, but also because the effectiveness and sheer firepower of the SAW was a massive force multiplier.

The M249 SAW made by FN Herstal was a clumsy weapon, weighing almost 22 pounds fully loaded—a bitch to carry on any movement—but it was worth the extra effort, especially in urban terrain, because it could fire eight hundred rounds of 5.56 mm bullets per minute. That's a devastating amount of firepower.

Raney was on point for his squad, the lead man in the element, usually the most dangerous position to be located. The squad moved up to an outcrop of smaller buildings on the outskirts of the mosque when Raney noticed one of the adjoining buildings led into the main mosque.

It was 0200 hours. Light reflected off the roads and burned gently from the intermittent glow of scattered streetlights and illumination from some of the surrounding houses. It made it difficult to see with the naked eye, and if the Marines switched to their infrared (IR) night vision devices, the ambient light would wash out their vision almost entirely.

Raney's squad first cleared a small outcrop of houses and then closed in on the mosque. Raney moved to the back of the mosque and saw a door with the key still jutting out of the lock. He turned the key, unlocked the door, and swung it open sharply. The room beyond was dark, but Raney detected a silhouette of someone coming toward him.

With his M16-A4 at the ready, Raney set his sights on the target—center mass, aiming squarely for the torso. He hesitated and lowered his weapon just inches as the target continued running, but it was right in front of him.

Raney fired a single shot. He knew instantly he hit his target as a loud, high-pitched scream echoed through the room.

Raney thought to himself, "Oh, fuck. I shot some bitch."

As Raney moved into the room, the woman ran toward another door that served as the exit. She pushed open the second door, which slammed into a man sleeping on the floor, and ran into the other room.

The other squads had converged in the main prayer room of the mosque where they turned on their white lights to search and assess the situation. There, the woman that Raney had shot was lying in her mother's arms, crying uncontrollably. She was in her early twenties, wearing a traditional black burka and hijab, and was now grasping her right elbow tightly.

The mosque's imam was trying to comfort the two women.

With the mosque now flooded with Marines from the other squads, Grillo came in to assess the damage and Doc began to provide first aid to the injured woman, bandaging the elbow with a compression dressing to stop the bleeding.

All of the lights were on inside the mosque. The Marines began to clear all the rooms for weapons and IED-making materials. Grillo started directing the other Marines to continue the search. Minutes later, he came over to check on Raney who had been rooted in place, still shocked by what he had done. His lieutenant's face bore a look of disappointment. Raney knew he had screwed the pooch on this one—badly.

Raney watched two Marines from another squad digging the bullet he'd shot out of the wall. The round had gone clear through the soft tissue of the woman's arm and lodged itself into the concrete.

When Raney returned to The Bank, he sat alone, wracked with guilt for shooting an unarmed woman.

From his time growing up in Tacoma, Washington, Joseph Raney had been brought up in the parochial school way of thinking that men take care of women, treat them with respect, and keep them safe. He had clung to that code—and now he'd live with the fact that he'd violated it and had harmed an innocent woman who was in what probably was to her the safest place in the world.

Raney replayed the scene over and over in his head that night and wondered why he had been so jumpy and had shot his weapon. Was it the unknown? The fact the whole situation unleashed so quickly? Was it that he felt nervous without his SAW gunner next to him for backup that night? He didn't find the answers, at least not that night.

As Marines will, his squad mates compounded his anxiety and guilt about the incident by giving Raney a new call sign—"PID." It stood for Positive Identification. It wasn't an affectionate handle. It was a reminder to him not to shoot anyone unless he could see his target clearly.

When I arrived, I found Foster and a security team on site. The Marines who had raided the mosque already had headed back to their firm bases. The injured woman had been moved outside the mosque and was standing amongst a group of other Iraqis, still holding her bandaged arm. I tried to communicate with her brother, but we didn't have an interpreter on site yet, so we put her inside Somerville's Humvee.

She sat there for two hours until we sorted out the situation.

Friction.

I went across the street to an apartment building occupied by the MSPF unit who had a Human Exploitation Team (HET) embedded with it. I asked if First Lieutenant Stephen Peacock was around.

Peacock was a former enlisted Marine from Anchorage, Alaska. At thirty-four, he came with a lot of experience and common sense. I was counting on him to help us deal with the situation as time ticked by and daylight crept closer. I didn't like hanging out in the middle of Rutbah during daylight under normal circumstances, let alone after my boys had raided three of the city's mosques—we had to clear the scene as soon as humanly-fucking-possible to eliminate what could have potentially boiled over into a worsening situation of local hostility.

Peacock knew a local doctor nearby who he'd run into occasionally while patrolling in zone. My Terp, Ford, explained to the brother and injured woman we were going to the local clinic to find her a doctor.

A small team of security accompanied Peacock, Ford, the wounded woman, her brother, and me on the trip to the clinic. It was almost 0400. We banged on the door to rouse the doctor. After several minutes, he cracked the door and peered through a slit with a wary look. Ford told him what had happened to the girl.

The doctor and Ford started going back and forth in what appeared to be a heated conversation. Most Iraqis spoke in a very sharp, loud manner punctuated by overt hand gestures. Despite our offer of money for his services, the doctor told Ford there was nothing he could do to help her. He said our best option would be to have her brother drive her to Ramadi General Hospital and get her to the emergency room for a proper exam. Ramadi was more than four hours away by car.

We were bewildered that the doctor refused to treat the woman—he was completely worthless to us.

"I guess there's no such thing as a Hippocratic-fucking-oath in Iraq," I thought, as I slammed the screen door in his face and pulled my team out.

On the spot, Peacock and I formulated a plan to tell the brother to get her to Ramadi General Hospital and gave him $1,500 to cover any potential fees needed to get her to Ramadi right away. The brother assured us that he had a car and was going to drive her there immediately once they got their things together.

With the situation controlled—to a degree—we all returned to our firm bases and tried to make sense of the night. Despite the unfortunate gravity of the situation and shooting the woman at the mosque, our raids yielded fantastic results. I saw the evidence of that when I walked into the main room of Building 500. Dozens of AK-47s were laid out neatly on the huge Persian rug that covered the floor, along with RPGs and other contraband all captured from the mosques by the Marines of Echo Company.

The sweat from my soaking-wet camouflage blouse had just begun to air out, and I unlaced my boots. I was planning on getting a couple of hours of sleep. My plans for rest, however, were derailed when one of the radio operators came into my room and told me we had gotten a call from the 15th MEU's operations center: I was to report to CKV to see Colonel Beaudreault.

I put my gear back on and told Somerville to get a convoy for a run to CKV.

I also told him that I wanted to do a quick patrol over to The Bank to check on the Marines before we pushed to CKV.

As our four-vehicle convoy approached The Bank, small arms fire began to crack around us, and the Marines on the roof scanned the area to see where the shots originated. At the same time, a squad across the street returned fire. Then, all of the Marines converged their fire on the buildings from where the muzzle flashes emanated.

We pushed to the west side of the street next to The Bank and took cover. We were in a bad position and had no direct observation of the enemy from our vehicles. The firefight lasted only a few minutes, and we quickly exited the Humvees and made our way inside.

I briefed Lee on the events and my planned trip to CKV, and told him he was in charge—he had no idea why I was going, but I'm sure his imagination had already been running overboard. Somerville had pulled the convoy to the front side of The Bank to mount up. As we did, rounds started biting the ground around us.

I scrambled toward my Humvee, the back door of which had already been opened up for me.

A couple of shots cracked around me, and the Marines in the gun truck and on the rooftop of The Bank returned fire. I dove for the cover of the heavily armored Humvee. With little grace under fire, I smacked my head on the edge of the door as I made my way into the back seat, jamming my Kevlar helmet down onto my brow.

The convoy sped out of the kill zone, and we drove west on MSR Michigan toward CKV. The driver kept looking over his shoulder at me. He finally piped up, "Hey sir. You know you're bleeding?"

I said, "What the hell are you talking about?

He said with certainty, "Yes, sir. You've got blood all over your face and nose."

The A-Driver, who occupied the right front seat, also turned around and chimed in, "He's right, sir. You're fucking bleeding."

I didn't feel anything, but I took off my helmet to assess the reported damage.

It turned out that my helmet had pressed my protective eyewear down so hard, that it cut deeply into the bridge of my nose. It looked worse than it was. The Marine sitting next to me took some paper towels and wiped the blood off of my face for me, like a mother licking a napkin to wipe smeared chocolate ice cream off of her kid's face.

Marines take care of their own.

During the forty-five-minute drive to CKV, my imaginary "career reduction light" continually flashed as I thought about facing the 15th MEU CO. I had raided all three mosques when he had granted permission to raid just one. Plus, one of my Marines had shot a civilian woman. I had no plan of diluting the truth to the MEU CO.

When we arrived, I told Somerville to get the boys some chow and hit the store while I handled things with the colonel.

As I walked into the COC, I sensed the eyes of officers and men staring at me, sitting behind their computer workstations in nice, clean uniforms with cans of cold soda on their desks. I knew I looked like hell. I was completely filthy, physically and emotionally drained, not to mention severely sleep deprived, after weeks of continuous patrolling.

It bothered me a little, I suppose. They looked at me like I was some mangy animal defacing their territory. But they all knew who I was—I was the CO of Echo Company, and we'd been out in the city for weeks cleaning house. Tough shit.

A Marine I knew grabbed me and said, "Hey, Scott, man. Come here. You're bleeding, brother!" The gash on my nose had come open again without my knowledge, and blood was trickling down my face. Hindsight being what it is, I guess maybe that's why all of the Marines gawked at me.

After I got patched up, I went to see the 15th MEU operations officer, Paul Nugent. He was one of the coolest and collected guys I'd ever met, and I was glad he was willing to listen to the events before I met with the boss. I knocked on his thin door, made out of a piece of plywood, that was already half-opened. He told me to come in. His first concern was if I was OK. I told him I was fine, just tired.

He asked me about the previous night, and I explained in detail all of the decisions. Major Nugent said, "Sounds good, Scotty. I think the Colonel just wants to talk to you."

He escorted me into the CO's office. The colonel was calm. He was tall and physically fit with salt-and-pepper hair, cropped short. He spoke in a low, relaxed voice for such a large man. Everyone called him a "soft talker." I never knew if that was really his nature or just the way he made sure that everyone was actually listening to him.

I went through the events in detail with the CO. I admitted that I decided on my own to hit all three mosques based on the reliable information, and the fact I had Marines positioned ready to strike.

There was a short silence. I was certain the CO was about to drop the hammer on me for deviating from his orders.

Instead, he said, "Scott, don't worry. You did the right thing. I made the call, not you. You got it?"

"Yes, sir."

I was relieved. I felt fortunate to have such loyal leaders taking care of me. I still felt like the whole night was replaying like a movie, fast-forwarding to certain parts in my head in no specific order as a result of the sleep deprivation I was fighting off.

Colonel Beaudreault asked if there was anything I needed out in zone and told me to keep up the good work. Despite the shit-storm that I had created for my boss to deal with, his leadership that day made a distinct and lasting impression on me.

I was grateful for his understanding and support and left feeling relieved about the decision I made. My gut had been right that night, but I never liked making decisions based on that alone.

CHAPTER 24

Crush

I didn't have to be a tactical genius to figure out that if I took the weapons and ammunition out of the hands of the enemy, my Marines would get shot at less. There were still some soldiers and Marines, however, who thought that local Iraqis were entitled to keep at least one AK-47 in each home—as if keeping a fully automatic assault weapon under a bed was a birthright of all Iraqis.

Bullshit.

If any of my units raided any home or building and found weapons, the weapons came out with us. Whether or not the Iraqi National Ministry of Defense wanted to enforce the policies was a moot point to me as an operator on the ground.

Once during routine clearance operations, we found an AK-47 in the home of a frail, seventy-year-old woman with a full magazine right next to it.

I asked her, "Is this yours? Do you own this?"

She said sheepishly, "Yes."

I politely asked her to pick it up and show me how it worked and to insert the magazine.

She had no idea how to do it.

It was a known tactic from city to city in Iraq for insurgents to stash guns in as many houses as they could to use at their discretion. Therefore, an insurgent scumbag could walk around town and blend in with the locals by not toting a rifle around. If he ran into a Marine unit patrolling along he would simply duck inside a nearby house, intimidate the shit out of the residents, grab a weapon he'd hidden inside, take a few crack shots at a patrol, and ditch the rifle back in the house. He then fled out the back door and blended back in with the crowd.

We developed a tactic to deal with this.

First, we'd set up a cordon at the edges of the city or zone we operated in and establish entry control points. We'd search all vehicles and persons coming in and out, choking off their supply lines.

Second, we'd bring in the dogs. They'd sniff out any weapons caches that were buried or hidden underground, in fields, walls, cars, dumpsters, or dead animal carcasses that scattered the landscape. Trust me, if there was a place to stash weapons and ammo, the insurgents used it. They were very creative. The military working dog teams, however, were better at finding them than the insurgents were at hiding them. Advantage, us.

Third, I ordered every Marine who went out on patrol to seize every single weapon, no matter where they found it.

One day, I overheard one of the Marines humorously refer to my tactic as, "Captain Huesing's Going Out of Business Sale." He wasn't far off. Just like a used car salesman, my theory was, "Everything must go!"

If it sounds easy, it wasn't. Implementing it was even harder. My men were already carrying more than fifty pounds of gear on patrol—body armor, ammo, helmets, weapons, batteries, radios, food, and water.

We had a saying, "Ounces equal pounds and pounds equal pain."

A fully loaded AK-47 weighs more than eight pounds. Pain.

If they got into a firefight, they still had to fight their way out, and could then be carrying up to three rifles that added up to almost twenty-five extra pounds. More pain.

Nonetheless, the Marines in Echo Company embraced it. There were days when they'd bring home dozens and dozens of rifles and RPGs along with boxes of ammunition even from zones deemed "clear" by intelligence reports. The weapons continued to pile up to our collective astonishment.

By the time Echo Company slid into a routine in Rutbah, we had figured out where the hot spots of enemy activity were. I decided to take action and drafted a concept of operations and pushed it up to Major Nugent for review. Two days later, the 15th MEU approved the plan.

My concept was simple, but it required a lot of manpower and support from adjacent units. I envisioned the area to the west of Building 500 to be a "crime scene" so to speak, since that was where we'd been receiving the most frequent small arms fire over the past few weeks.

Like any good police force, we had to seal off the crime scene. We did just that.

The area we would be clearing was roughly two square kilometers, or one hundred forty football fields put together, jammed with more than two hundred houses. Streets lined with dilapidated, abandoned vehicles that were so narrow you could barely drive a compact car down them—let alone Humvees. Most of the area's residents were families with small children.

Echo Company could not stop manning our existing observation posts; therefore, we had to rely on support from other units. It was my intention to go in at dawn and cordon off the entire area. I intended to go in heavy—supported by six General Dynamics LAV-25s and twelve Humvees, mounted with heavy weapons and machine guns. We were joined by two teams of military working dogs, Human Exploitation Teams, four Terps, and medical support vehicles.

Helicopters, including Bell AH-1W Cobra attack gunships, would fly overhead and provide aerial reconnaissance and close air support. In addition to this ensemble of firepower, a platoon of over sixty dismounted Marines from Echo Company would go house-to-house and clear thoroughly.

The reinforced platoon staged for the operation at Building 500 right across the street from the zone we were about to enter. The Marines checked their gear and readied their teams. Small unit leaders reviewed the pocket-sized strip maps that detailed the zone they'd be operating in.

They were set.

Once we had communications with the Light Armored Reconnaissance crews with Chippewa, the helicopters, and the mounted patrols, we were ready. I gave the command to execute just before first light.

The massive, eight-wheeled, LAV-25s rushed into zone and assumed the high ground and major avenues of advance. Simultaneously with the mounted Humvee patrols, the LAR infantry scouts hopped out of the back of the vehicles with rolls of two-inch, white, cloth engineer tape and began to rope off the entire perimeter from vehicle to vehicle. Under cover of darkness, they stretched the cloth tape four feet off of the ground and tied it from bumper to bumper. Additional Marines from the mounted patrols covered all of the access points along the streets.

We had sealed off the crime scene, and no one would be allowed in or out.

We estimated that it would take around six hours to clear the zone once we had it sealed.

The infantry Marines reached their release points at the south end of the zone. They moved north, conducting a systematic search of every single house.

It was a laborious process. Each house took a great deal of time to clear. It took even longer if the home was occupied since we needed the Terps on site to explain what was happening and enable us to conduct tactical questioning.

If there were women alone in the house, this posed another issue. It was improper for a female to have strange men in the home without the husband or a male family member present. Some of the women had no issues with it, and they would gather up their children and sit in the kitchen while we conducted business. Some even offered us tea and bread.

I found this interesting when we operated in Rutbah. It always made me think, from a tactical perspective, that women were actually the best sources of information. They stayed at home all day. They knew the comings and goings of everyone in their neighborhoods. Not to mention they liked having the MNF around to provide security since they knew the local police weren't worth a shit when it came to protecting the common good.

I thought that we failed miserably by not having more female Terps and female Marines on patrols with us in Iraq. The Lioness program (female Marines attached to forward units) came of age late in the Iraq campaign, and was primarily designed to have female Marines at entry control points to conduct searches of women as they went through the checkpoints so as not to offend the sensitivities of anyone. I think if we'd had more female Marines supporting us on patrols the information we gathered might have been more substantial.

For the Iraqis, the experience of having their houses raided must have been unsettling at best, and terrifying at worst. We'd show up heavily armed at four o'clock in the morning and then scour every room looking for contraband.

To the average American, having his or her home raided in the fashion we conducted business would be incomprehensible—something most would only see on an episode of *Cops* and that only happens to drug lords and gangs. But that wasn't the case in Iraq. They weren't all bad people, but this was our job and how it had to be done.

I moved with the lead squad on foot, and as we progressed we continued to deplete the arsenal that the insurgents had been stashing away amongst the locals. We collected hundreds of AK-47 assault rifles, countless RPGs, and an unbelievable amount of loose ammunition.

In the end, we got shot at less, there were fewer IEDs, and the entire city was safer.

Not a bad day's work.

CHAPTER 25

Governance

It galled me to no end when I'd have to sit and listen to officers negotiate with the local sheiks or city officials in Rutbah. It was all new to me. We never dealt with it in Ramadi, at least at my level. Our mission was clear there: kill or capture the enemy.

I couldn't fathom how our military invariably got bogged down in such bureaucratic deliberations with self-appointed officials in Rutbah. Our senior officers spoke to the local officials about governance, roads, power, water, sanitation, and rebuilding—things that military officials probably didn't know much about themselves.

For over a decade in Iraq, the Marines had perfected the art of blowing things up, but had scarcely learned much, if anything, about building things up. It wasn't what we trained to do.

I don't know if our people ever stopped to think about the fact that the men with whom they had these allegedly in-depth conversations might have the equivalent of a third-grade education, at best. They knew their city, yes, but they didn't have the education to implement any of the grandiose ideas that we were proposing. They never came to fruition anyway, at least not during our time in Iraq. Maybe it was a game to make local leaders feel important, give them a sense of authority and an air of legitimacy, and get them to buy in to our presence.

It boggled my mind to think how we were ever going to get our ideas of governance and infrastructure to work. How? By trying to impose our western ethos on a culture that couldn't even manage to pick up its own trash, or refrain from shitting and pissing in the middle of public streets? How could they comprehend how to rebuild an entire city? They couldn't. Not the way we had envisioned it for them. It was a game, I suppose, to make them feel important. It gave them a sense of false authority, and it legitimized our existence in the town.

It is hard to explain the lawlessness and disorganization that pervaded the whole country. It wasn't that there weren't laws meant to govern people's actions—there were. Plenty of them. It's just that nobody seemed to care. They did what they wanted, and the barely functional police could do little to stop them.

To compound the problem, it was impossible to get a straight answer from Iraqis, whether it was from local sheiks at a meeting or from people we met on the streets during patrols. It was perfectly acceptable to lie.

They did not do it maliciously—it's just what they do. It's hard to explain and even harder for most Americans to comprehend because it was ingrained in their culture. It was a way to maintain status and prestige in their culture. There was no real way to stop it. We just had to deal with it and factor it into any discussion we had with them and any decision we made.

There was another steadfast rule in Iraq: the guy with the biggest stick won. Iraqis respected power, authority, and force. They responded to it. When we tried to transition to support and stability operations, the Iraqi Government could not grasp the concept, and it never seemed to take root—either the military was too inept at instituting it, or Iraqi politicians just didn't want any part of it.

There were times when I asked myself, "How can we possibly expect a few meetings and a boatload of platitudes about effective governance and democratic values to transform a country overnight?"

American culture is an impatient one. We want, we expect, everything right the hell now. Fast food, fast cash from ATMs, email, online shopping with next-day delivery from Amazon. Now.

We should have considered that we were dealing with a culture that had developed over thousands of years and a country and people who had no experience with government as we understood it. Instead, we expected fast government, fast stability, and fast democracy. It was American hubris at its worst.

Considering all these problems, it seemed a risky move to shift to the SASO paradigm when we did—essentially replacing the "Iron Fist" with the gentler "Velvet Glove." It was useless to try to win the support of the people, stabilize the country, and rebuild the cities without crushing the insurgency and keeping at bay countries like Iran and movements like ISIS, which had their own plans for Iraq. To do so, we should have staked a claim in the country and built permanent bases there like we did after World War II in places like Germany and Japan in order to keep the bad guys out. Politicians and senior leaders were too concerned that we might be viewed as occupiers—playing the role of the ugly Americans—rather than what we were: defenders. And the call was made to withdraw from Iraq. It's still biting us in the ass.

Friction.

■   ■   ■

2 February 2007

Colonel Beaudreault requested that I attend a local governance meeting on the west side of Rutbah. Staff Sergeant Jeromie Slaughter, the platoon sergeant for 1st Platoon, had gathered a squad to provide security for us to move to the Government Center. The movement was less than a thousand meters away from Building 500; we moved by foot. Slaughter set up the patrol route, and we stepped off early that morning to make the meeting on time.

Some of the Marines joked. "Hey, the CO is coming out with us. What do you think the chances are we get shot at today?"

The other Marines laughed.

It was their respectfully sarcastic way of reminding me of the fact any patrol I accompanied would take contact from the enemy. I'm not sure if it was dumb luck or if the insurgents actually knew who I was and wanted to take me out. Either way, it happened. It was about to happen again.

We departed from the back side of Building 500 and made our way north, skirting up Stacy's Mom, one of the streets named in jest after a trendy 2003 pop song. As we made our way up the street in a staggered column, we could see the Marines from 2nd Platoon on the rooftop of The Bank that sat to our left.

The Bank actually had been a functioning bank. It was now a prominent terrain feature on the corner of MSR Michigan and Stacy's Mom that provided superior overwatch of the city and that two of my platoons used as a firm base.

The 15th MEU commander allowed me to use The Bank on one condition: that I turn it back over to the locals in better shape than I found it in. I stressed this point on more than one occasion to the Marines in The Bank. It didn't really sink in. We provided them paint and told them to repaint the interior. They weren't in the mood to take on any do-it-yourself projects after patrolling all night, however. Incessant bitching ensued.

It was always dark and dreary inside The Bank because the thin ten-foot windows were sandbagged from top to bottom. It was crowded, too, and cots were jammed into just about every corner, nook, and cranny. The rooftop was a maze of fighting positions covered with desert camouflage netting, and intermittent walls of sandbags and old windshields from destroyed Humvees that served as protection and observation into the zone.

■　　■　　■

Days earlier I made a surprise inspection at The Bank. I stopped my vehicle convoy outside.

I told the driver, "Wait here; I'll only be a few minutes."

As I made my way inside The Bank, I asked one of the Marines where Grillo was.

He said, "Sir, I think he's upstairs on the second deck."

I made my way up trying not to grasp the handrail—it dangled loosely from the concrete wall by a few screws. I found Grillo and one of my combat engineers standing by the front wall of the building, engaged in some sort of project.

As I came closer, I saw they had placed a series of small C-4 plastic explosive charges on the wall with duct tape. The engineer was about to fuse the explosives and connect it all up with det-cord. When it went off, it would have blown a massive hole in the front of The Bank.

I motioned to Grillo to come to me. "What part of '*Leave The Bank better than we found it*' didn't you understand?"

Grillo explained that he wanted to build a better fighting position on the second deck, but the wall to which the engineer had rigged the explosives obstructed its fields of fire. It was a textbook case of what Marines refer to as, "good initiative—poor judgment."

The tactical advantage The Bank provided our company was far too valuable to lose, and I didn't want the MEU CO to evict us because we weren't good tenants.

I shut the whole project down immediately, had them remove the demolition charges, and told them never to try something like that again—ever.

■　　■　　■

As our patrol came within one hundred meters of The Bank, we began to take small arms fire from the northeast, and the Marines quickly pushed into the row of buildings that sat along Stacy's Mom. They began to return fire but they really had no idea where the shooting started. It was dangerous, but not uncommon for the Marines to return fire where they thought they had seen muzzle flashes. Doing so violated our policy of positive identification before you fired, and could have resulted in either civilians being hit or blue-on-blue casualties.

A machine gun crew on the rooftop of The Bank opened up too, spraying rounds into the buildings across the street from us. I quickly got on the radio and told them to cease fire.

When the firing abated, we emerged from the houses in which we had taken cover. The only confirmed kill we could see was a dead goat lying in the middle of Stacy's Mom, bleeding out.

I thought, "Great. We killed someone's goat. I'm going to have to pay for that too, I suppose."

Self-imposed friction.

In Rutbah, the MNF had caused so much damage that paying the locals CERF money had become routine. Every morning, they lined up outside of Building 500, knocked on the gate, and told how the Marines had damaged something they owned. We paid up in American dollars. It was like I was a walking, talking ATM—they all wanted some of the American cash that seemed to flow freely.

Heading down MSR Michigan, we noticed an unusual amount of activity on the street, mostly men congregating around the local shops, all looking at us keenly as we moved toward the Government Center.

We made security halts along the way, during which I questioned some of the locals about the firefight, hoping to get some information. No one seemed to know anything.

We approached a group of young Iraqi males. They were posturing like tough guys as we advanced. One had his hands tucked in the back of his pants, underneath a lightweight jacket he wore. He was young, maybe sixteen years old.

I told him forcefully in Arabic, *"Arini Yadaik!"* Show me your hands.

He just stood there with his gaze fixed on my Marines and me. We had our rifles at the alert but were not pointing them directly at the boys.

I repeated the command. The boy still didn't comply. Defiant. Then he bolted. To me, it confirmed he had a weapon. I shouted, *"Kiff! Kiff!"* Stop! Stop!

I instinctively took off after him. I had a habit of doing this, much to my Marines' frustration.

Lance Corporal Zach Shores followed close behind me for cover. Another veteran of the battalion's 2004 deployment to Ramadi. Shores was big—six-two and more than 200 pounds. He was scruffy and surly, and exuded a "Don't-give-a-shit-about-it" attitude most of the time. In a firefight, however, he was as dependable and as dangerous as they come—a killer.

I pursued the boy as he made it around the corner, yelling at him again to stop.

This time, he did, and then he turned to face me—his hand still in his coat. I trained my M4 on him, ready to shoot if he drew a weapon. I could see him looking around for an escape route, sensing he was about to dart into an alley.

He made a move.

I fired two shots.

Not aimed at the boy. I drilled two rounds into an air conditioner unit that was on the ground ten meters away from him in a vain effort to get him to comply. I had just violated our own policy of never firing warning shots.

The boy took off.

Shores grabbed me and said, "Sir, he's gone. Fuck him. Let him go. It was nothing. Let's get back to the squad."

As we moved back, I could still feel the effects of the adrenaline rush. I was out of breath and sweating. The men in the street looked at me coldly, scornfully.

When we made it to the Government Center several minutes later, my Marines set up a security perimeter with the others who were already on site. The place was packed. It seemed that every Iraqi and his brother were there for the meeting.

For the next hour, I sat watching the local officials arguing with our key leaders. I'm sure it was the same shit they always argued about—mindless and incessant discussions about how great the city could be if we worked as a team. It was a circus show.

I couldn't remember a word because the whole time all I thought about was that kid.

After the meeting ended, I made my way out into the courtyard. I saw Staff Sergeant Slaughter sitting on the elevated, concrete sidewalk, his feet dangling over the side. I walked over to him and sat down. I took off my helmet and stared at the ground.

Slaughter was twenty-nine years old and from Sante Fe, Texas. Married with two kids. He stood five-six. He was rough and built like a fireplug and constantly had a big, thick dip of Copenhagen snuff tobacco in his lower lip. He always had an air of seriousness about him, maybe because he was on his second combat tour in Iraq.

A sense of vulnerability and uncertainty hit me as I sat there.

Slaughter sensed it. "So, sir. How'd the meeting go?"

I said, "Same shit."

He dug deeper. "What's going on, sir? You alright?"

I didn't normally divest my emotions with the Marines, but when Slaughter asked me I felt an overwhelming need to share with him.

"Staff Sergeant, what the fuck would have happened if I had shot that kid? I don't know what I was thinking. I just can't get it out of my head. Why did I even shoot my rifle if I wasn't going to shoot him?"

Slaughter didn't hesitate to respond. "Sir, you did the right thing. It wasn't worth it either way. It's this place. It's a fuck story, and it gets to everyone. That includes you. You're good, sir."

I felt that Slaughter was right. At least that's what I wanted to believe at the time. He was, though. I thanked him for listening. He gave me a quick head nod. I told him to get the boys together and get ready to go.

That moment weighed on me for days. That young kid, cocky as he may have been, would never know how close he was to death. Either way, Slaughter and Shores were right.

I never saw the gun.

■ ■ ■

Later that week, on the morning of 7 February to be precise, I led a patrol with one of the squads in 1st Platoon. It was routine. We kept an eye out for suspicious activity. We met with the locals. I handed out Tootsie Roll candies to the kids that I kept in a small pouch that I had attached to my gear. We were back in Building 500 after a couple of hours.

When we entered the compound, I saw a group of 15th MEU command element vehicles parked out back. My first reaction was, "What did we fuck up today?" It was my gut reaction whenever higher command showed up unannounced to our position.

I walked inside the house and made my way up the stairs to the COC on the second floor

When I came to the top of the stairs, I saw Colonel Beaudreault standing at the large table in my COC.

He turned to me with a solemn look on his face, and said, "Scott, I'm not sure if you've heard yet, but Sergeant Major Ellis was killed this morning in Barwana."

It felt as if someone punched me in the stomach. I couldn't breathe. I felt dazed.

Colonel Beaudreault explained that Ellis and some others had been killed at an Entry Control Point (ECP) in Barwana by a suicide bomber.

■ ■ ■

The 2d Battalion, 4th Marines, staff had gone down to the ECP in the morning to promote a Marine from Golf Company that day.

The battalion headquarters and three other companies worked in Barwana, two hundred miles northeast of Rutbah, conducting operations to secure the area. They'd been there for several months and had not encountered any heavy fighting, only sporadic small arms fire from time to time, punctuated by an occasional mortar attack.

The insurgents must have been conducting surveillance on the ECP for weeks in order to see if there was a moment when the Marines might let their guard down—gauging their reactions and looking for an opportunity to strike. They were always watching. We knew that.

They probably figured out fast that if they tried to attack in a conventional fashion with rifles, RPGs, and mortars, they surely would have had their asses handed to them tenfold. They would need to attack in a different way if they wanted to be sure to make their mark. They chose a suicide bomber.

They'd studied the routines of the Marines at the ECP, and, when they saw the large entourage that was the battalion staff gather at the ECP, they must have figured that someone important was there. Sensing an opportunity, they made their move.

The ECP sat on the east side of the Euphrates River on the south end of Barwana. The ECP wasn't much, just an old building reinforced with rows of sand-filled HESCO barriers. The rows formed lines for pedestrians to walk through, long lanes constructing a security checkpoint like those at an airport. The locals would walk through—men in one lane, women in another—and be searched at stations set up along the lanes. Female Marines searched the women in order to avoid offending cultural sensitivities. It was crude, but it was effective.

On this day, it was all routine—until it wasn't.

Without warning, there was a flash. Dark, gray dust billowed up followed by a deafening explosion. Sand and debris fell around the ECP, on top of the barriers and those standing close by.

Ellis, who had been talking to some Marines close to where the bomb went off, was killed instantly.

Another Marine and a Terp also died. One Marine from Golf Company lost both of his legs in the attack. Others were severely wounded.

When the quick reaction force responded to the scene, it was already too late. It was a horrific aftermath.

It would have been much worse had the bomber not made an error. He had detonated his vest just before the search point. The HESCO barriers, therefore, absorbed most of the blast and the shrapnel that followed—limiting its path of intended destruction. Had the bomber made it much further through the checkpoint that day, his bomb could have killed or wounded dozens more people.

A few weeks later, a patrol led by Captain Scott Gehris, the commander of Weapons Company, came across a weapons cache. I knew Gehris well. We shared a stateroom on the *Boxer*. From Bowers, Pennsylvania, he had a stoic demeanor. When he did manage to smile—and that wasn't often—it was just out of the corner of his mouth.

Among the contraband they confiscated was a fanny pack that lay near some explosives and some monofilament line. After they had confiscated the cache, Gehris and his men figured out how the bomb that had killed Ellis and the others was constructed.

The bomb maker had loaded the fanny pack full of explosives and projectiles, such as ball bearings and nails. They fused the device inside the fanny pack that fastened around the bomber's waist and tied the fishing line to the detonators at one end and his elbows at the other. When the killer arrived at the search point, he would, as instructed, raise his arms. Doing so would pull the line taut and trigger the detonators.

■   ■   ■

I couldn't believe Ellis was gone. He was an amazing Marine. I loved talking to him, and I did every chance I got. Throughout my entire career, I classified Sergeants Major in one of two ways: the great and the average. Ellis was one of the great ones. I was not alone in my assessment. Everyone in Echo Company and the rest of 2d Battalion, 4th Marines, admired and loved him.

Making his death all the more painful was the fact that Ellis was on his final deployment. He'd made no bones about his plan to retire after we returned home.

My Marines acted differently after that day. On patrol, they were edgy and more cautious, especially around the locals. Each of them must have thought if it could happen to our senior enlisted leader, it could happen to anyone.

CHAPTER 26

Wreckage

It was a strange day. The sky was overcast as rain came down sporadically when a fourteen-man squad from Nicholson's platoon went out on a dismounted security patrol.

Nicholson was with the patrol. Most leaders, including myself, made it a point to go out on at least one patrol, if not more, during the day in order to gauge the atmospherics of the town and to see how our Marines were performing.

I'd often get strange looks from other Marines when I'd tell them I'd go out on patrols with my Marines. In response, they'd delve into stories about how their COs had "never left the FOB" or never came out from behind their computers. I always took these stories with a grain of salt—maybe these guys had an ax to grind with their COs—but if there was an ounce of truth to the stories, I found it detestable.

I have an unequivocal distaste toward any commander who would not lead his Marines from the front. It seemed an abrogation of the heavy responsibilities of leadership and an insult to his Marines, as if sharing in the dangers they faced was somehow beneath him. I always felt it was my place to be with my Marines. Even more so, I felt privileged to be with them. I like to think they welcomed it, too. Nicholson was cut from the same bolt of cloth in this regard.

The men in that patrol later said that they felt uneasy that day as they walked slowly in a staggered formation along MSR Michigan. It was one of the busiest streets in town, but there was very little traffic. The number of cars parked along the road seemed too numerous.

All but three Marines in the patrol had turned west with the main element. They had stopped short to check the rear, or six o'clock position, of the formation.

Lance Corporal Raymond Bowen joined the Marines from his hometown in Joliet, Illinois, at nineteen. His parents, brothers, and sisters were so proud of him when he joined, but like many families, they were nervous he was heading to Iraq. Bowen was a SAW gunner with 2nd Squad, 2nd Platoon, and this was his first deployment.

When he joined the Marines, I don't think he ever expected he'd have to make such life-changing decisions.

Bowen was at the tail end of the patrol when he noticed a light-colored, four-door sedan speeding up toward the formation, going about thirty to forty miles per hour. Iraqis knew when Marines were on the road they had to slow down and wait for us to signal them to pass. For some reason, this car was not slowing down.

The Marines began to wave their arms at the vehicle that was now no more than one hundred meters away, motioning for it to stop.

They yelled, "*Kiff! Kiff!*" Stop! Stop!

The vehicle continued to close in on their position. The Marines now trained their weapons on the front of the car. It continued to speed forward.

With the vehicle showing no sign of stopping, just a few car lengths away, Bowen feared for his life and his fellow Marines. He looked through the sights of his SAW, aimed at the car's grille, and squeezed the trigger. A quick rip and a bright muzzle flash from the barrel of the SAW erupted, and the car came to a screeching halt short of where Bowen stood. The driver made a quick U-turn and sped off.

Nicholson heard the loud, distinctive gunfire from the SAW at the rear of his patrol and moved quickly to gain better situational awareness.

Nicholson's attention was drawn to a group of Iraqi men standing near the corner of a building not far from where Bowen now stood. The men were yelling frantically. Their apoplectic shouting became more panicked as they stood over a wounded man. They motioned to the others.

Nicholson quickly ordered the patrol to form a 360-degree defensive perimeter and took some of his Marines over to the group of agitated men. His heart sank as he saw what they were standing around: a young Iraqi man, no more than twenty years old, lying in the street. He had been hit in the head by a bullet.

Bowen couldn't force himself to look at the scene. He posted outward for security, already assuming the worst.

Nicholson immediately called for his Corpsman, HM3 Nate "Doc" Dicks. Lance Corporal Christopher Muscle, a combat aidsman, also rushed over to provide medical care. They placed the man into the bed of a pickup truck that sat close and began to examine him. Part of his skull was missing, and blood pooled rapidly in the grooves in the bed of the truck.

As Doc Dicks checked the man for any other wounds, Muscle reached into his medical bag and pulled out an airway tube which he slid carefully into the patient's mouth. As Dicks and Muscle worked on the man, Nicholson got on the radio and called for an urgent CASEVAC to fly the patient to the shock trauma facility located at CKV.

When the team arrived, they rushed the patient to the helicopter-landing zone at TCP 2 and loaded him into the back of a U.S. Army H-60 helicopter for the flight.

Forty minutes later, when the man arrived at the shock trauma center, the medics pronounced him dead on arrival. Later, Doc and Muscle told Nicholson that what had happened was what Bowen feared: the man had been struck by one of Bowen's bullets, which had ricocheted off the speeding car. The errant bullet had hit the man in the front of his head, causing massive damage. There was nothing anyone could have done to save him.

Hours later, his grieving father was paid the Diya, a condolence payment for the accidental death of his son. It was $2,500. He took it willingly and went on his way.

After returning to The Bank with the other members of 2nd Squad, Bowen ran through the incident in his mind. He knew that, because he had squeezed the trigger, the man's death was his responsibility. He was despondent that the man was dead, but he was certain that he had done the right thing. He had been protecting his squad from a clear threat, a speeding car that would not stop. The sheer randomness of it bewildered him. The ricochet could have just as easily hit a building or the ground.

But it didn't.

Despite the dark cloud of grief that hung over him, Bowen continued to go on patrols and do his job. None of the other Marines ever asked him about the incident. They knew how difficult it must have been for him, what a burden it had to be to bear.

After that day, Bowen didn't remember any other patrols.

But this was one he'd never forget.

Despite the fact that we paid the dead man's father $2,500, there is no price you can put on a human life. I know this. I never look back and think about how much more training we could have given the Marines to avert these tragedies, because we did. We trained. We ran scenarios. Shoot. Don't shoot. We held classes. We did our best with the time we had.

The bottom line is that war is a tough, uncertain business, and bad things happen to everyone involved even with the best-laid plans.

It's never clean.

I'll never think that the lives of the innocent men and women of Iraq who died in the crossfire of that war didn't matter. They did. They meant something to me. They meant much more to the families they left behind.

Many Iraqi locals were decent and kind to us as we disrupted their way of life. I guess they figured it was the price they'd have to pay for us helping them out. They gave us small cups of black spiced chai when we were cold. They generously fed us stacks of Iraqi flatbread they cooked in large clay ovens. It was dry and flavorless, but the closest thing to home cooking we had at times. Many willingly gave us information to help fight the insurgents whom they desperately wanted us to kill so the madness around them would end.

Despite the kindnesses that many showed to us, the Qur'an advocates "an eye for an eye." It dominates Arab culture. It bothered me because it meant that there was always the potential for retribution.

There were dreadful thoughts that went through my mind after something like that happened—especially while we were still fighting. Although I knew the event constituted a tragedy, I asked myself, "Was the man who died shooting at me days earlier? Was he innocent or an insurgent? Did his family use the condolence payment to buy weapons to fight against us in retaliation?"

At the end of the day, I buried those thoughts deep inside for another time. I had a job to do.

■ ■ ■

Weeks later, Echo Company Marines shot at another moving vehicle. Three men drove their car down the alleyway behind Building 500 without their lights on. This was a violation of curfew, and it was curious for them to be driving so slowly—and with no lights.

The Marines opened fire, putting several well-aimed shots through the windshield of their car.

A quick reaction squad moved quickly on foot after the shots rang out, swarming the vehicle.

Of the three men inside, only the driver had been shot. Two 5.56mm rounds had grazed his right shoulder. He bled mildly and winced in pain as the Corpsman treated the two long gashes across his arm with an antiseptic.

We detained them and turned them over to our interrogators from HET. The men were shady, and the Marines were well within their rights under the ROE to engage the vehicle. Turned out the men were on the command's wanted list. The Marines made the right call that night.

■　　■　　■

Our departure date from Iraq was finally announced. We would begin turning over our battlespace in Rutbah with 1st Battalion, 2d Marines. We were ordered to turn over Building 500 to its rightful owner and were told to make sure it was in top shape before we left for CKV.

We didn't.

It was a significant—and oddly emotional—event rooting out three months' worth of trash, gear, sandbags, equipment, radios, and all our personal gear from Building 500. We filled in the hole behind it with everything we didn't need—gear, dirty uniforms, trash, shit, torn cammie netting—then we set it on fire. Flames from it reached high into the night sky as we departed. The 15th MEU TOC came across the net and advised us that there was a huge fire in our zone.

The radio operator blurted without a verbal filter before replying, "Yeah, no shit, it's our fire." Then, he keyed the handset, acknowledged the message, and politely let them know it was ours.

For the most part, the Marines were ready to go, but they also had become accustomed to living so close together, under such austere conditions, for so long, that the reality took a while to sink in. After being extended on the deployment twice already, they braced for the impact of another letdown. This time, however, there would be no letdown.

We were headed home.

CHAPTER 27

Liberty

As we cruised home, there were no gratuitous stories of killing or destruction or death. I suppose I expected to overhear the Marines telling stories of the fighting, filled with bravado—but they were relatively absent from conversations and routine shipboard gossip. I think most of us had already begun tucking away what we had seen and done. No one was ready to talk about it.

■   ■   ■

Everyone was excited to get home. The loud whooshing of the Navy's Landing Craft Air Cushion (LCAC) hovercraft as they lumbered onto concrete ramps at Kuwaiti Naval Base was deafening. They kicked up sand and blew saltwater mist in our faces. We didn't care. We wanted to get aboard and start the trip back home. When we boarded, we saw that the crew of the ship, who had been floating around for almost nine months waiting for us, had draped "Welcome Home" banners all over the ship. It was uplifting to know that our naval brethren felt this way about us.

Our ride back to the States would be a long one—five weeks. We worked out in the gym on the ship. We slept until we were hungry and ate until we were sleepy. There really wasn't much else to do. Unlike other combat deployments where I flew home, I was grateful to be locked away at sea for weeks on end. It allowed me to decompress. I think it did the same for a lot of the Marines.

■   ■   ■

We stopped in Perth, Australia, as our first liberty port. Most of the commanders and senior staff braced for impact, expecting a flood of liberty incidents: drunkenness, fighting, and run-ins with local authorities.

To our astonishment, during our three days in port, we didn't have a single incident. I was never able to put my finger on the source of this strange anomaly of good behavior. Maybe most were so keen to get home that they weren't willing to jeopardize it by committing some half-cocked antics in a foreign country. Either way, we were proud of their conduct and fortunate not to have to deal with the headache of sorting out any troublemakers.

The ESG continued to sail on to Hawaii where we made another port call. A week later, we were off the coast of southern California. Echo Company boarded the helicopters and flew off the *Boxer* and landed at Camp Pendleton—eager to greet our families after a deployment we'd never forget.

■   ■   ■

As we flew off the ship, I thought that all the battles and the bloodshed were in our wake. I could not have been more wrong.

CHAPTER 28

Tribute

Marines die in combat. It is inevitable. But the inevitability of death does not make it any less painful, any easier to accept. Every day, I remember that men I knew are now gone. Gone forever—and there is nothing that anyone can do to change that.

Since 2004, I have had to attend more memorial services than I care to remember. I respect those who choose a life of faith, but I have never been deeply religious as an adult. Perhaps this combination has left me looking at things through a different lens.

As I sit during memorial services, I don't fantasize the dead are looking down on me or are keeping me safe. Nor do I think that angels lift the deceased to Heaven during the eulogy.

I'm unmoved by the usual stage at the memorial services—the upside-down rifles, suede combat boots, aluminum dog tags, and Kevlar helmets—but the somber expressions of grieving parents and heartwrenching faces of crying spouses and children break my heart. It is then that I'm on the verge of tears and find myself consciously looking away, trying to think of something mundane. I count the smooth rivets on the airplane parked conspicuously nearby or try to identify the state flags on display as they wave gently in the wind. I felt like an asshole at times for not paying attention to the service or worse, not allowing myself to grieve like everyone else.

But that's how I dealt with it.

I think about parents who have to bury their kids and children who now have to go through life without a parent. I know that receiving a folded flag and a loved one's medals help provide closure to these Marines' families. Whenever I see a commander doing that, I can only think what a horrible, heartbreaking moment that is.

That is the haunting reality that stays with me.

■   ■   ■

June 2007

The Marines of Echo Company and the rest of the battalion prepared to greet our Gold Star families that were traveling to southern California for our final memorial service.

Corporal Brian McKibben drove from Camp Pendleton to San Diego International Airport with his platoon sergeant, Staff Sergeant Jeromie Slaughter. During the forty-five-minute drive, they tried to figure out what the hell to say or talk about with the Matus family when they picked them up.

At the security checkpoint, the TSA agents made them both remove the medals from their uniforms. They were setting off the sensors, they explained. McKibben and Slaughter placed their medals into a crappy little plastic dish commonly reserved for wristwatches, cell phones, pocket change, and jewelry.

Slaughter was infuriated at the lack of respect the inspectors afforded them. And he was right: it was the ultimate insult to men who had just returned from combat, purging the world of so many insurgent scumbags.

McKibben was anxious about meeting Donna and Gary Matus. Would they want to know all of the details about their son's death? What do I tell them? How am I going to react? He was at a loss to answer any of those questions.

Slaughter's mind and heart raced at the prospect of talking to the family. He became almost breathless thinking about what he would say. He thought, "What would I want someone to tell my parents if it was me?"

Both men's worries vanished the moment the Matus family walked out of the gate and into the airport. They instantly took to Slaughter and McKibben and greeted them affectionately as if the two Marines were members of their family.

McKibben and Slaughter were relieved that they talked more about Matus's childhood—and told many funny stories about him as a kid—than they did about their son's death.

There was a moment when McKibben described, in part, what took place that day on the roof of Building 500. "Matus took a bullet for me that day," he said. The family never pressed him for more details.

■   ■   ■

The battalion held an elaborate party at the beach at Camp Del Mar aboard Camp Pendleton the day before the formal memorial service. It was organized by the City of San Clemente, which had adopted our battalion, and it was magnificent. Food trucks and tents, drinks, giveaways, prizes, kids' activities, you name it, we got it. The city came out in full support. I was awestruck at the willingness of complete strangers to give so much to help us on that special day.

I saw the Sanchez family immediately. You couldn't miss them.

Forty-two members of his tribe traveled together from New Mexico to southern California to attend the service. They all wore white T-shirts that had a picture of Emilian on the front. I introduced myself to his mom and dad, David and Jennie Sanchez. It was hard for me when I walked up to them, not knowing exactly what to say. They were being swarmed by the other Marines, and I almost felt as if I was in their way. But we spoke. They smiled and were happy to be surrounded by their son's friends—the Marines he fought and died for that day in Iraq.

I saw Judd Libby, Corporal Libby's father, out of the corner of my eye and made my way over to him. He tightened his lips and nodded his head in approval to let me know it was OK as I approached him.

He asked if I minded going on a walk.

We moved slowly away from the crowd, toward the surf. I was certain about what Judd was going to ask. I was ready. Emotionally, I had been through so much that day, but there was no doubt that I had to be there for him, whatever his questions were.

Judd asked me about 6 December. He wanted to know what happened. He was not probing, just curious about the unknown. I told him the important details about that night and was honest about how bravely his son fought.

We headed back toward the crowd. Judd walked casually with his hands in his pockets, looking down at the packed wet sand as the ocean rolled onto the beach. He asked me, "Can you tell me if he suffered?"

I turned to him and said without hesitation, "No, he didn't suffer."

That day on the beach was one of many essential steps in the healing process for us. It's a process that never really stops, however.

■　　■　　■

15 June 2007

It was a warm, sunny day when the Magnificent Bastards of 2d Battalion, 4th Marines, honored our fallen brothers. We held the last memorial at Camp San Mateo, a smaller camp aboard Camp Pendleton, on the elaborately decorated parade ground behind our battalion command post. It was lined with all fifty state flags that ruffled slightly in the wind as it blew through the base of the mountains surrounding the camp. Aluminum bleachers were set up to accommodate the hundreds of attendees.

We had the customary memorial displays. Eight dressed wooden pedestals with eight upside-down M16-A4 rifles, their bayonets thrust into a sandbag at the bottom, holding them tight. Combat boots sat at the base of each pedestal with a camouflage-covered Kevlar helmet on top of the buttstock of each rifle. Dog tags of each Marine dangled over the rifles' pistol grips. Every pedestal had a hand-drawn, charcoal portrait of the eight Marines that died on our deployment in 2006 and 2007. Three were from Echo Company.

The tribute we paid to our fellow Marines that day was a fitting ceremony. After the oral homages, music played softly over the speaker system as the crowd filtered slowly out from the bleachers.

Marines were the first to gravitate to the eight battlefield crosses on display. Individually or in groups of three or four, they stood before the memorials and placed their palms on the tops of the helmets that rested on the rifles. Some reached down and gently rubbed the aluminum dog tags between their thumbs and forefingers—pressing the tags into their palms.

Some wept.

Other Marines swarmed around their broken comrades, wrapping their arms around their backs, supporting each other and trying to fight off their own tears. Some of the Marines stood paralyzed by emotion in front of the pedestals, unable to leave.

I watched from afar at first. Then, I felt compelled to rush to the men and hug them myself. Heat and emotion welled up inside me, and I blinked hard to fight back the tears. I sniffed sharply and swallowed against the tightening muscles in my throat. I was heartbroken, too.

Watching my Marines in pain was hard.

I had always tried to safeguard them from the danger and pain during our time in Iraq, but there was nothing I could do now to protect them from this.

The Marines lingered at the memorials for a while and were given respect from the families and friends that watched this immense display of affection and loyalty.

As they had while we were in Iraq, the families supported us that day, even though our job was to be there for them. I am sure seeing us so vulnerable hit them hard in contrast to the hard-charging warriors they watched go off to war. They descended upon us with hugs and support as we stood there weakened by our grief.

They put their arms around us, still saying, "It's all right."

The kindness of the families overwhelmed me. Some touched me gently on my back as they brushed past compassionately. Comforting me. I felt comfort. I felt as if I were immersed in a large pool, floating in warm, gentle water as the Marines and families moved around me. It was their love and support that surrounded me.

■ ■ ■

I still keep in touch with all of the families of the men I lost. I ordinarily call around Memorial Day. Some of the other Echo Marines call on Mother's Day or at Christmas time. We know they are still hurting, and we want to let them know we are still thinking about them and their Marines.

Sometimes, before calling, the boys have dulled their own pain with too much liquor, but the families always answer and listen. They know how inextricably linked the Marines are to their sons and always will be.

The families like staying connected to the Marines, too. It gives them comfort knowing that the Marines are still thinking about them.

We will forever be a part of an irreplaceable family.

CHAPTER 29

Risk

After all of the bloodshed and pain everyone endured over a decade in Iraq, I hoped that the closing chapters of this story would provide a happy ending of sorts. I envisioned writing the final parts after a ten-year reunion trip I planned to take in 2016 with my interpreter, Big Sam, and a few other Marines. We'd walk the ground we fought on a decade before, reminisce about the firefights we had endured, and take a moment to honor the Marines we lost.

I imagined writing success stories about how the cities had improved and how democracy was flourishing. I would provide "then and now" photos of streets once cluttered with piles of trash and rubble and charred vehicles that were now clean and clear and full of traffic, proof that life had come back to the cities and the people were thriving.

All of this—the democracy, the prosperity, the thoughts of a new Ramadi and a restored Iraq—was only a pipedream.

Instead, darker echoes resonated through Ramadi and Al Anbar Province. In May 2015, the city fell to the Islamic State in Syria (ISIS) and other radicals who imposed a reign of terror on the city.

I don't think that too many of us were heartbroken about the unfolding events in Ramadi and Iraq as a whole; many of those who fought there weren't really surprised. I think we almost anticipated it in fact because the United States was unwilling to establish a permanent presence in Iraq.

Often, I get asked what I think about the situation in Iraq in general, and the rise of ISIS specifically. I dismiss out of hand any rhetoric about "hitting the reset button" on the Middle East and how the solution to ISIS is to bomb Iraq into a "glass factory."

There are so many decent and kind Iraqis who want to lead a normal life that it's not fair to punish them because ISIS or any radical Islamist faction seems to represent the country as a whole. They don't.

I usually tell people that what has happened in Ramadi and Al Anbar Province over the past few years is a stark reminder of why we should have stayed in Iraq. I also say that what those of us who served struggled with then and now was the fact that we never really understood the political strategy that the United States was pursuing and the political endgame it was trying to achieve. It would have been nice to have something simple laid out, so we could have told ourselves and our families, "Yeah, this is what we are fighting for, this is what we're out here to do…" and either we succeeded at it or we failed.

But to date, I have never really had a metric for success of our purpose in Iraq. I suppose the only metric I have for myself is that I brought as many Marines back home safely with me as I possibly could.

■   ■   ■

Sadly, the dark echoes of our time in Iraq still resonate with many of Echo Company, who battle with the effects of post-traumatic stress (PTS). Including me.

I never refer to it as a disorder.

A good friend of mine, Charles Adam Walker, taught me that. He wrote an article called "Postcombat Residue" in the December 2013 issue of the *Marine Corps Gazette*. It shaped the way I look at PTS today.

Adam uses a prophetic analogy, likening the effects and residue of combat to those on a stained, well-used coffee mug. Indelibly tainted, yet still capable of performing its intended use day in and day out—but the residue will always remain.

■   ■   ■

I thrived on a lifestyle of high-risk behavior since I was a kid. I loved to live on the edge most times.

I never hesitated to take a dare or perform a ridiculous stunt. I was jumping off the high dive at age four. I played BB gun wars with my neighbors. My first car in high school was a Yamaha sport motorcycle. I used to race it fast, going over 145 miles per hour on occasions on abandoned sections of freeway in Illinois. I fought. I ran from the cops. I drank at parties. I skipped school. I fought some more.

Being in the Marines seemed to be a natural fit. They were the biggest group of risk-takers I'd ever met.

I always sought out the risk and adventure even when I wasn't in combat. When I was a lance corporal, I jumped eighty-five feet off a ship into the Red Sea just for fun. I climbed rocks. I fought. I still rode a motorcycle. We'd go out into the desert and shoot guns. I drank with the other Marines and officers. Sometimes we'd drink and shoot guns. It was a totally acceptable lifestyle. Mine was pale in comparison to some.

No one ever thinks it will catch up to you.

■   ■   ■

July 2011

I was at my computer in my house in San Marcos, California, when suddenly my skin buzzed, and my entire body became hot and flushed. I began to tremble. My vision narrowed and the room began to close in around me. I stood up from my chair and nearly fell over. My left arm began to hurt.

I said to my seven-year-old daughter in the other room, "If Daddy falls down, I want you to call 911, OK?" She was terrified but stood alert. I knew she would do it.

I stumbled into the living room and called my wife at work. I told her to call 911. I thought I was having a stroke or a heart attack. I had no idea what was going on.

Within minutes, the paramedics arrived. The team began to take my vitals and hooked me up to a mobile EKG machine. The warm pressure that had overtaken me subsided a bit. My vitals were strong.

The left side of my face drooped. I couldn't make a smile or raise my left eyebrow. I was sure I'd had a stroke. I was forty. The medics calmly informed that what I was going through was a panic attack.

When my wife came home, the paramedics were packing their gear up. They told her to drive me to the emergency room.

We drove south on Interstate 5 to the Balboa Naval Medical Center in San Diego. The rush came over me again in the car. My breathing was short. I felt pressure all around me. I leaned forward and placed my face close to the air conditioning vent on the dashboard, sucking in the cool air. My wife called the emergency room at Balboa and told them we were ten minutes away.

The team at the ER ran brain scans, heart scans, EKGs, EEGs and everything else they could. The attending doctors told me I had suffered an anxiety attack, and Bell's Palsy had caused my face to droop. They said it would get better. Within three or four days, it did. They gave me some sedatives to calm me down. They helped.

Two days later, I pulled my Jeep over to the side of the freeway while driving to work. It was happening again. A ringing sensation started all around me, accompanied by an overwhelming sense of pressure. I didn't want to black out on the highway, so I pulled over to the shoulder of the road and took a couple of the pills the ER doctors had prescribed for me. I waited it out for twenty minutes, enough time for the pills to kick in.

I'd have several more episodes like that over a few months and then nothing. I was back to normal. The doctors said it was stress related.

They said it was my body trying to tell me to slow down from the life-style of fast-paced, risky behavior I relished. I didn't listen.

I still took pills to calm my nerves, mostly when I knew I'd be in a big crowd or an unfamiliar place. I was already taking pills for the pain in my neck. I had to have emergency spinal surgery in 2008 to repair two damaged cervical discs that had ruptured and impinged on my spinal cord as a result of my fall on 6 December 2006 at ECP 8. Two more spinal surgeries followed, in addition to the litany of steroid injections I got from the Navy doctors who used me like a human voodoo-doll.

Sometimes I'd kick-start the pills with a glass of vodka or Scotch. I'd ignored the pain for years before the surgery, numbing it with the meds and booze. Why stop now? I kept taking risks I didn't need to. I raced my motorcycle at high speeds often under the effects of the pills and somehow made it back home in one piece. I took different pills to put me to sleep once I got there.

Everything I took was prescribed from the U.S. Navy and my doctors. Most of the time, I was away from my wife. I was on deployment or stationed away from home, and only came home on the weekends. She never really saw the pattern.

It caught up with me.

■　　■　　■

I came to. Dazed. All of the airbags in my brand-new Jeep had deployed. There was a strange chemical smell around me. Yellowish dust covered the inside of the car. I tried to exit; I couldn't move out of the seat. The Jeep sat buried, nose-first, in a rocky drainage ditch on the opposite side of the road. I had crossed over the double-yellow lines on a sharp curve at 0200 hours. My Jeep was totaled. I was lucky to be alive and uninjured.

In my drunken, drug-induced state, I apparently had the muscle memory to put on my seatbelt. It had saved my life.

It was the day after Christmas. I had poured glasses of single malt Scotch down my throat all day. I kept drinking when I went to a party alone later that night. Had more pills. There was a rowdy group there—hardcore bikers and fighters. They were all a good ten or fifteen years younger than me. I wrestled with one in the front yard. It wasn't much of a match, but I loved the feeling. The challenge. The risk.

None of them stopped me from getting behind the wheel. None of them were Marines. I lived less than two miles away. I could make it. No problem.

I managed to dial the phone. My wife arrived within minutes and pulled me out of the car and took me home before the cops showed up. A passerby had called the cops anyway when they saw the Jeep smashed in the ditch. My buddies tried to tow it out before they showed up.

I sat at home—a complete mess—while my wife went back to the scene of the accident. The rest of my family was fast asleep—they never even knew the cops had shown up and brought my wife home. She'd talked them out of giving me a ticket that night—giving them a pitch about me being a disabled veteran and combat Marine. A miracle. I vaguely remember talking to them and thanking them in my driveway, spilling a cup of hot coffee as I slurred my gratitude to the officers.

My wife dragged me into the house to my bedroom. I was so fucking hammered. I rambled on incoherently until I passed out. I think it was the only time she ever saw me come to tears. I don't even want to know what I said to her that night. I'm thankful she never told me.

There are plenty of Marines who will say how stupid I was for doing that. I was. There are plenty of Marines who will say they never drink and drive. Some don't. I never really did, not like that night. But most do and just haven't been caught. I was lucky. Nothing more.

After that, I didn't touch a drop of alcohol. I was physically averse to it after the accident that nearly killed me, or worse, that could have killed someone else. Aside from having a sore abdomen and shoulder from where the seatbelt caught me, the biggest pain was the shame. It washed over me. It still does. I have never been more ashamed of anything I have ever done more than what I did that night.

It had caught up to me.

I don't have nightmares. I don't lament over the dead bodies or graphic scenes of war. The killing.

It's not the gunfire, or firefights, or any of that stuff for me.

It's the friction.

It has been a part of my entire adult life. But the friction is relatively absent now in the physical sense that it had been in combat. I function well. At least I think I do. I don't sleep much. I don't drink. I exercise fanatically and follow a strict diet to maintain my fitness level. I'm probably just more centered now with everything else orbiting me.

But it's there, and I don't even know it. Most of the time.

CHAPTER 30

Unseen

Many events—not necessarily limited to combat or war—cause PTS. Some veterans who have experienced the most terrifying and gruesome facets of combat are often the most affected. They fall into a higher percentage of those dealing with PTS through their experiences.

Especially grunts.

There are plenty of guys on active duty with PTS right now. I was one. They can be compared to high-functioning alcoholics. They have a problem but get through the day without being found out. They're still great Marines. They still do their jobs. They're successful.

They push it to the side.

There are others who discount it or, worse, ignore it. Some believe it's only a problem that "the weak of mind" experience or concoct as excuses to justify their quick tempers or explain their lack of concentration. Some posture as if they're impervious to it. They can dismiss it all they want. But it's there. And it catches up to you one way or another.

Combat is strange, chaotic, and sometimes an exhilarating experience—all wrapped up in one, at times. I would go into situations that were so volatile and dynamic on the battlefield that I rarely thought about the worst outcome—but they happened. I pressed forward vigilantly in my mission to help others, or destroy those that opposed it. I did this with the safety of my fellow Marines surrounding me, like a giant, yet lethal, protective bubble, guarding me. Every Marine took care of one another as their main concern.

For some, it is often a challenge to deal with the fact that when they return home that "protective bubble" is no longer around them physically. It creates a sense of vulnerability, abandonment, loneliness, and anxiety for some. Marines miss the brotherhood, too.

It manifests itself in many ways. Some drink and do drugs. Some overeat. Some seclude themselves. Others check the locks on their doors at night three or four times before going to bed. They sleep with loaded weapons. The list is endless. Whatever form it takes, they are looking for a way to insulate themselves in the absence of that bubble.

Marines will always have a calling. They'll away have a sense of duty and courage to run toward danger when others run from it. It's cliché, but true.

Marines, especially, still find themselves on edge in the absence of danger. They're programmed for life in some cases to protect, fight, and remain alert, even when there is a limited threat. Their minds are still telling them they are living on the edge.

For some, it is too much to cope with.

■　　■　　■

2 November 2015

Shortly after midnight, local police were called to the scene of what appeared to be a single-vehicle collision on a cold night in Minnesota. A car had veered off the road and slammed into a tree. When they arrived, what the police discovered was not what they had expected. There was much more to the story. Simon Litke sat in the driver's seat. He had shot himself in the head.

The paramedics rushed him to the local hospital. It was too late.

Litke had gone out earlier in the night. He had some drinks with friends—and then a few more. He'd even texted some of the Echo Company Marines minutes before. There were no indicators to his family or friends as he drove down that dark road. No one imagined it would unfold the way it did.

Tragically, less than seven years after leaving the Marines at the age of thirty, Litke took his own life after battling with the effects of post-traumatic stress (PTS). He was trying to cope like so many do with drugs and alcohol, trying to fight off the demons that haunted him and all that his mind could never "un-see."

We'd lost Lance Corporal Andrew Marrari the same way in 2009. He was only twenty-four at the time.

On the plane to Minneapolis, Minnesota, to attend Litke's memorial service, I held back my personal emotions and unsubstantiated contempt as I sat there. I thought about all the passengers—lemmings packed on that plane around me—random, unknown people—concerned about getting their complimentary snacks and what the in-flight movie was going to be. They had no idea how good they had it. They would never begin to understand the sacrifices of men like Litke and everything he had gone through, both in and out of the Marines.

It was groundless disdain, but it welled up inside of me.

13 November 2015

It was a clear Friday afternoon when friends, family, and more than eighty Marines from Echo Company gathered and stood in the crisp, thirty-five-degree Fahrenheit weather outside the American Legion Post for Litke's memorial service. In total, there were more than four hundred people there that day to honor Litke and his warrior spirit.

I was planning to speak at the service but hadn't prepared any words.

I wasn't sure what I would say. The pain and emptiness of it all left me at a loss.

I struggled.

Instead, I pulled a piece of paper from my coat and unfolded it as I stood on the stage in front of the crowd of fellow Marines, strangers, and his grieving parents. It was an essay Corporal Litke had written on his way back from Iraq. I made all the Marines write one. Originally, I only planned on giving a copy of it to his mom and dad.

I decided to read what Litke had written:

Combat Essay by Corporal Simon Litke, 2007

It wouldn't do my squad justice to say that one story, good or bad, is all that I could come up with for this story. First, I'd have to say that it gave me great satisfaction to watch my squad excel during our time in Iraq. To see the Marines come together as a team as well as on their own is all I could have ever asked for as a leader; all that any leader can.

I mulled it over in my mind for hours before I decided what to write about. This is one of the proudest moments as a squad leader that I can remember. In the early morning hours of January 21, 2007, and our first day in Building 500 in Ar Rutbah, Iraq.

I was awoken [sic] after only an hour or so of sleep to a scream that will haunt my dreams forever. *"Corpsman Up!"* Hearing the scream Corporal Scott and I threw our gear on feverishly and as we did, tripped on each other in the commotion as we desperately tried to make our way to the site of the casualty that was on the rooftop of the building at the time.

By the time we reached the landing of the staircase, every possible scenario had run through my mind as to what could have happened. Nothing that I thought of could have held a candle to what I saw at the top of those stairs. I saw what every leader dreads; one of my Marines was down. I could take this story down that road and the grim details of that event—but I won't. Instead, I want to tell the good thing that I saw that day related to this horrific and tragic event.

HN "Doc" Lleva, our squad Corpsman surpassed every expectation I ever had set for him. When he first came to the unit, I thought that our squad had gotten the proverbial short end of the stick in getting one of the most junior, inexperienced, Corpsmen in the unit. Frankly, that was one of my main concerns. I really wasn't terribly worried that my Marines would falter because I had the best team leaders in the company. I was, however, scared shitless that my Corpsman would freeze when we needed him the most.

On that day, as much as I felt God damned me, I saw a blessing in Doc Lleva. His performance under those unfortunate conditions may have been my proudest moments as a squad leader. I want to add that I think this deployment was challenging and I believe that it was a fitting culmination to my Marine Corps career.

Everyone in the American Legion hall stood quietly as I folded up the letter and slipped it into the inside pocket of my suit coat. The quiet pause didn't last long. The Marines who had been toasting Litke all day let loose with applause and several loud, "Ooh-Rahs" to lighten the mood. Litke's mother, sitting in the front row, looked up at me and mouthed, "Thank you," as she wiped tears out of her eyes.

■　　■　　■

Even in the aftermath of Litke's loss, he continued to take care of those around him—just as he had always done for his fellow Marines.

Litke was an organ donor.

Today Litke's heart beats in the chest of a sixty-three-year-old man, his lungs breathe for a forty-seven-year-old woman, his kidney functions in the body of an eight-year-old girl, and his liver thrives in the body of a thirty-eight-year-old man. Even though our hearts were breaking, we all knew that Litke lived on.

Those dark echoes resonate with all of us who served. Some still don't hear them. They are only a fraction that represent over twenty veterans that take their own lives every day.

Echo Company stays closely bonded. It's our chemistry that flows through us perhaps, interconnecting us, as only Marines will know.

Marines who served under some of the worst conditions at a time when there was great uncertainty, and most certain danger.

We'll never lose the permanence of what we saw—never be able to "un-see" some of the worst actions of humanity, never ignore the echoes of what was heard. But Echo Company will always have a sense of pride that we helped so many who could not help themselves—the true spirit of what Marines do.

Gratitude

I cannot begin to fully express my thanks and acknowledgements to the following friends who contributed to this book. It is, in essence, their story. They sacrificed with me in combat and supported me at home, both while I fought and while I wrote. They all shared their stories, hearts, and expertise with me to tell this story.

To my wife, Kimberly—You fell asleep alone so many nights while I fought and while I wrote this book. I know it was never easy, but you you were there for me through it all and raised our beautiful daughter, Bailey, in my absence.

Ed Vasgerdsian—You guided me, mentored me, and provided hundreds of hours of your time to help me with this project. I will forever be in your debt.

Sylvia Mendoza—My friend and first editor who transformed this story to truly make it shine.

John McLaughlin—You provided countless stories and contributions to this book. Your words and conversations did much to help me tell this story.

The Libby, Sanchez, Matus, and Litke families—The memories and stories you shared with me were instrumental in honoring your Marines. I'm humbled that you trusted me with them.

Kimberly Downing—Your story reflects what thousands have gone through during the Long War and continue to do today. I am so honored that you shared it with me.

Richard "Bam-Bam" Rasmussen—My thanks to you for being a sounding board, amazing friend, better warrior, and for filling in the gaps in time.

Jared Norrell and Miciotto Johnson—I offer you my humble appreciation for supporting me then and now. Your words and contributions helped pave the way for this book.

The Red Origami Dragon—An inspiration in more ways than I can count. A muse and motivation, tucked inside my desk, that kept me writing and telling this story when I waned.

Joe Vallely—My agent, who always provided sage guidance, unvarnished advice, and vast experience to make this happen—I am extremely grateful for the "supporting arms."

Scott Belliveau—My project editor who worked tirelessly with me for weeks on end to take this story to an exceptional level.

Finally, to Marji Ross and Alex Novak, who believed in this amazing story from the beginning and supported me throughout the process with your patience and enthusiasm. Thank you for welcoming me into the Regnery family.

Special Thanks

To all of the contributors of this book, I respectfully offer my personal "Thank You" for all that you provided. You shared your pain, your tears, and your time with me to tell this story. I will never forget your amazing stories, unshakeable commitment, and words of encouragement along the way.

Big Sam

Raymond Bowen

Jack Coughlin

Jeff Downing

Kimberly Downing

Ryan Downing

Dale Dye

Jonathan Espinoza

Ford

Jared Flannagan

Thom Foster

Scott Gehris

AJ Goldberg

Jay Grillo

Colin Heaton

Dianne Layfield

Bobby Lee

Robert Litke

Chris Libby

Geni Libby

James Livingston

James Mackenzie

Donna Matus

John McLaughlin

Christopher Muscle

Brian McKibben

Jonathan Neris

Seth Nicholson

Jared Norrell

Paul Nugent

Mike Perkins

Joseph Raney

Charles Sasser

Matt Scott

Peter Somerville

Calvin Spencer

Drew Sturrock

Patrick Van Horne

Nick Velez

Giles Walger

Charles Walker

Bing West

Now

I would love to know where every one of my Marines are today, what they are doing, and how they've grown. I'd like to reach out and remember all the fantastic soldiers, sailors, civilians, and Iraqis who supported us during our time as we fought. I'd like them to know I still think about them all, even the ones whose names I don't know, because they impacted my life so deeply.

I want them all to know that I am still here for them.

For those Marines who have left the battlefield you need to know one thing: that protective bubble will always be there. It may now be a phone call, a drive, or a long flight away, but make no mistake about it, we will always be here to protect you.

Longhorns

Samawi "Big Sam" Al Helli—Big Sam received his undergraduate degree from the University of Baghdad. He moved to Chicago after being sponsored to the United States by "Bam-Bam." He went on to get two master's degrees. He is awaiting approval for his U.S. citizenship.

Raymond Bowen—Bowen deployed again with 2d Battalion, 4th Marines. Later, he turned down a $40,000 re-enlistment bonus and left active duty. He served as a Marine Reservist until 2013. He now works as a journeyman boilermaker and lives in Joliet, Illinois, with his wife and young daughter.

Derek Carpenter—After leaving Echo Company, Carp deployed to Afghanistan and spent five more years in the infantry. In 2013, he earned a coveted slot with Marine Corps Special Operations Command (MAR-SOC) and is a critical skills operator, still fighting the War on Terror. He lives in southern California with his girlfriend and two beautiful children.

Jonathan Espinoza—Espo is a gunnery sergeant serving on active duty. Since 2007, he has deployed twice to Afghanistan and has had a successful tour on recruiting duty in El Paso, Texas. He is working on attaining his bachelor's degree. He is currently stationed in Miami, Florida, where he lives with his wife and two children.

Kimberly Downing—Since 2007, Kimberly has worked as a nurse for the VA in Des Moines, Iowa, feeling constantly honored to take care of veterans. She struggled for years taking care of her Marines when they couldn't settle down and were in and out of trouble. Kimberly is now a travelling nurse with five beautiful grandchildren. She still feels blessed that her boys all came home and is continually honored to be their mother and wife. She always thanks me for that phone call each time we speak. I remain humbled.

Jeff Downing—Jeff is a Des Moines, Iowa, firefighter. He's with his family again boating and camping and enjoying family cookouts. Getting together and talking about their past experiences helps them grow as a family.

Ryan Downing—Ryan left the Marines in 2007. He has been happily married for eight years now and has three children and is a full-time law enforcement officer in Iowa. It took him years to process all of the things he witnessed and endured as an eighteen-year-old and to adjust back to civilian life. He is eternally grateful to his mom and wife for guiding him back to where he needed to be.

Ford—In 2008, Ford immigrated to the United States. He went on to finish his college degree in Information Technology. He moved to Chicago with Big Sam in 2013 and received his U.S. citizenship. As the threat of ISIS rose in 2015, Ford went back to Iraq as a high-level interpreter-translator for the U.S. Department of Defense. He currently lives in Florida.

Thom Foster—Foster made another deployment with 2d Battalion, 4th Marines, to Okinawa, Japan, and then went on to the Marine Corps Recruit Depot in Parris Island, South Carolina. He was promoted to sergeant major and is currently the command sergeant major at Marine Aviation Weapons and Tactics Squadron One (MAWTS-1) in Yuma, Arizona.

Jonathan "Jay" Grillo—Grillo left active duty in 2008 and is now a U.S. marshal living in Plattsburg, New York, with his wife and baby girl.

Dianne Layfield—For more than fourteen years, Dianne has been surrounded by support and comforted by her son's memory. She has supported organizations such as the Fallen Heroes Funerals, Gold Star Families, Operation Moms, and Veterans Hospitals, and organized massive contributions to help veterans. She was instrumental in the passage of federal legislation meant to keep protestors one thousand feet away from fallen heroes' memorial services and legislation in California that authorized Gold Star license plates.

Bobby Lee—Bobby Lee married his college sweetheart, Meghan, and they have three beautiful children. He went on to take company command and serve in Afghanistan. He received the Bronze Star Medal for bravery. Now a major, he is currently serving as an advisor at the Expeditionary Warfare School training young captains.

Geni Libby—Geni Libby retired from the McDonald's Corporation and is happily living in Castle Hill, Maine. She leads a quiet life now and enjoys reading and staying close to home. The Marines from Echo Company call her often and let her know that we are always thinking about her.

Judd Libby—Judd is retired and lives in Caribou, Maine. He struggled for years after the loss of Dustin but is doing well and still keeps in touch with many of the Marines of Echo Company for support.

James "Mac" Mackenzie—After 2007, Mac went on to lead a scout sniper platoon with the 31st Marine Expeditionary Unit. He deployed again to Afghanistan on another combat tour and retired from the Marines in 2015. He is pursuing his undergraduate degree and lives in Spokane, Washington, with his wife and four children.

Donna and Gary Matus—The Matuses still live in the country house that their son grew up in in western Wisconsin. Gary hunts and fishes, and Donna is semi-retired and works from home.

Brian McKibben—McKibben is still on active duty as an infantryman and is currently the assistant operations chief for 2d Battalion, 8th Marines. He continues to serve proudly and is happily married with three beautiful children stationed in North Carolina.

John McLaughlin—Shortly after returning from Iraq, McLaughlin was selected from Echo Company to lead an Advisory Team for the Iraqi Army and returned months later. He was hand-selected to lead a USMC Silent Drill Platoon at the prestigious Marine Barracks in Washington, D.C. He served as a company commander in 2d Battalion, 9th Marines, and then left the Marines after ten years of honorable service. McLaughlin, his wife, and their twin daughters live in Dallas, Texas, where he is currently pursuing his MBA while working as senior leader at a national real estate management company.

Christopher Muscle—Muscle was inspired as a combat lifesaver in the Marines to continue his medical training. He has pursued a career as a full-time firefighter where he is one of the youngest ever to attain the rank of lieutenant within his department. He went on to get his bachelor's degree and is currently working on his master's degree. He lives in Argyle, Texas, with his wife and two amazing boys.

Jonathan Neris—Since 2006, Jonathan continued to serve in other units in the USMC as a marksmanship instructor, an intelligence specialist, and finished his service as a recruiter in Chicago, Illinois. After ten years of honorable service, Jonathan is now in the civilian world. He currently works as a welder and resides with his wife, son, and daughter in Illinois.

Jared Norrell—Jared completed his career in the U.S. Army and retired honorably in 2012. He has an MBA and currently serves as the president at Lyman Ward Military Academy in Alabama where he lives with his family.

Mike "Dolby" Perkins—Mike lives in southern California with his wife and two children. He retired from the Marines in 2015 and is flying commercial aircraft for Southwest Airlines.

Joseph Raney—Raney left the Marines and moved to the Tacoma area and went to work in the private sector. He struggled with PTS and has benefited from connecting with other vets. He is happy now with his family and three beautiful children. He still misses the Marines of Echo Company everyday—he feels they're still a part of him.

Richard "Bam-Bam" Rasmussen—"Bam-Bam" went on to be a flight instructor in Florida in 2007. He earned a master's degree in Military Studies from the Marine Corps in 2011. He returned to the operating forces flying CH-53E Super Stallion helicopters until 2015. He currently serves as the Marine Corps Air Station Miramar, California, Airfield Operations Officer. He lives in southern California.

Calvin Spencer—Spencer left active duty in 2009 and studied culinary arts and graduated from Le Cordon Bleu. He was the head chef at a prominent restaurant in Long Beach, California, before co-founding Bastard's American Canteen with Nick Velez in 2012, where he manages the entire food selection and menu for their thriving business.

Matt Scott—Matt transferred to 3d Battalion, 5th Marines, and made another deployment overseas. He was honorably discharged from the Marines in 2010 and began his studies at UCLA. Matt lives in southern California and is a private security contractor for the U.S. Department of State.

Peter Somerville—Somerville left active duty in 2008. Since then, he has worked for several nonprofit organizations and political campaigns, including advocacy for veteran causes. He now lives in Arlington, Virginia, and works for a tech startup providing funding for veteran-owned small businesses.

Drew "Tex" Sturrock—Tex is a singer and songwriter in Tyler, Texas. He is married and has two beautiful daughters. His motto is, "Find the silver lining in everything you do—life, love, and laughter."

Nick Velez—Nick is the president and co-founder of Save the Brave, a certified non-profit foundation that connects veterans through outreach programs that struggle with PTS. He is the owner of two successful restaurants, affectionately called Bastard's American Canteen, in both Downey and Temecula, California. He's pursuing his bachelor's degree.

Index